$7.95

RACE AND ETHNICITY
Essays in Comparative Sociology

PIERRE VAN DEN BERGHE

The study of race relations in this country, while still focused principally on the Negro American, is shifting increasingly toward a more comparative approach. Pierre van den Berghe has been a key figure in bringing about this shift, for he is one of the few scholars in the field who applies theoretical and integrating skills to cross-cultural and comparative studies in race relations. Here he has assembled in one volume essays spanning more than a decade of field work and research in Mexico, Guatemala, and South and East Africa (including work on overseas Indians). The result is a book that no one interested in the exciting possibilities of a more comparatively oriented study of race relations will want to miss.

RACE AND ETHNICITY

Essays in Comparative Sociology

Pierre L. van den Berghe

Basic Books, Inc., Publishers • New York • London

To the women in my life:
Denise, Irmgard, Gwendoline,
as members of
an oppressed majority

PIERRE VAN DEN BERGHE is Professor
of Sociology at the University of Washington. His books include *Race and Racism*
(1967) and *South Africa: A Study in Conflict* (1968).

Contents

RACE
AND
ETHNICITY

Introduction

The papers collected here stretch over a dozen years of research and publication and are representative of my intellectual evolution during that period. In a sense they are milestones (or perhaps better pebbles) in a scholarly biography, and I decided therefore to let them stand or fall as they were originally published without the benefit of a "face-lifting" job to make the earlier ones conform more closely to my present position. Since, however, most readers will presumably be more interested in the substantive content of the articles than in the evolution of my thinking, the pieces have been arranged geographically and topically rather than chronologically. Let me simply state that, although I would not repudiate any of the main arguments contained in the following essays, some of my earlier functionalist formulations (particularly in the pre-1963 pieces) seem a bit naïve in retrospect. This is perhaps most evident in my treatment of the "paternalistic" type of race relations.

Believing as I do that scholarship is intimately linked with one's life experiences, I am taking this opportunity to indulge in a bit of autobiography. My earliest recollection of ethnic problems goes back to my primary-school days in Brussels. Since my mother tongue was French, I went to a French medium school in Belgium's bilingual capital. My mother is Parisian, and my father, although born in Ghent in the Flemish part of the country, comes from a family which had become francophone one or two generations before his. This accounts for the ambiguity between my French first name and my Flemish surname, although my case is by no means exceptional in Belgium.

3

Happily, the situation has changed drastically since then, but a quarter of a century ago, the so-called upper classes in Belgium were still predominantly French-speaking, and fluency in French was a prestige symbol. Many of my snobbish classmates in school regarded Flemish as an inferior "kitchen language" to be used only with domestic servants and peasants. However, because of the official bilingualism of Belgium, all schools were (and still are) forced to teach both national tongues. A twisted form of snobbery developed, whereby to be good in Flemish carried a social stigma as it indicated that you were really a Fleming trying to pass for a francophone Belgian. As it happened that I was spending most of my summer vacation with my paternal grandparents in Ghent, my Flemish was better than that of most of my schoolmates, and thus I had my first encounter with ethnic prejudice.

At about the same time, I had much more humiliating experiences in France whenever I went to visit my maternal grandparents. In the French bourgeoisie any dialect other than "educated" Parisian French is regarded as inferior and excites hilarity; and of the many dialects, the Belgian and Corsican accents are regarded as the ugliest and funniest. This ties in with the *grande nation* complex of the French vis-à-vis the *petits belges*. Thus my maternal relatives almost invariably greeted me with an amused remark as to how much of a Belgian accent I had, and my French playmates ridiculed my "belgicisms," as when I said "septante" instead of "soixante-dix." Even my Parisian mother was said to have become contaminated by the "bad" Belgian accent, since she lived in Brussels.

This period in my life also coincided with World War II and with the Nazi occupation of France and Belgium when feelings of ethnic hostility against the German invaders ran high. A whole underground culture of anti-German prejudice developed almost overnight, consisting mostly of jokes and unflattering animal similes at the expense of the foreign oppressor. Throughout my childhood, then, ethnic conflicts were a salient part of my day-to-day experiences, and my international parentage often put me in a "marginal" position.

The next formative experience was when, at the age of fifteen,

I returned to the then Belgian Congo, where I had been born during one of my father's study trips but which I had left before my first birthday. Until then, I had not consciously encountered racism. The Congo to me meant a few photographs of myself as a baby in the family album and an adventuresome past that always elicited interest when I was asked my place of birth. This often brought forth some joking as to why I was not black. The Congo also meant to me collecting silver paper from chocolate wrappings "for the missions" and feeding small change into an ingenious collection box whereon sat a broadly grinning black figurine which obligingly tilted its head in thanks when a coin was dropped.

My socialization as a would-be colonial began as I stepped on board the ship that was to take me from Antwerp to Lobito in Angola. Although I did not realize it at the time, the situation was really an extremely interesting one for the study of the genesis of racial prejudice. The crew of the ship was European except for the catering staff of waiters and cabin attendants, who were all Congolese. This was my first conscious and direct contact with blacks. Passengers were almost entirely Belgians, half of whom were "old colonials" returning to the Congo after several years during which the war had kept them in Europe, and the other half "new colonials" going out for the first time. The latter group typically reacted to the strange situation of being waited upon by Africans by showing, if anything, greater courtesy than they would have used with white servants. Some even addressed the Congolese as "Monsieur," whereas, to a white waiter, they would have said "garçon." Three or four days later, by the time we had reached the Canary Islands and when the process of shipboard acquaintance had started, there was already a subtle change in attitude. By the time we reached Lobito, most new colonials had become as racist as the old ones and were referring to the same Congolese as "macaque" ("rhesus monkey," a favorite form of abuse of Belgian colonials toward Africans). The few who still resisted the process of racist indoctrination were condescendingly assured that they too would lose their illusions when they got to know "them" well.

The next two and a half years gave me the opportunity to observe at first hand the operation of a colonial regime at the height of its exploitative efficiency and arrogant power. I lived in a thoroughly segregated world where Africans were tolerated only as servants and even then treated at best as shadowy nonentities or at worst as the victims of a steady stream of abuse and brutality. Africans, I was told, were dull-witted simpletons, grown-up children whose minds had not evolved beyond age ten or so, really just one step from the apes, a kind of compromise between a European moron and a trained chimpanzee. The more liberal upper-class Europeans pontificated on the "civilizing mission" and the white man's burden. The missionaries wanted to save their black brethren from darkness and ignorance. The cruder plantation, road, and factory foremen dispensed their daily quota of kicks and whippings (with the "chicotte," a hippopotamus- or oxen-nerve whip). It was, broadly speaking, a world in black and white but with a few shades of gray. The mulattoes were cleverer than the blacks, but pretentious and deceitful. The Indian merchants were just like Jews, only worse. The Greeks and Portuguese were whites, but just barely, and they were responsible for all the "poor mulatto children" who did not fit anywhere.

At seventeen, I left one racist society to enter another. From the Congo, I went to the United States to enroll at Stanford as an undergraduate. As a student of political science and sociology, I became interested in the comparative study of race relations in Africa and in America. I was immediately struck by the differences in patterns of contemporary United States race relations and the colonial regime which I had known in the Congo. On the other hand, I noted more similarities between the African colonial regimes and the slave plantation regimes of the Western Hemisphere. This eventually led to my conceptualizing race relations in terms of two ideal types, the "paternalistic" and "competitive." Later, I applied that scheme to South Africa for my Harvard doctoral dissertation.

It was at Harvard in the late 1950's that this long-standing interest in race and ethnicity matured into a professional specialization. In 1959, I had the opportunity to do my first piece of actual field work in Chiapas, Mexico. Seven years before, I had spent a summer as a student in Mexico City and had been struck by the nearly total absence of racism in Mexico. And in 1956, while at the Sorbonne, I had collaborated with Roger Bastide on the analysis of a questionnaire study of racial attitudes in São Paulo, Brazil. Now was the chance to take a closer look at ethnic relations in a Latin American context and to gain some experience in field work before going out to South Africa. My task was facilitated by the fact that B. N. Colby, with whom I collaborated on this project, had preceded me in the field and established valuable contacts with key informants.

A few months after my Mexican field work, I submitted my doctoral thesis on South Africa written under the joint director-ship of Talcott Parsons and the late G. W. Allport, and it was accepted. This thesis was based purely on library research, and I reversed the usual sequence of events by leaving for South Africa to check up on my thesis after getting the latter approved. Of my research experiences in South Africa I have written at length in one of the pieces in this collection. Trying as these two years were, they contributed greatly to the evolution of my thinking away from the functionalist approach to which I had been exposed at Harvard and toward the conflict model of plural societies. While in Durban, I came especially under the influence of Leo and Hilda Kuper and became more intensively exposed to the works of other Africanists in the conflict tradition such as Max Gluckman, M. G. Smith, and Clyde Mitchell. While in Paris, of course, I had already become familiar with the works of French Africanists such as Georges Balandier and Paul Mercier in the field of multiethnic relations in African cities, and these contacts were renewed in 1962 when I spent a few months in Paris working on my South African materials. It was out of those two traumatic but enriching years in South Africa and these pro-fessional contacts that I began to take a more holistic view of race and ethnic relations not as phenomena *sui generis* but as special cases of social segmentation in plural societies.

The next five years of my career were spent in the United

States, teaching and working on my South African data, with a summer's field work in Guatemala in 1966. There, I collaborated with Colby again and worked in an area not far from the site of my 1959 Mexican research, putting the pluralism framework to the test of a Latin American situation.

In 1967, the Rockefeller Foundation supported a year's visiting professorship at the University of East Africa in Nairobi, where I became especially interested in the position of the East Indian minority in East Africa. This tied in with my South African experience insofar as the community of "Caneville" which I studied there had a predominantly East Indian population. Thus I gained a more comparative view of overseas Indian communities. My year in Kenya was followed by a brief summer trip to Mother India herself, and in 1968–1969 I took up a one-year visiting professorship at the University of Ibadan in Nigeria. In fact, I had intended to go to Ibadan the year before, but because of the political uncertainty of the situation in the summer of 1967, the Rockefeller Foundation advised me to go to Kenya first.

In contrast to Kenya, where the racial caste structure of the colonial days still pervades most aspects of life and makes for a high degree of racial hostility between Europeans, Asians, and Africans, I found Nigeria almost totally devoid of racism. However, I found myself in a situation of acute conflict and one which has an important (though by no means exclusive) ethnic dimension. While in Nigeria I studied the social structure of the University of Ibadan, including the ethnic aspect of it.

Both before and after these two years in Africa, I spent several weeks in Belgium, where the linguistic quarrel has gained in intensity over the years, and thus relived at a quarter-century's interval my first childhood experiences in the field of ethnic relations. There I found that a customs official in the Flemish part of the country whom I had addressed in French looked at my American passport, frowned at my Flemish surname, and chose to reply to me in "neutral" English rather than speak the "other" national language of Belgium. If I have reached one conclusion in the course of my academic nomadism, it is that problems of ethnic particularism and hostility are not limited to the so-called developing countries.

The reader may ask why, having become an American citizen and having spent over ten years in the United States, I did relatively little work on American race relations. I think the answer is that, precisely because I intend to make the United States my permanent home, and because I am so deeply disturbed by the all-pervasive racism, black and white, in that country, I cannot afford to become more deeply involved in the issue than I already am. If I were to do research in that area, I doubt that I could stand to live in the States much longer. Like the proverbial psychiatrist in the hospital who must periodically go back to the outside to test his sanity, I feel a powerful urge to leave the United States every couple of years.

This is also an opportunity to restate my current theoretical and epistemological position on the analysis of race and ethnic relations.[1] It became increasingly clear to me over the years that the subject had no claim to a special place in a general theory of society. In other words, race and ethnic relations are not sufficiently different from other types of social relations—nor, conversely, do various types of race and ethnic relations have enough that is exclusively common—to justify special theoretical treatment. If the subject has established itself as one of the standard specializations in sociology, it is mainly because of its immense practical consequences all over the world. Consequently, the specialty has been generally characterized by a level of theoretical sophistication which is, if anything, lower than the altogether modest state of the discipline as a whole. Especially in American sociology, the "race and ethnic field" has been little more than a timid and rather ineffectual handmaiden to the meliorative and reformist attempts of the well-intentioned liberal establishment. With disconcerting disregard for the epistemological issues involved, most scholars in that field have swung their position and their "objective" findings with the ideological winds. They have salvaged their pretense to objectivity while shifting from the racist Social Darwinism of the teens to the environmentalism and social determinism of the 1930's. Now, the scholarly weathercock seems to take another turn. Genetic determinism of behavior is slowly becoming *salonfähig* again, and white "liberal" academics, yielding to subtle blackmail and their guilty consciences, outdo each other in pandering to the currently fashionable black racism.

It should be obvious from these remarks that I regard myself and my colleagues, not as objective scholars engaged in a dispassionate search for knowledge, but rather both as products of the society we are studying and as blundering and ineffectual influences thereon. We are not studying a reality "out there." We are, willy-nilly, plunged in the racist stew of the American society which produced us (if I may now speak as an American). Any claim to scientific objectivity in the matter is, in my view, a complacent delusion.

It should be stressed here that the term "race" will consistently be used in these chapters to mean *not* a subspecies of homo sapiens but a group of people who in a given society are socially defined as different from other groups by virtue of certain real or putative physical differences. What makes a society multiracial is not the presence of physical differences between groups, but the attribution of social significance to such physical differences as may exist. As will become clear in comparing the chapters on Latin America with those on South Africa, the distinction between societies where the important criteria of group membership are physical ones and those where they are cultural —that is, the distinction between multiracial and multiethnic societies—is an important one. It is true that systems of race and systems of ethnic relations have much in common, but multiracial societies are in the nature of the case more rigidly ascriptive ones than most of the multiethnic societies. Some of the world's most rigid systems have not ostensibly been based on race, notably the Hindu caste system (which may, however, have originated in a racial system), but a disproportionate number of the world's most rigid systems of social stratification have been racial, and indeed racist, in character.

Keeping, then, the analytical distinction between race and ethnicity in mind, it is equally important to stress how much these two bases of social segmentation have in common, not only with each other, but with other criteria of group membership, notably caste, class, age, and sex. The analogy between caste and race has a long history of academic polemic, and there would be little profit in reactivating the controversy here. The reader will find that I have accepted the "minimum" definition of caste as ascriptive, endogamous, and hierarchized groups and thus have applied the label to multiracial societies.

On the other hand, the analogy between sexual and racial discrimination and prejudice has not been stressed as much as it deserves. If one defines racism as the theory that there is a causal link between physical traits on the one hand, and social behavior, character traits, and intelligence on the other hand, it becomes evident that antifeminism very frequently assumes a quasi-racist guise. Certainly in Western societies there is a widespread belief that temperamental differences between men and women are rooted in sexual physiology rather than in the socialization process. Although the detailed modalities of etiquette and role playing differ, there are profound similarities between being black and being a woman in American society. For example, playing the "dumb blonde" role is much like "playing the nigger," and the folklore of cunning and deception to circumvent the tyranny of the superordinate group shows much in common between the Victorian woman and the plantation slave. If it were not for the network of binary affective ties which links the vast majority of men and women, the sexes might well become as polarized as the "races."

The similarity and the interplay between class relations and ethnic and race relations are also striking. Racial and ethnic groups are frequently stratified, and, at the same time, they are never the only bases of stratification in complex societies. Thus both race and ethnic relations have to be understood in the context of a broader system of stratification.

The study of race and ethnic relations remains a fascinating one if only because it often reveals in especially extreme form certain social processes, such as conflict and competition, which might not otherwise be as evident. However, if that study is to make an important contribution to the discipline of sociology as a whole, it must meet certain conditions.

1. Race and ethnic relations must be studied *historically,* that is, as part of the development process of a given society. It should

be axiomatic that one cannot understand the present if one does not know the past, but much of the work in that area has lacked time depth. How, for example, is one to understand the present situation of Afro-Americans if one does not know about the plantation slavery system? Yet how many American sociologists studying contemporary race relations in the United States have delved firsthand into the mass of documentary evidence about southern plantations, and how many American historians have conveniently swept that vital aspect of the growth of the *Herrenvolk* Republic under the rug?

2. Race and ethnic relations must be studied *holistically,* that is, in the context of the total society in which they take place. "Race" or "ethnic" relations are, in last analysis, a special type of relations of *power* and relations of *production:* they can be understood only in the larger framework of political and economic institutions. This again seems too obvious to need belaboring, but the narrow focus of many studies has limited the usefulness and indeed the validity of their findings. For example, studies of residential segregation by race in cities based on demographic indices tell us something about the morphology of segregation and are of course interesting in their own right, but they can scarcely get at the causality of the situation.

3. We must approach the subject from a comparative, a *crosscultural,* perspective. This must necessarily be the case if we want to generalize. Every situation is a mixture of unique and repeated elements, and one of the first tasks in trying to discover regularities is to establish what the range of both crosscultural and intracultural variability is in the phenomena one is trying to account for. A vastly disproportionate amount of work has been done on a few Western or Western-dominated societies, and we know very little indeed about intergroup relations in other parts of the world, such as traditional African societies. The conventional focus of anthropology on the culture group (or some subsection thereof) as the unit of analysis has deflected attention from relations between groups, and the vast ethnographic literature, with half a dozen exceptions, gives us only a few glimpses of ethnic relations in non-Western societies. Even in the contempo-

rary African situation, the word "tribalism" is bandied about by scholars, journalists, and others, but very little actual research is conducted on the nature of ethnic relations in the multinational states of Africa. For complex and different reasons, both African and foreign scholars find the subject too hot to handle except at the polemical level, when they accuse each other of tribalism, neocolonialism, racialism, and other heinous crimes.

4. This leads us back to the point already made concerning the problem of "objectivity" and "value-freedom." I doubt that any scholars working in this area (or indeed in many others) are "value-free" on the issue of racialism, for example. A couple of generations ago most scholars were racists; today most are anti-racist, but hardly any are neutral on the issue. Nor do many of them put up a creditable performance of keeping their private value judgments out of their scholarly writings. How many studies have been devoted to the heightening of racial tensions, for example, compared to those devoted to the reduction of racial tensions. Surely, from a theoretical perspective both subjects are equally seminal. Ideological commitment on this issue is so powerful that it takes great courage for any scholar not to suppress evidence which might be interpreted as supporting racism.

Under the circumstances, it seems to me that the only honest thing to do is to drop the positivist credo of "objectivity," to make our ideological position and our value premises explicit, and, indeed, to subject ourselves to a kind of "socioanalysis" similar to the psychoanalysis required of the psychiatric clinician. Is it not preferable to reach a state of conscious, disciplined, explicit subjectivity than one of naïve pseudo objectivity?

In conclusion, I should like to mention in its broad outline the conceptual approach of "pluralism" which a group of us, mostly Africanists, have developed in the last few years in an attempt to deal more systematically with multiethnic and multi-racial societies. Here is not the place to present my position *in extenso,* as I have done so elsewhere.[2] I should stress that I am not using the term "pluralism" in the same sense as have a number of French and American political scientists in the

Tocquevillian tradition. They have meant by pluralism a condition in which competing interest groups interpose themselves between the state and the individual to create a democratic polity. This theory is an extension of economic liberalism and is based on the assumption that the clash of opposing self-interests produces by some magic the greatest good for all. I should also emphasize that pluralism is not a theory, but merely an analytical concept to help us deal with heterogeneous societies.

Plural societies are those that are segmented into two or more groups that have distinct and duplicatory sets of institutions, except in the political and economic spheres where the institutions are shared. The primary criterion of whether a society exists or not is political. If several groups share a common polity, however differentially and unequally, they constitute a plural society. However, plural societies are seldom if ever held together by political power alone; the various groups also typically share a common system of economic exchanges. In both the political and the economic spheres, very frequently the "sharing" of institutions is highly unequal. Many if not most plural societies are politically and economically dominated by one of the constituent groups, and that group is frequently a minority. Thus colonial societies and other large multiethnic empires are plural societies. Some multinational states, like Switzerland, Belgium, Canada, and more recently most of the African and some of the Asian states, have attempted to institutionalize more democratic forms of pluralism, but these attempts have often been disrupted by open conflict and plagued by instability. Tyranny over and economic exploitation of the majority by an ethnic minority is the more common and more enduring form of the plural society. Conflict and competition between groups are endemic, and coercion and economic interdependence rather than consensus are the bases of such social integration as exists.

Many of the world's polities exhibit some degree of pluralism. At present a majority of the world's states are larger than the national groups that constitute them, and "pure" nation-states are the exception rather than the rule. Even relatively homogeneous states like France, Italy, and China have their ethnic minorities. But some states, like India, Nigeria, or the Soviet Union, are much more pluralistic than others, like the United States or Spain.

In the majority of cases the deepest lines of cleavage in a society are the cultural ones. People of different ethnic groups tend to have far fewer and more "superficial" relationships with each other than they do with people from the same ethnic group. The multiple barriers of language, values, customs, expectations, and so on limit mutual understanding. Also, the frequently unequal character of the interaction makes for conflict or avoidance of contact; or, if the relationship is between equals, it is often defined in competitive terms. There are, of course, different degrees of cultural pluralism, ranging all the way from totally unrelated cultures, such as the Zulu and Afrikaners in South Africa or the Spanish and the Maya in Central America, to distinct but related cultures, as between Anglo- and Franco-Canadians or Flemings and Walloons in Belgium, to minor subcultural differences as, for example, in dialect between regions or social classes.

It is important, beyond distinguishing degrees of cultural pluralism, to differentiate between cultural and social pluralism. The two usually go together, but not always. Cultural pluralism is usually accompanied by social barriers to interaction which may take the form of prohibitions against eating together, or strict rules of endogamy, or rigid rules of etiquette, or the maintenance of physical distances, or various avoidance patterns. Usually, these social barriers tend to break down in situations where the process of acculturation has diminished the cultural distinctiveness between groups. In some especially rigid systems of stratification, however, such as the Hindu caste system and the color bar in the United States and South Africa, the social pluralism may persist even though cultural assimilation may have almost completely obliterated the cultural pluralism. Thus Afro-Americans belong to all intents and purposes to the American variety of western European culture, notwithstanding an Africanist mystique to the contrary. Yet they remain a clearly distinct caste in American society with a separate set of duplicatory institutions, such as black churches, professional organizations, political pressure groups, and so on. Here is a case of maximal social pluralism accompanied by minimal cultural pluralism. This lack of complete correspondence between cultural and social pluralism makes the distinction analytically useful.

Pluralism, then, is in the last analysis a set of properties characterizing heterogeneous societies. The concept of pluralism embraces both ethnicity and race and puts them in the broader context of the total society. To understand the structure of a plural society, the first steps in the analysis are to map out the lines of cleavage between the groups, to specify the institutional areas that are shared between these groups and those that are not, to establish the form and content of relationships between members of these groups, and to define in which ways these intergroup relations differ from relations within the groups. This procedure is equivalent to studying the entire society, Q.E.D.

I am not suggesting, of course, that less ambitious and more limited studies are worthless; but even when a scholar concentrates on a more narrowly focused topic, he must, if he is to interpret his data correctly, understand the total social context; that is, he must, at least in its broad outline, know the structure of the plural society he is studying and be familiar with the temporal evolution of intergroup relations. As a minimum, he must have a clear picture of the relations of power and the relations of production in that society. Otherwise his study of race or ethnic relations will dangle like a stringless puppet on a dark stage.

So far, I have spoken exclusively of the sociological dimension of race and ethnicity. I am not denying that the subject also has an important psychological dimension. In a couple of the chapters that follow, I have been concerned with racial and ethnic attitudes, a social-psychological topic. But there is no question that my central concern and interest has been that of a sociologist. I can only hope that my psychological colleagues will not take umbrage and will not interpret my choice of emphasis as a denial of the relevance of their specialty. I am simply suggesting, as did Durkheim at the dawn of sociological enquiry, that the sociological and the psychological are two discrete levels of explanation.

NOTES

1. For a more extensive and systematic presentation of my position and critique of present trends in the field, the reader should refer to my *Race and Racism* (New York: Wiley, 1967), especially Chapters 1, 6, and 7.

2. Cf. *ibid*. The first treatment of "pluralism" in the present meaning is to be found in J. S. Furnivall, *Colonial Policy and Practice* (Cambridge: Cambridge University Press, 1948). The approach has been used by M. G. Smith in the Caribbean and Nigeria, Leo Kuper and van den Berghe in South Africa, J. Clyde Mitchell in Central Africa, B. N. Colby and van den Berghe in Guatemala, Leo Despres in Guiana, Burton Benedict in Mauritius, and others. For a recent statement of that "school," see Leo Kuper and M. G. Smith, eds., *Pluralism in Africa* (Berkeley: University of California Press, 1969).

Part I

GENERAL AND
THEORETICAL

1

Paternalistic versus Competitive Race Relations: An Ideal-Type Approach

Our general contention is that manifestations of racial prejudice have historically polarized around two ideal-types which we shall call *paternalistic* and *competitive*. The choice of labels is always a difficult one. Rather than use arbitrary symbols and thereby hinder readability, we adopted two words which are in some way descriptive of our two types. Obviously the common-sense meanings of the labels do not exhaust the content of the two types.[1]

The Paternalistic Type: Its Characteristics

The paternalistic type is incompatible with a complex manufacturing economy and with large-scale industrial capitalism. The most congenial form of economy is agricultural, pastoral, or handicraft. Mercantile capitalism and a large-scale plantation agriculture geared to the export of staple products (cotton, coffee,

This chapter is a revised version of Chapter 2 of my doctoral dissertation, "The Dynamics of Race Relations: An Ideal-Type Case Study of South Africa," (Harvard University, 1959). An earlier version of the theory was presented in my article, "The Dynamics of Racial Prejudice: An Ideal-Type Dichotomy," *Social Forces* 37 (December 1958): 138–141.

rubber, sugar, and the like) are also compatible with the paternalistic type. This type of economy coincides with an "intermediate" level of differentiation in the division of labor. By "intermediate" is meant here a degree of specialization which has gone considerably beyond a "primitive" division of labor based primarily on sex and age criteria, and yet which is not as complex as in the case of large-scale manufacturing industry.

Typically, in this intermediate stage of the division of labor, the mass of the labor force still consists of a fairly unspecialized, servile, or quasi-servile peasantry. But there is already considerable differentiation. Handicraft production is in the hands of full-time specialized artisans. Trading is concentrated in the hands of a merchant class, though the latter is often not very powerful. A rudimentary professional specialization is present. Warriors, priests, judges, and officials constitute the ruling group. This intermediate stage corresponds to what Weber called the "traditional" type of authority and is exemplified by most large-scale premodern societies. This stage implies both urbanization and fairly advanced social stratification. In paternalistic interracial situations with which we are concerned, the division of labor is along racial lines. A servile or quasi-servile racial caste (serfs, slaves, indentured laborers, "recruited" labor, *peones,* and so on) performs the heavy manual labor, in particular the agricultural tasks.[2]

The dominant upper caste confines itself to such occupations as war, the priesthood, the professions, government, supervision of labor, and commerce. The upper caste is, in fact, a ruling aristocracy, usually a small minority of the total population. This ruling caste is fairly homogeneous in social status. Class distinctions within the ruling caste are secondary to the paramount caste distinctions between the racial groups.[3]

A wide and unbreachable gap exists between the castes, as indicated by living standards, income, occupations, education, death rates, for example. There is a horizontal color bar with no intercaste mobility. Intracaste mobility is possible but limited, as there is little status differentiation within the castes. A slave can be manumitted, or gain a privileged position as house servant,

bigot which have come out of research in the United States are, we think, more typical of a competitive situation when the ethos of the culture is opposed to prejudice. This is not to say that no high F's will be found in a paternalistic situation, but rather that in a paternalistic society the authoritarian syndrome will not be a good predictor of racial attitudes, opinions, and behavior. It would also be a misunderstanding of our position to interpret us as saying that psychological variables are not operative in the paternalistic type of prejudice. In fact, we suspect that there might be a corresponding psychological syndrome in the paternalistic type. Roger Bastide, a psychoanalytically oriented social scientist, has suggested that paternalistic master-servant relationships are an extension of the nuclear family situation.[6] He suggests an ambivalent oedipal relationship between master and slave in the plantation situation and an incest taboo between white mistress and male slaves. We are not equipped to pass judgment on such interpretations. But although our own primary theoretical focus is sociological, we do not deny the operation of psychological factors or the existence of individual differences in the paternalistic situation.

An important note of caution should be added here. The romantic myth of the kindly master who led an existence of genteel leisure on his plantation amid the happy singing of his slaves should, of course, be dismissed. Violence and aggression do occur in the paternalistic type. But they take different forms than in the competitive case. They generally originate from the lower caste and are not directly and specifically racial in character. Slave rebellions and nationalistic, revivalistic, or messianistic movements are typical of the paternalistic type and indicate a lack of complete integration of the society. Such movements are usually repressed with utmost vigor by the upper caste, because if they are allowed to develop, they tend to lead to a violent and cataclysmic overthrow of the "old regime," as exemplified by the Haitian revolution.

Generally speaking, however, the paternalistic type of prejudice can be said to be "adjustive," "functional," or "integrative" for the social system. This statement implies, of course, no value judgment. We simply mean that, barring external influences and other disruptive factors such as industrialization, the more the racial ideology is believed in and practiced in a paternalistic society, the more integrated and stable the social system is. In other words, the more the hierarchal norms have been internalized in the personalities of both upper- and lower-caste members, the greater the stability of the social system, everything else remaining constant. But this inherent stability of the paternalistic type is accompanied by inherent inflexibility and inadaptability; that is, when the system is attacked from the outside, as is colonialism today, or when internal developments such as industrialization are incompatible with paternalism, the whole social system collapses altogether or evolves into a competitive situation.

Examples of the paternalistic type of racial prejudice are the slave plantation regimes of the ante-bellum United States South, of the West Indies, of Brazil; the encomienda or hacienda system in various parts of Spanish America; the colonial regimes of the various European powers in Africa, some of which, such as the former Belgian Congo, have survived in fairly pure form to the recent past. All the preceding examples were taken from Western societies because the cases are more familiar. But paternalism is not limited to Western societies. In Ruanda-Urundi (Central Africa), for example, the Watuzi, a group of pastoralists famous for their tall stature, have imposed their domination over an overwhelming majority of shorter and physically quite distinguishable Bahutu. The latter, who were already tillers of land before the Watuzi conquest, have become the serfs of the Watuzi; the situation is typically paternalistic.

Likewise, paternalism as a type of relationship is not limited to interracial situations, as we shall see later.

The Competitive Type: Its Characteristics

In our ideal-type dichotomy, the competitive type is the polar opposite of the paternalistic type. Generally, the competitive type is found in the large-scale manufacturing economy based on industrial capitalism. However, competitive prejudice has existed in preindustrial societies. The case of the Jews in medieval Europe, though not racial according to our definition of the word, was competitive. The problem whether the competitive type is linked with capitalism, as a Marxist might contend, is not easy to settle empirically. Ethnic relations in the Soviet Union and Soviet policies toward the "nationalities" are not easy to investigate. However, the USSR has known waves of anti-Semitism indicative of competive prejudice. At any rate, urbanization seems a prerequisite for a competitive situation, and, empirically, the latter is very much associated with an industrial and capitalistic society.

The division of labor is complex and based on rational and universalistic criteria as required by a differentiated manufacturing economy. The bulk of the labor force is no longer unskilled, and technical competence and efficiency become paramount criteria of selection. Hence any rigid racial division of labor based on ascription and particularism cannot be maintained without entailing serious economic dysfunctions. Racial criteria of selection are not altogether absent, however. Indeed, they can be operative, due to prejudice, but they can be maintained only at a cost to the efficiency of the system of production, and the tendency is toward a breakdown of the industrial color bar. As a corollary of the factors above, there is much mobility, both social and spatial. Any complex industrial economy based on "organic solidarity" requires a spatially and socially mobile labor force; one that is responsive to the demand for labor and skills. Again, social mobility is hampered by racial prejudice, but only at a cost to the production system, and the tendency is toward "*la carrière ouverte aux talents.*"

In typical form, the competitive situation is accompanied by a caste system, but the distance between the castes in education, occupation, income, living standards, death rates, and so on, tends to diminish; that is, the color bar tends to tilt from a horizontal to a vertical position, though the vertical position has never been fully achieved. Within each color caste, there is more and more class differentiation. In other words, the status gap *between* castes tends to diminish and the status range *within* the castes tends to increase. With the tilting of the color bar, an upper-class lower-caste person may have a higher education, occupation, living standard, and the like, than a lower-class upper-caste person. Hence, there often comes about a status panic of lower-class persons from the upper caste, who feel threatened by rising lower-caste members as soon as class status and caste status cease to have a one-to-one correspondence. Though threat to status is probably not the whole story, it goes a long way to account for the higher virulence of competitive prejudice among poor whites in the United States, for example.

The dominant caste, in the competitive situation, is usually a majority which has within itself great status and class differences. The upper caste is not a homogeneous ruling group, as in the paternalistic case. On the contrary, a large segment of the upper caste engages in manual labor and hence is in direct competition with members of the lower caste. The sheer numerical ratio between the castes makes this situation inevitable. A certain percentage of the population must engage in manual occupations, and only a minority can be "on top."

In some interracial situations where miscegenation has been so extensive as to blur physical distinctions, and where the criteria of group membership are at least partly cultural rather than purely racial, the rigid color-caste system has broken down in part. This has been the case to some extent in most of Latin America. In Mexico, for example, a mestizo or Ladino can be a full-blooded Indian, provided he speaks fluent Spanish and is acculturated to Hispanic ways. But that still does not make him a "Spaniard." Prejudice is still present, though it is a mixture of ethnic and racial prejudice, and a quasi-caste system exists, though in much less rigid form than in the United States.

The competitive type is usually accompanied by ideological conflict, at least in a Western, "Christian," "democratic," and "liberal" sort of society. This conflict was the central core of Myrdal's analysis of the United States' situation.[7] Whether the ideological conflict is simply a superstructural reflection of the more basic incompatibility between the production system and prejudice, as the Marxist line of argument would run, is an open question, and one which cannot easily be settled empirically.

The form of government found in a competitive situation is generally a restricted or partial democracy from which the lower caste is excluded by various means and to a greater or lesser degree. The lower caste has generally no definite legal status. Discriminatory legislation can be passed, but usually without explicitly mentioning race as the basis of exclusion. Devious devices such as poll taxes, rezoning, and the like are used. Extra-legal sanctions against the minority are resorted to, such as lynching in the southern United States. The law generally is on the side of the general value system of the society and hence opposed to the prejudice norms. In terms of Max Weber's typology, the form of authority found in the competitive type is "rational-legal."

Racial roles and statutes are ill defined and in a constant state of flux. In terms of Parsons' pattern variables, they are based on achievement, universalism, specificity, self-orientation, and affective neutrality. There is no elaborate etiquette. Rather, members of the lower caste are in constant doubt as to the behavior expected from them. Conversely, members of the upper caste are in constant difficulty as to how to address educated lower-caste members, for example. The old etiquette is no longer applicable, and no new one has been evolved.

Unequal caste status is constantly assailed by the leveling forces discussed above. Since etiquette has broken down as a mechanism to maintain intimate unequal contacts, spatial segregation is resorted to in order to minimize interracial contacts which threaten to become equal and which are replete with uneasiness, ambiguity, and tension because of mutual prejudices.[8] Suspicion, hatred, antagonism prevail between the racial groups. Competition, real or imaginary, for status, for jobs, for women, or the threat of competition, poisons race relations. Miscegenation is severely condemned and infrequent. If it takes place at all, it will assume the form of transitory or commercialized contacts between the fringe members of both castes (as between poor whites and Negro prostitutes in the United States). Lasting concubinage is not institutionalized. A few cases of intermarriage will occur, at the cost of much disapproval, and usually among fringe groups (such as artists, bohemians, political radicals, low-class white immigrants).

Forms of aggression are numerous and originate both from the upper and from the lower caste. The basis of such aggression involves specifically racial issues. Besides the more violent manifestations of prejudice, such as sabotage, bombing, lynchings, race riots, and pogroms, other forms of resistance and antagonism are organized mass protests, strikes, passive resistance, and the like. The lower caste often seems to turn also to in-group aggression as a response to frustration. Typical of the competitive situation is a recurrent pattern of increase and decrease in prejudice which is in contrast with the relatively stable level of prejudice in the paternalistic case. In the competitive case, prejudice against groups seems to build up to a point of dangerous tension in response to such conditions as rapid influx of lower-caste migrants or rising unemployment. The slightest incident will then trigger off interracial violence. Such a gradual building up of tension seems to precede most race riots, pogroms, waves of terrorism, and the like.

Naturally, competitive prejudice, irrespective of these cyclical trends, can operate at an average level which is lower in one society than in another (anti-Semitism is stronger in Germany than in France, but still there has been a Dreyfus affair in France. Anti-Negro prejudice is stronger in the United States than in Brazil, but is far from absent in the latter country).

Stereotypes held about the lower caste are colored by fear. Lower-caste members are held to be aggressive, "uppity," insolent, oversexed, dirty. In short, they are despicable and dangerous as well as inferior. Clearly, stereotypes and prejudice are reciprocal. Lower-caste members describe upper-caste members as overbearing, bullying, brutal.

It appears that competitive prejudice is linked with authoritarian personality variables in members of the upper caste. This relationship is probably even closer when the values of total society are opposed to prejudice. In the United States, this aspect of prejudice has been widely studied, and the link between competitive prejudice and sexuality, sadism, anality, and so on, has been established. Scapegoating and frustration-aggression are clearly not complete explanations of prejudice even at the psychological level, but the relevance of these psychological mechanisms is beyond question. One may speak of a personality "need," or, as Allport puts it, of the "functional significance" of prejudice for the high F's.[9] It is still an open question how this relationship between authoritarianism and competitive prejudice holds when the values of the society are not openly against prejudice. Fragmentary evidence from the southern United States suggests, however, that the relationship becomes lesser. In other words, conformity to prejudicial norms in the southern United States accounts for a good deal of anti-Negro prejudice.[10]

One point stands out clearly from our description of competitive prejudice; it is a highly maladjusting or dysfunctional phenomenon in an industrial society. Again, no value judgment is implied. Not for a moment would we assert that the paternalistic type is any "better." By "maladjusting" we mean that the higher the level of competitive prejudice is, the less smoothly the social system will operate. Competitive prejudice, then, is a luxury which can be bought only at a price.

The reason for this built-in maladjustive factor in competitive prejudice lies primarily, we think, in the functional prerequisites of an industrial society which conflict with prejudicial norms. Mobility of labor and rationality of recruitment based on achievement and universalism are all in conflict with racial prejudice which is ascriptive and particularistic. Competitive prejudice finds itself in the inherently paradoxical position of operating both within a rational-legal system and against it.

Some empirical examples of competitive types of prejudice are the anti-Negro prejudice in the United States since the Civil War, the anti-Asiatic prejudice in California, anti-Semitism in Europe and the United States, anti-non-European prejudice in South Africa in recent years, and anti-Negro prejudice in Brazil, at least in the large industrial centers such as São Paulo, Santos, and Rio de Janeiro.

The Two Types of Prejudice:
A Summary and Analytical Schema

Such a broad description of the two types of prejudice as we have presented is rather unmanageable for analytical purposes. We shall now attempt to isolate the main variables, classify them for purposes of analysis, and present a schema contrasting the two types side by side to ensure that they do indeed constitute polar opposites and differ on the same dimensions.

We propose to classify the main variables of analysis into dependent, independent, and social control variables. Since these terms call to mind the experimental model, we should immediately emphasize that we are using them, for lack of better words, only in an analogical manner, not in a strict experimental sense. As variables interact, the words dependent and independent are interchangeable. In the present context, they are only meant to clarify the starting point of our analysis and to disentangle somewhat the relationship between variables.

We shall call "dependent variables" those that are directly concerned with race relations and prejudice, such as stereotypes, patterns of segregation, psychological syndromes, for instance. They are the variables which we shall attempt to "predict" ex post facto from the independent variables. The latter are broader social structure variables—the social framework in which prejudice expresses itself. They are the type of economy, the division of labor, the social stratification, and so on. Lest we be accused of economic, sociological, or some other form of determinism, we must again emphasize that the primacy we give to these independent variables is strictly heuristic and in no way precludes reciprocal causation.

A third set of variables we shall call "social control" variables, though we depart again from the strict experimental model. By "social control" we mean here deliberate attempts to modify, restore, or preserve an existent set of social conditions. This set of variables includes primarily governmental action in its executive, legislative, and judicial forms.

Table 1–1 presents the schema.

The Two Types of Prejudice in Relation to Other Theoretical Schemes

We have already indicated explicitly our borrowings from Parsons and from Weber. Weber's traditional type of authority tends to coincide with our paternalistic type of prejudice, whereas his rational-legal type of authority both coincides and conflicts with competitive prejudice. Weber's third type of authority, the charismatic one, is unstable and rarely found in a pure state. Insofar as charisma is revolutionary and unstable, it is incompatible with our paternalistic type. An example of competitive prejudice under a system which had strong charismatic elements is anti-Semitism under National Socialism in Germany. But anti-Semitism was already present in the rational-legal Germany of pre-Hitler days. Hence, charisma and the competitive type are not incompatible, but the relationship is not a necessary one.

In our use of Parsons' pattern variables, we have seen that they polarized along our two types. The pattern variables are conceived of by Parsons as being *independently* variable, however. That such is the case in many of the possible applications of the scheme, we shall not dispute. But in application to racial roles, there does not seem to be independent variation.

Our dichotomy is obviously related to some of the classical distinctions in sociology. Our competitive type coincides largely with the type of social solidarity which Durkheim called "organic." However, the reverse relationship between paternalism and mechanical solidarity does not hold. Most cases of paternalistic prejudice are found in a functionally differentiated, though preindustrial, society with a division of labor which we have termed "intermediate." Such a level of differentiation in the division of labor already contains strong "organic" elements and no longer represents a primitive "mechanical" level of solidarity, at least not in anywhere near a pure state.

Redfield's "folk" versus "urban" distinction likewise bears only a partial relationship to our own typology. Although the competitive type is associated with urbanism, and although paternalism is compatible with a folk society, the paternalistic situation

TABLE 1-1

	Paternalistic	Competitive
	A. Independent Variables	
1. Economy	Nonmanufacturing, agricultural, pastoral, handicraft; mercantile capitalism; plantation economy.	Typically manufacturing, but not necessarily so. Large-scale industrial capitalism.
2. Division of labor	Simple (primitive) or intermediate (as in preindustrial large-scale societies). Division of labor along racial lines. Wide income gap between racial groups.	Complex (manufacturing) according to rational universalistic criteria. Narrow gap in wages. No longer strictly racial.
3. Mobility	Little mobility either vertical or horizontal (slaves, servants, or serfs "attached" in space).	Much mobility both vertical and horizontal (required by industrial economy).
4. Social stratification	Caste system with horizontal color bar. Aristocracy vs. servile caste with wide gap in living standards (as indexed by income, education, death and birth rates). Homogeneous upper caste.	Caste system but with tendency for color bar to tilt to vertical position. Complex stratification into classes within castes. Narrower gaps *between* castes and greater range *within* castes.
5. Numerical ratio	Dominant group a small minority.	Dominant group a majority.
6. Value conflict	Integrated value system. No ideological conflict.	Conflict at least in Western, Christian, democratic, liberal type of society.
	B. Dependent Variables	
1. Race relations	Accommodation. Everyone in his place and "knows it." Paternalism. Benevolent despotism.	Antagonism. Suspicion, hatred. Competitiveness (real or imaginary).
2. Roles and statuses	Sharply defined roles and statuses based on ascription, particularism, diffuseness, collectivity orientation, affectivity. Unequal status unthreatened.	Ill defined and based on achievement, universalism, specificity, self-orientation, affective neutrality. Unequal status threatened.
3. Etiquette	Elaborate and definite.	Simple and indefinite.

TABLE 1-1 (continued)

	Paternalistic	Competitive
4. Forms of aggression	Generally from lower caste: slave rebellions, nationalistic, revivalistic, or messianistic movements. Not directly racial. "Righteous" punishment from the master.	Both from upper and lower caste. More frequent and directly racial: riots, lynchings, pogroms. Passive resistance, sabotage, organized mass protests.
5. Miscegenation	Condoned and frequent between upper-caste males and lower-caste females. Institutionalized concubinage.	Severely condemned and infrequent.
6. Segregation	Little of it. Status gap allows close but unequal contact.	Much of it. Narrowing of status gap makes for increase of spatial gap.
7. Psychological syndrome	Internalized subservient status. No personality "need" for prejudice. No high F. Pseudo tolerance.	"Need" for prejudice. High F. Linked with sexuality, sadism, frustration. Scapegoating.
8. Stereotypes of lower caste	Childish, immature, exuberant, uninhibited, lazy, impulsive, fun-loving, good-humored. Inferior but lovable.	Aggressive, uppity, insolent, oversexed, dirty. Inferior, despicable, and dangerous.
9. Intensity of prejudice	Fairly constant.	Variable, and sensitive to provocative situations.

C. Social Control Variables

	Paternalistic	Competitive
1. Form of government	Aristocratic, oligarchic, autocratic. Either centralized or feudal. Colonial.	Restricted or partial democracy.
2. Legal system	Lower caste has separate legal status. Law on side of racial status quo. Weber's traditional type of authority.	Lower caste has no separate legal status. Resort to extra-legal sanctions. Weber's rational-legal type of authority.

is also found in urban societies. As regards Toennies' *Gemein-schaft-Gesellschaft* dichotomy, the correspondence to our two types is perhaps closer. The paternalistic type has many *Gemein-schaft* characteristics, and a *Gesellschaft* society is most compatible with the competitive type.

Subject to the reservations mentioned above, Table 1–2 schematizes the relationship between our dichotomy and the distinctions reviewed above.

TABLE 1-2

	Paternalistic Type	Competitive Type
Max Weber's types of authority	Traditional	Rational-legal (occasionally: charismatic)
Parsons' pattern variables	Ascription, particularism, affectivity, collective orientation, diffuseness	Achievement, universalism, affective neutrality, self-orientation, specificity
Durkheim's forms of solidarity	Mechanical-organic mixture	Organic
Toennies	*Gemeinschaft*	*Gesellschaft*
Redfield	Folk or urban	Urban

Applicability of the Paternalistic-Competitive Distinction and the Problem of "Mixed Types"

We must first answer the question: Is our scheme synchronic or diachronic? The answer is that it is both. Historically, at least in Western societies since the first period of overseas expansion in the fifteenth century, the general tendency has been away from the paternalistic type and toward competitive prejudice. In that sense, then, our scheme is diachronic and evolutionary. But each of the two types can also be viewed as an existing situation in a given society. There is no *necessary* evolution from one type to the other. A competitive situation can prevail without having been preceded by a paternalistic one, as with Jews in medieval Europe; conversely, a paternalistic system can endure, barring disruptive factors, without leading to the competitive type, as between Watuzi and Bahutu in Ruanda-Urundi until the eve of independence.

There is another sense in which our scheme is to be regarded as synchronic. The two types of prejudice can coexist in different segments of the same society and toward different groups. One example comes to mind to illustrate this point, though it is not a case of racial prejudice. In medieval Europe, the prejudice against Jews in the cities was competitive, while the feudal lord-serf relationship in the rural areas was paternalistic.

We have already hinted that our scheme was applicable cross-culturally to non-Western societies. The argument that racial prejudice is a recent development limited to Western societies, and intended to rationalize the economic exploitation of subject peoples, is only a half-truth. True, the pseudo-scientific theories of racial differences have attained their most thorough elaboration in the Western world with the writings of Gobineau and the popularization of Social Darwinism. That such theories provided convenient justifications for the exploitation of "native" labor and slaves in the European colonies is likewise incontrovertible. But the exploitation preceded the development of the theories, and a simplistic view that the theories were devised with the Machiavellian purpose of justifying the colonial system is untenable. The main point, however, is that racial prejudice is much older than Gobineau and not limited to the Western world. Whenever phenotypical differences have existed between groups of people, racial prejudice seems to have arisen. The Bantu groups of Central Africa regard the pygmies who live among them as intermediate between chimpanzees and men. The Japanese express contempt for the bearded Ainu of Hokkaido. The Chinese expressed bewilderment at the sight of the first Europeans who landed in their country and compared the Europeans to monkeys because of their hairiness. In India, there is considerable evidence that the caste system originated in racial differences between Aryan conquerors and Dravidians, though, of course, race alone does not account for the florescence of caste. In short, physically distinguishing characteristics are generally seized upon to perpetuate group differences and establish the superiority of one group over the other.

Not only does our scheme apply to non-Western societies. It also applies *mutatis mutandis* to forms of prejudice other than racial. The competitive ethnic and religious prejudice against Jews in Europe and the United States is an example of nonracial prejudice. Similarly, the paternalistic syndrome can be found in a wide variety of contexts: between the factory owner and his workers; between the company or ship commander and his men. In this study, however, we shall limit ourselves to specifically racial prejudice.[11]

The problem of "mixed types" is crucial in any ideal-type scheme. As ideal types are logical constructs, it is important not to reify them. The fact that no empirical situation coincides exactly with one of the types does not invalidate a typology. But, as in any scientific theory, heuristic usefulness is a paramount consideration. A distinction should be made here between schemes that are constructed in terms of a continuum between two or more poles and schemes based on what we may call a "true typology." The first sort of scheme admits of all intermediate positions on the continuum; even a normal distribution where most cases are found in the middle of the continuum, and none at the extremes, is compatible with this sort of scheme.

A true typology, in the restricted sense in which we use that term, implies an empirical polarization of cases around the extremes and qualitative rather than quantitative differences. "Mixed cases" must be inherently unstable and tend to move toward one of the ideal types. We believe that our dichotomy satisfies this condition. Societies have moved from the paternalistic to the competitive type of prejudice and hence must have gone through a "mixed" stage. But the social system as a whole tends to continue to evolve until the competitive situation is rather closely approximated. It cannot remain in a stable intermediate position between the polar opposites. Mixed types at the total society level of analysis can only be transitory. But there is another sense in which mixed types can occur. Subsystems in the society can belong in different types, as in the case of medieval Europe mentioned earlier. Different groups in the same society can be the object of different types of prejudice. Also, in the case of a society in transition, different segments of the total society (as rural versus urban) can be in different stages in the process of evolution. The isolated rural areas will tend to remain paternalistic longer than the industrial centers, for example. All these possibilities can make the over-all characterization of a total society a complex matter. But again, this does not invalidate the criterion of polarization. It is only a question of defining the boundaries of the social system or subsystem under analysis.

NOTES

1. The labels *paternalistic* and *competitive* will be used in conjunction with the term "prejudice" when the psychological reference is emphasized and with the term "race relations" when sociological or social system factors are stressed.
2. In agreement with Dollard, Warner, Myrdal, and others, we shall call "caste" a group which satisfies all three of the following criteria: (1) endogamy, (2) membership therein by birth and for life, and (3) a position of superiority or inferiority vis-à-vis other such groups.
3. Professor Parsons suggested to us an important distinction between social stratification as a product of internal differentiation in the social system and social stratification imposed from the outside. In the latter case, the hierarchy is likely to be rigid. In fact, most caste or quasi-caste systems, such as estates, have their origin in conquest. The greater the disparity in physical characteristics, level of organization, technology, and so forth between conqueror and conquered, the greater is the likelihood of a caste system to arise. Of course, a caste system may perpetuate itself long after these differences have been blurred, as exemplified by India.
4. Cf. Robert E. Park, *Race and Culture* (Glencoe: The Free Press, 1950), p. 183; Bertrand W. Doyle, *The Etiquette of Race Relations in the South* (Chicago: University of Chicago Press,

1937); and Pierre L. van den Berghe, "Distance Mechanisms of Stratification," *Sociology and Social Research* 44 (1960): 155–164.

5. John Dollard, *Caste and Class in a Southern Town* (New Haven: Yale University Press, 1937); Abraham Kardiner and Lionel Ovesey, *The Mark of Oppression* (New York: Norton, 1951).

6. Roger Bastide, *Sociologie et Psychanalyse* (Paris: Presses Universitaires de France, 1950), pp. 241–245.

7. Gunnar Myrdal, *An American Dilemma* (New York: Harper, 1944), pp. 21, 39, 84–89, 460, 614, 899.

8. If one conceives of spatial distance and social distance as alternative mechanisms of social control in a racial caste situation, certain theoretical considerations follow. Both mechanisms are based on the ascriptive criterion of race and hence involve a "cost" in efficiency, at least in the sense of economic rationality. To quote Linton, "The ascription of status sacrifices the possibility of having certain roles performed superlatively well to the certainty of having them performed passably well." (Cf. Ralph Linton, *The Study of Man* [New York: Appleton-Century, 1936], p. 129.) But social distance involves a great measure of functional differentiation insofar as the members of the various castes perform tasks that are largely complementary. Spatial distance, on the contrary, involves a large degree of segmentation without differentiation, insofar as tasks, facilities, and functions are duplicatory rather than complementary. If the considerations above are correct, they may in part account for the greater degree of in-built maladjustment in the competitive type of race relations. An industrial competitive type of society which "needs all the differentiation it can get" can afford the luxury of segmentation even less than a preindustrial paternalistic society. Yet the tendency is toward spatial segregation as a substitute for social distance. This is one of the inherent paradoxes of the competitive type.

9. Gordon W. Allport, *The Nature of Prejudice* (Cambridge: Addison-Wesley, 1954), pp. 285–286.

10. Thomas F. Pettigrew, "Regional Differences in Anti-Negro Prejudice," (Thesis, Harvard University, 1956).

11. This limitation of our subject matter is heuristic rather than substantive. We do not believe that racial prejudice is fundamentally different from the other forms of prejudice. We con-

ceive rather of racial prejudice as a special case of a more general phenomenon. But the relative permanency of physical characteristics makes for a more rigid definition of groups and for more clear-cut and enduring situations than in other forms of prejudice.

2

Distance Mechanisms
of Stratification

Many observers and students of race relations have pointed to an apparent paradox in the practice of segregation in the southern United States and elsewhere. Although the majority of southern whites believe in school segregation between Negro and white pupils, they have no objection to entrusting their children to colored servants.[1] At the height of Jim Crowism in the South, Negro nurses in charge of white children were admitted without question to "white" railway carriages, public parks, and the like.[2] Although many white southerners would not think of inviting a Negro university professor to dinner in their home, they do not object to having their food cooked and served by a colored servant. To cite a more macabre illustration from another culture, Indian medical students in South Africa are not allowed to watch a postmortem examination performed on a white corpse, but that very corpse is sewed up after the autopsy by a black hospital attendant.[3]

Incongruous though such attitudes and practices may seem, the paradox is only apparent. As observed by several social scientists, the key to the problem is *social status*.[4] As long as the social status of the races is unequal, segregation need not be enforced.

Reprinted from *Sociology and Social Research* 44, no. 3 (January–February 1960): 155–164.

In the field of social therapy, the importance of the status variable in changing prevailing stereotypes and attitudes has been demonstrated by many empirical studies.[5] Contact per se does not reduce prejudice, but equal-status contact does, barring conditions of competition whether real or perceived. In this chapter we shall attempt to draw more general theoretical conclusions from these observations and findings.

The central concept to be used here is that of *distance* as a mechanism of stratification. Some form of distance is presumably a functional prerequisite in any social situation involving authority, hierarchy, or stratification. For analytical purposes, forms of distance can be classified as *spatial* (of which segregation is a notable instance) and *social* (such as etiquette and sumptuary regulations). No formal definitions of the two terms are required, as the meaning of the first term is self-evident, and the second term already has a long history in social science.[6]

Presumably, a combination of both forms of distance will be present in any hierarchical or authoritative situation, though in various combinations. Distance is a major mechanism of social control for the maintenance of authority and hierarchy. If everything else remains constant, close physical or social contact can be achieved only at a "cost" in authority and hierarchization.

In order to illustrate the generality of these propositions, three examples will be given before drawing the implications of the concept of distance for the field of race and ethnic relations.

In the relations between the sexes in Western culture, gallantry is a form of social distance. It has been repeatedly observed that, at least in Western societies, the lower the status of women is in relation to that of men, the more punctilious the rules of gallantry are. In Italy, Spain, Portugal, and Latin America, where the status of women is the lowest of all Western countries, both gallantry and spatial distance (chaperonage and the like) are the most developed. The reverse is true of the Anglo-Saxon and Scandinavian countries. Other European nations occupy an intermediate position; modern France, for example, still practices much gallantry (though hand-kissing is rapidly disappearing), but relatively little segregation of the sexes. The hope of some American women to revive gallantry while preserving a measure of status equality with men seems to be a forlorn Utopia. Similarly, as the status gap between the sexes decreases, differences in dress become less (sumptuary regulations are also a form of social distance). In the Islamic countries, the relatively low status of women is accompanied by a great amount of segregation.

The problem of authority of adults over children in the family, whether nuclear or extended, offers another illustration of the principle of distance. In order to maintain such authority, a combination of spatial and social distance is at work. Though spatial distance is minimal, some form of "segregation" in sleeping or eating arrangements is generally present. But social distance is of paramount importance here. Homans and Schneider have indicated that the child must show respect and restraint toward the adult who has authority over him—his father in patrilineal societies, his mother's brother in the matrilineal case.[7]

The military is another illustration of the institutionalization of distance. Since the military hierarchy is very rigid, a high degree of both spatial and social distance separates commissioned officers from the lower ranks. In the case of a peacetime army, spatial distance between officers and men is very great indeed. Living quarters, dining halls, recreation facilities, and the like are segregated. Whatever physical contact officers and men have is ritualized under a rigid etiquette known in the U.S. Armed Forces as "military courtesy." This etiquette, which most enlisted men (excepting a few old "accommodated" N.C.O.'s) find irksome and superfluous, is probably a "safety margin" intended for wartime conditions, when spatial distance breaks down to a large extent. Besides close physical contact under battle conditions, one of the two main kinds of *social* distance to which the Army resorts, namely, uniform differences (a form of sumptuary regulation), is also reduced in combat. Battle uniforms are nearly identical for all ranks in modern armies. Hence, etiquette remains as the principal mainstay of authority under the conditions which constitute the very raison d'être of military organizations. It is, therefore, little wonder that "military courtesy" should be cultivated in peacetime to a degree which appears excessive to most people concerned.

In the illustration above, we have indicated that spatial and social forms of distance can be not only complementary but also alternative to each other. As a further indication of this, it may be pointed out that the Navy, in which spatial distance aboard ships in peacetime is by necessity lesser than in peacetime Army units on land, has an even more rigid etiquette than the Army. Furthermore, sumptuary regulations (another device of social distance) are much more pronounced in the Navy than in the Army. Whereas Army uniforms have become "democratized," the difference between the uniform of a sailor and that of a Navy officer is still very great. Given a like requirement for authority as between Navy and Army, it may be said that the Navy "compensates" for its lesser degree of spatial distance with a greater degree of social distance.

We can now turn to some implications of the considerations above for the field of race relations. In the previous chapter we have suggested a typology of racial prejudice.[8] We distinguish two ideal types which we call *paternalistic* and *competitive*. The paternalistic type is characterized among other traits by the existence of a rigid and elaborate etiquette of race relations and the relative absence of segregation. In the competitive type, the reverse relationship between spatial and social distance prevails: the etiquette is ill defined and not complex, whereas segregation is pronounced.

In the paternalistic situation, where the type-role between members of different racial castes is the master-servant relationship, close physical and emotional ties between the castes prevail.[9] Doyle and Park were among the first social scientists to recognize the crucial importance of etiquette in such an "accommodative" sort of race relations. Park defines etiquette as a social ritual which maintains social distance. Etiquette, concludes Doyle, makes a measure of cooperation possible by preserving rank and order of precedence between the groups in presence. Myrdal speaks of etiquette as one of the primary mechanisms of social control that permit intimacy of contact coupled with status inequality.[10]

When, because of a complex of factors such as social and geographical mobility brought about by industrialization and urbanization, the paternalistic type of race relations breaks down, etiquette ceases to be an effective mechanism to preserve distance between the racial castes in presence. One of the requirements for an effective functioning of etiquette is that the roles be unambiguous; this condition ceases to prevail when the traditional master-servant ties are disrupted. As the situation evolves toward what we have called the competitive type of race relations, segregation is introduced as an alternative means of maintenance of the caste hierarchy.

In the context of race relations, segregation and etiquette emerge, then, as two primary mechanisms of spatial and social distance, respectively. Both are aimed at preserving a caste hierarchy of socially defined "races."[11] Insofar as etiquette and segregation in this case are both based on the ascriptive criterion of "race," they involve a cost in efficiency, at least in the sense of *Zweckrationalität*. There is, however, an important respect in which etiquette and segregation are functionally different from each other. Etiquette involves a great measure of functional differentiation in the sense that members of the various castes perform tasks which are largely complementary. Segregation, on the contrary, involves a large degree of segmentation without differentiation insofar as tasks, facilities, and functions are duplicatory rather than complementary. If the "separate but equal" doctrine is applied, the cost of segregation is maximized. This fact is one of the reasons why the separate but equal precept has remained a Utopia, even when interpreted in purely physical terms, quite apart from subjective, psychological considerations.

If these considerations are correct, we can see that segregation involves an even greater cost in the efficiency of the social system than etiquette. Indeed, etiquette in a relatively stable, preindustrial, paternalistic type of society can perform a definitely adjustive function. To the extent that roles are ritualized and unambiguous, and that everyone "knows his place," race relations will be relatively stable and peaceful.[12] On the other hand, segregation in an industrial competitive society is inherently dysfunctional for the social system as a whole. The extent of functionality as between the two types of prejudice is one of the major differences between the paternalistic and the competitive types.[13]

We can now turn to two brief illustrations of etiquette and segregation as alternative mechanisms of color-caste hierarchization. It is a well-known fact that segregation in the southern United States increased markedly after the Civil War. In the antebellum paternalistic South, the type-role between whites and Negroes was the master-slave relationship.[14] This is, of course, not to say that *all* Negroes were slaves and *all* whites, or even a majority of whites, were slaveholders. But most Negro-white contacts up to Emancipation were of the master-slave variety. There was some spatial segregation between whites and Negroes, particularly for field slaves. But house servants lived in very close spatial contact with their masters, as chambermaids, concubines, "mammies," body servants, and so on. They often lived in the "big house" of the plantation as members of the patriarchal household; they worshiped in the same churches as their masters; white and Negro children played together.[15] It is far from our intention to romanticize the past and evoke images of happy singing slaves. But the fact remains that masters and slaves lived in comparatively close spatial symbiosis and that most whites did not look with horror on physical contact with Negroes. Miscegenation was widely tolerated and frequent, though, of course, intermarriage was unknown.[16] Nevertheless, there existed a rigid caste line, which, in the relative absence of segregation, was maintained by a complex etiquette. The Negro had to "know his place," exhibit the proper marks of subservience, use the appropriate titles in addressing whites. Ideally, he internalized his lower-caste status and accepted his master's estimate of his own worth.[17]

Of course, much of that etiquette has survived Emancipation in the South, particularly in the rural regions of the Black Belt. The Civil War, however, disrupted very abruptly the old master-slave relationship, with the result that the South moved from a paternalistic to a competitive type of race relations. With the subsequent migration of Negroes to cities and the rise of industrialization in the South, the old etiquette, which was based on stable, highly particularistic, and personalized ties, became rapidly incompatible with the changing situation. The increased mobility of Negroes, both spatially and socially, made the crystallization of a new etiquette difficult.[18] Whatever was left of the old etiquette was only a vanishing survival of another era. If the color-caste order was to be maintained, new mechanisms had to be devised.

One of these new mechanisms was the lynching of Negroes, which increased very rapidly at the end of the Civil War. Another mechanism was segregation. In his history of segregation, C. Vann Woodward rightly points out that the main wave of Jim Crowism did not set in until some twenty years after the end of the Reconstruction era. But some important aspects of segregation were introduced during the Reconstruction period, notably segregation in churches and in schools.[19]

The lull in the implementation of segregation between the end of the Reconstruction period and the wave of Jim Crowism of the 1890's is to be accounted for, in large part, by the fact that the "Redeemer" politicians were mostly members of the old slave-owning aristocracy, with a strong tradition of paternalism. With the downfall of this upper-class white rule, segregation and political disenfranchisement followed. Extralegal segregation anticipated even the most drastic Jim Crow laws.[20] A whole set of rationalizations was developed to justify segregation. Negroes were considered unclean, smelly, lascivious, and hence the thought of close physical contact became abhorrent to most whites. Miscegenation was seriously condemned and probably much less common.[21]

A dramatic illustration of etiquette and segregation as alternative mechanisms of caste hierarchy is provided by the housing situation in American cities. In the older cities of the South, such as Charleston, South Carolina, which had a sizable Negro population before the Civil War, there is relatively little racial segregation in housing. Many Negroes live in back alleys near "white" houses, in what were formerly servants' quarters. In these cities, which are little industrialized, the traditional etiquette of race relations is still operative. This situation contrasts markedly with the high degree of residential segregation in the newer industrial cities of the South and in the Negro ghettos of the northern cities. In these cities, conditions of rapid migration and industrialization prevent the establishment of a rigid racial etiquette.[22]

From this very cursory examination of the racial situation in the southern United States, we would suggest that etiquette and segregation are two main mechanisms of caste hierarchization in a multiracial society.[23] Segregation, the more "costly" of the two major mechanisms, was introduced as an attempt to salvage the color-caste system, which was undermined by the decay of the old etiquette. If these conclusions are correct, it would be safe to predict that the present attack on segregation in the United States must lead to a decline in the importance of color as a criterion of hierarchization.[24]

Another illustration of the shift from etiquette to segregation is the case of South Africa. The Cape Colony in the seventeenth and eighteenth centuries had a paternalistic slaveowning type of society similar in many ways to that of the southern United States, though on a much smaller scale. Masters and slaves lived in close, intimate physical contact. Miscegenation was common, and interracial concubinage was institutionalized. Masters and slaves worshiped together. Household servants often lived in the same house as their masters; female slaves did sewing and embroidery work together with their mistresses in the family parlor.[25]

Yet, there was a rigid color-caste system, which was maintained by an elaborate etiquette of race relations with a wealth of terms of address.[26] With the abolition of slavery in 1834, the discovery of the diamond and gold mines later in the nineteenth century, and the large-scale industrialization and urbanization since the Anglo-Boer War of 1899–1902, South Africa has moved steadily toward a competitive type of prejudice. Although, as in the southern United States, relics of the old system of race relations can still be found, etiquette as a mechanism of caste hierarchy has been seriously undermined, and racial segregation has been substituted for it.

Since 1948, the apartheid policies of the Nationalist government have received much publicity. Because of space limitations, it is impossible to review all the segregation legislation passed by the South African Parliament. Apartheid, to be sure, represents a post-World War II intensification of the segregation doctrines, but it is merely a new label for a long-standing practice in South

Africa. The apartheid program is the culmination of a trend that started with the establishment of Native Reserves under a British administration in the middle of the nineteenth century. By now, the wave of color-bar legislation and extralegal segregation has covered most aspects of life.[27]

Contrary to the recent trend in the United States, South Africa has been moving toward increasing segregation in the last decade. But powerful economic and ideological forces militate against the long-range success of apartheid. In both countries, the built-in dysfunctional nature of racial segregation in an industrial society is well illustrated. Though segregation was introduced in both cases, at least in part, in response to changing conditions of industrialization and urbanization, segregation conflicts with certain functional prerequisites of any industrial society. Among these necessary conditions are mobility of the labor force, "rational" criteria of recruitment based on achievement and universalism, and functional differentiation, all of which are impeded by racial segregation.

Besides economic forces, segregation also undergoes a powerful ideological onslaught in the United States. South Africa, in spite of her relative cultural isolation, cannot escape a similar onslaught on apartheid. It seems, thus, that racial segregation, at least in a Western industrial society, truly contains the "seeds of its own destruction."

In summary, we have suggested that: (1) some form of distance, whether spatial or social, is basic to any situation involving authority, hierarchy, or stratification; (2) etiquette (social distance) and segregation (spatial distance) are basic mechanisms of hierarchization in a racial caste situation; (3) these two mechanisms have tended to vary in inverse relation to each other during the transition of multiracial societies from a paternalistic to a competitive type of race relations; (4) whereas etiquette in a preindustrial, paternalistic society can be an adjustive mechanism, segregation in a competitive industrial society is inherently dysfunctional; (5) given the failure of both etiquette and segregation as mechanisms of color-caste hierarchization, physical appearance or race must decrease in importance as a criterion of status, at least in Western industrial societies. This does not mean, however, that racial prejudice will disappear in any foreseeable future.

NOTES

NOTE: We are indebted to Professors Talcott Parsons and Gordon W. Allport for stimulating advice and criticism, but the responsibility for the views contained in this chapter is entirely our own.

1. Cf. Charles S. Johnson, *Patterns of Negro Segregation* (New York: Harper, 1943), p. 118.
2. Cf. Robert E. Park, *Race and Culture* (Glencoe: The Free Press, 1950), p. 241.
3. Cf. G. H. Calpin, *Indians in South Africa* (Pietermaritzburg: Shuter and Shooter, 1949), p. 105.
4. Cf. Park, *op. cit.*, pp. 181–182, 232–233; Gunnar Myrdal, *An American Dilemma* (New York: Harper, 1944), p. 582; G. W. Allport, *The Nature of Prejudice* (Cambridge: Addison-Wesley, 1954), pp. 234, 276, 319–323; J. Greenblum and L. I. Pearlin, "Vertical Mobility and Prejudice," in R. Bendix and S. Lipset, *Class, Status, and Power* (Glencoe: The Free Press, 1953), pp. 480–500.
5. Cf. M. Deutsch and M. B. Collins, *Interracial Housing* (Minneapolis: University of Minnesota Press, 1951); Allport, *op. cit.*, pp. 261–268; D. M. Wilner, R. P. Walkley, and S. W. Cook, "Residential Proximity and Intergroup Relations in Public Housing Projects," *Journal of Social Issues* 8: 45–69; F. T. Smith, "An Experiment in Modifying Attitudes toward the Negro," *Teachers College Contributions to Education*, no. 887 (1943); M. Jahoda and P. S. West, "Race Relations in Public Housing," *Journal of Social Issues* 7: 132–139.
6. Cf. Park, *op. cit.*, p. 183; E. S. Bogardus, *Sociology* (New York: Macmillan, 1954), p. 536.
7. Cf. G. C. Homans and D. M. Schneider, *Marriage, Authority, and Final Causes* (New York: Free Press, 1955), p. 58. Interestingly enough, the authority relationship seems to preclude a close affective relationship to the same person. This finding is further corroborated by Bales's polarity between the "idea-man"

and the "best-liked" man in his small-group studies. Cf. T. Parsons, R. F. Bales, and E. A. Shils, *Working Papers in the Theory of Action* (Glencoe: The Free Press, 1953), p. 147.

8. Cf. Pierre L. van den Berghe, "The Dynamics of Racial Prejudice: An Ideal-Type Dichotomy," *Social Forces* 37: 128–141; see also Chapter 1 in the present volume.

9. One of the important corollaries of these close ties is the prevalence of miscegenation under a system of institutionalized concubinage. Cf. van den Berghe, *op. cit.*, p. 139.

10. Cf. Doyle, *op. cit.*, p. 171; Myrdal, *op. cit.*, p. 612; Park, *op. cit.*, p. 183.

11. In the use of the term "caste," we follow the Warner-Dollard-Myrdal-Davis and Gardner definition. Cf. John Dollard, *Caste and Class in a Southern Town* (New Haven: Yale University Press, 1937), pp. 62–97; Myrdal, *op. cit.*, pp. 674–675; W. L. Warner, "American Caste and Class," *American Journal of Sociology* 42: 234. We dissent from Cox's usage of the term. Cf. Oliver C. Cox, *Caste, Class and Race* (New York: Doubleday, 1948), pp. 3–5, 427–428, 489–498, 539.

12. This is *not* to say that "efficiency" in the sense of economic rationality will be maximized.

13. Cf. van den Berghe, *op. cit.*, p. 141.

14. Cf. Myrdal, *op. cit.*, p. 592–593.

15. Cf. C. Vann Woodward, *The Strange Career of Jim Crow* (New York: Oxford University Press, 1955), pp. 24–25; Charles Wagley and Marvin Harris, *Minorities in the New World* (New York: Columbia University Press, 1958), pp. 89, 122.

16. Cf. Myrdal, *op. cit.*, pp. 124–126; L. Wirth and H. Goldhamer, "The Hybrid and the Problem of Miscegenation," in Otto Klineberg, ed., *Characteristics of the American Negro* (New York: Harper, 1944), p. 267.

17. Cf. Myrdal, *op. cit.*, p. 701; Wagley and Harris, *op. cit.*, p. 122.

18. Cf. Johnson, *op. cit.*, pp. 119, 139; Myrdal, *op. cit.*, pp. 611, 614.

19. Cf. Woodward, *op. cit.*, pp. 14–15; Doyle, *op. cit.*, pp. 122–123.

20. Cf. Woodward, *op. cit.*, pp. 29–30, 38–39, 51–52, 66–69, 81–84.

21. Cf. Wirth and Goldhamer, *op. cit.*, pp. 273–274.

22. Cf. Wagley and Harris, *op. cit.*, pp. 143–146.

23. Other mechanisms, such as sumptuary regulations, lynchings, and pogroms, may also be present, but are of secondary importance. Lynching in the American South, for example, seems to

have been resorted to mostly when and where other mechanisms had been unsuccessful in preserving the traditional caste hierarchy and when the breakdown of that hierarchy was perceived by the dominant caste as a threat. In that sense, lynching was a "last resort" mechanism.

24. This is, of course, not to say that *racial prejudice* will disappear, but rather that a rigid system of color caste will be seriously undermined, as, indeed, it already is.

25. Cf. C. G. Botha, *Social Life in the Cape Colony in the 18th Century* (Cape Town: Juta, 1926), pp. 45, 97; I. D. MacCrone, *Race Attitudes in South Africa* (London: Oxford University Press, 1937), p. 69; J. S. Marais, *The Cape Coloured People, 1652–1937* (London: Longmans, Green, 1939), pp. 162–167, 169.

26. Cf. Botha, *op. cit.*, p. 50; Sheila Patterson, *Colour and Culture in South Africa* (London: Routledge and Kegan Paul, 1953), pp. 139–140.

27. Cf. Calpin, *op. cit.*, pp. 23, 33, 91, 169–171; G. M. Carter, *The Politics of Inequality, South Africa since 1948* (New York: Praeger, 1958); E. P. Dvorin, *Racial Separation in South Africa* (Chicago: University of Chicago Press, 1952); Leo Kuper, "The Control of Social Change, A South African Experiment," *Social Forces* 33 (October 1954).

3

Hypergamy, Hypergenation, and Miscegenation

The term *hypergamy* has been used for a long time to describe a matrimonial practice found in some castes of Hindu society. Robert E. Park suggested many years ago the widespread occurrence of hypergamy when he spoke of it as "a principle of human nature"[1] in connection with miscegenation, but he did not elaborate on his insight. The most systematic theoretical treatment of hypergamy is probably Kingsley Davis' article on "Intermarriage in Caste Societies,"[2] although the author did not extend his analysis to class societies.[3] The theoretical literature on the subject, then, is still scanty. In the present chapter we shall point to the widespread occurrence of hypergamy and try to make explicit the structural consequences of, and conditions for, the phenomenon.

Hypergamy is a form of marriage in which a woman marries a man of higher social status than her own, or better, than that of her family of orientation. Since the term applies only to *marriage,* we must reluctantly coin the more generic word *hypergenation* to cover such practices as concubinage.[4] The main necessary condition for hypergenation is, by definition, status differential. The term "status" in this chapter will refer to relative prestige positions rather than to specific statuses corresponding to roles. When

Reprinted from *Human Relations* 13, no. 1 (1960): 83–90.

we speak of status differential, we shall refer not to the relative position of men qua men as opposed to women qua women, but rather to the relative ranking of particular men and women qua members of social groups such as families, clans, "races," classes, and castes. Our analysis is thus restricted to societies in which some form of social stratification exists.

As hypergamy (or, by extension, hypergenation) involves an upward flow of women, it must have an effect on the sex ratio of the various groups in the hypergamous system. Assuming an approximately equal sex ratio between the groups to start with, hypergamy must create a surplus of women at the top of the hierarchy and a scarcity at the bottom.[5] We may, therefore, expect hypergenation to be accompanied by polygyny, monogamy combined with concubinage, or, alternatively, a high rate of spinsterhood at the top of the social hierarchy. Conversely bachelorhood or polyandry is likely to manifest itself at the bottom of the status scale. Of course, not all instances of polygyny are traceable to hypergamy. Polygyny can also be achieved by altering the sex ratio through war, capture of women, and so on or by marrying girls at an earlier age than boys, a very common practice. But in stratified societies, polygyny is almost invariably a high-status phenomenon as far as the men are concerned. Barring exceptional imbalances in the sex ratio or great discrepancies in age of marriage between men and women, polygyny in stratified societies must involve hypergamy. The same argument holds for hypergenation and plural concubinage.[6]

Before examining a few empirical cases, we may advance a hypothesis accounting for the widespread occurrence of hypergenation. We have already seen that *status* is central to the very definition of hypergenation. We shall hypothesize that the principle involved in hypergenation is *maximization of status*. Hypergenation will tend to occur when it involves a gain in status for the woman and her children and no commensurate loss of status for the male partner. Under those conditions, hypergenation is a method whereby the "sum of status" for any given couple and its offspring is maximized.

Obviously, such a condition can exist only if the woman, on

becoming a wife or a concubine, gains more status than the man loses. In the extreme, "ideal" case, the woman and her children assume the higher status of the man, and the man's status remains unchanged. In other words, the husband-father is the "status-giver" to the entire nuclear family, and the wife and children gain full acceptance in the high-status group of the father-husband. This ideal case can probably be approximated only where marriage takes place, but the same general principle would apply to concubinage. Hypergenous concubinage can be expected to take place so long as it is "better" to be the concubine or the illegitimate child of a high-status man than the wife or legitimate child of a low-status man.

The hypothesis of maximization of status implies, of course, that high status is desirable, everything else being equal. However, this assumption is, we think, fairly incontrovertible, indeed almost tautological. In no way does the hypothesis imply that other factors such as romantic love cannot override status considerations in mate selection. Some of these factors may even operate in direct opposition to, and impose limits on, hypergenation. Maximization of status merely predicts a statistical trend toward hypergenation.

We may best begin our rapid review of a few empirical instances with the Hindu type-case of hypergamy. The traditional Hindu stratification system was based on a complex hierarchy of *varnas* or classes of castes, *jatis* or castes, and subcastes. Subcastes were usually divided into exogamous clans or lineages, the exogamous unit in some of the higher castes being termed a *gotra*. Where it existed, the custom of hypergamy sometimes applied at the level of the exogamous unit, as among the Rajputs. The exogamous units of a caste were ranked in relation to each other, and a girl should, in theory, marry into a unit of higher rank than her own. In other cases, hypergamy took place between castes or caste categories adjacent in status, as among the higher-ranking Nambudiri Brahmins and the lower-ranking Nayars and Kshattriyas of Kerala.[7] Of caste hypergamy Karvé writes: "In the patrilineal Rajput hypergamy of the north, a woman secured a higher status for her children by marrying a man of a higher caste. A man's children did not lose caste by marrying women who were their equals or slightly lower in rank."[8]

Another instance of hypergenation is the Chinese custom of "buying" girls from poor families as concubines for well-to-do men. Of course, concubines did not enjoy the same status as legitimate wives, but the birth of a son gave a concubine a permanent status in the family of her male partner.[9]

The case of the modern United States class system is better documented by quantitative studies. The American case is different from the East Indian one insofar as there is no explicit rule of hypergamy. Indeed, the primary tendency, in statistical terms, is toward class endogamy. When marriages occur across class lines, however, the tendency seems to be strongly toward hypergamy. Women marry "up" more often than do men.[10] Insofar as there is any "rule" for class marriage, it is a negative one: women should not marry "down." As the father-husband, primarily through his role in the occupational structure, is the status-giver to the nuclear family, the woman is lifted up to the status level of her husband, and the husband's status is not markedly affected by his marrying down. Similarly, the status of the children, so long as they remain in their family of orientation, is determined much more by the status of their father than by that of their mother.

Of course, the preference for class endogamy sets limits on the extent of hypergamy. Other things being equal, a man will prefer to marry a woman from a social background similar to his own. But women are better able than men to compensate for low status by physical attractiveness. Even then, certain limits are imposed in the sense that a wife has to be socially presentable.

Since the sex ratio is approximately equal in the United States (at least in the young-adult age group), and since polygyny and infanticide are not allowed, hypergamy makes for a greater probability of spinsterhood in the upper classes. Indeed, the upper-class old maid has become almost proverbial in American culture. Conversely, at the bottom of the class structure, the fact that hobos are predominantly male and unmarried is probably not unrelated to hypergamy. The enlisted ranks of the regular armed forces also have a relatively high proportion of unmarried lower-class males.

Western European culture seems to be similar to American culture in respect to hypergamy, with the exception that the practice of concubinage is more widespread, at least in Latin Europe. It is fashionable for an upper-class Frenchman or Italian, for example, to keep a mistress, usually of a lower social status than his own (*demi-mondaines*). Europe differs, then, from the United States in having more hypergeneration as distinguished from hypergamy and, hence, a disguised polygyny at the top of the class hierarchy. But hypergamy is also not absent in Europe, as in the marriages of nobles with rich bourgeois girls. In such marriages, the wife and children acquire the title and status of the husband-father.

A similar practice existed in pre-Meiji Japan where daimyo and samurai men married daughters of merchants, although the merchants were very low in the social scale.[11] Another form of hypergeneration in Japan was the taking of concubines of lower social status. Noblemen took samurai concubines, and samurai took commoners. Although the position of concubines was distinctly inferior to that of wives, children of concubines were often adopted.[12] Geishas, a group of women of relatively low status, often became the concubines and even wives of wealthy and respectable men.[13] Of much interest is the Japanese custom of *yoshii* or adoption of a son-in-law. If a man has no sons, he tries to adopt a son-in-law for one of his daughters. The son-in-law takes the name of his adoptive father (and his title, should the father-in-law be a daimyo or a samurai), inherits his property, and resides matrilocally in his adoptive family. The adopted son-in-law, in this case, is usually a poor younger brother in his own family of orientation who has no claim to inheritance from his father, since Japan adheres to primogeniture. Occasionally, he may even come from a family of lower status than that of his adoptive in-laws. The custom of *yoshii* thus provides a test in reverse of our hypothesis. Where the status-giver, in this case, is the wife through her father, marriage tends to be *hypo*gamous.[14]

Miscegenation in various parts of the world provides one of the

the most interesting and clear-cut instances of the principle of hypergenation, as Park suggested many years ago.[15] We shall, therefore, examine the case of racial mixture in somewhat greater detail. The extent of miscegenation between whites and nonwhites since the fifteenth century hardly needs to be emphasized. The Portuguese in Brazil interbred extensively first with the Indians and, later, with Negro slaves, as witnessed by the variety of physical types existing in Brazil today. In the Spanish colonies, the conquerors mixed so extensively with the Indian population that, today, the mestizo group outnumbers both whites and Indians in many Spanish-American countries. In the West Indies miscegenation was likewise very common. On most of the islands, whites have always constituted small minorities, and the mass of the population exhibits all shades of color from pure black to café au lait.[16]

In the United States, only an estimated 22 per cent of American Negroes are of pure African ancestry, according to Herskovits,[17] and this estimate does not include the many light-skinned mulattoes who have, in fact "passed" into the white group. The presence of a large Coloured group in South Africa is evidence of the extent of miscegenation in that country. Today the Coloured number some 40 per cent of the white group, and many Coloureds have passed into the white group.[18]

All the examples cited above have many characteristics in common. They all exhibited, until the nineteenth century, a type of race relations that we have characterized in another paper as paternalistic.[19] All were, at some time between the sixteenth and the nineteenth centuries, agricultural societies based on servile or quasi-servile (peonage, debt slavery, and such) labor. All, except South Africa, had an economy based on what Freyre has called "latifundiary monoculture"[20] with large plantations named *fazendas* in Brazil, *haciendas* in Spanish America, *habitations* in Martinique, and so forth.[21]

Likewise, the type of miscegenation that took place was similar in all cases. It was overwhelmingly the result of institutionalized concubinage between white men and women of color; that is, it constituted a clear-cut case of hypergenation.

Although most white North Americans and South Africans now look on miscegenation with aversion if not with horror, interracial concubinage in the colonial or slavery period was widely tolerated.[22] The widespread occurrence of racial hypergenation in similar circumstances has given rise to many explanations. The sex ratio has been invoked as a cause of miscegenation.[23] It is true that the first white colonists were predominantly males, but so were the Negro slaves who were imported from Africa. Furthermore, this sex ratio, over time, tended to approach unity, as was certainly the case in the ante-bellum southern white population of the United States. And yet miscegenation did not cease.

It has been argued also that miscegenation took place simply because female slaves were forced to submit to their masters. Though undoubtedly true in many cases, this factor does not account for the absence of miscegenation in the other direction: between white mistresses and male slaves.

In the Brazilian case, Gilberto Freyre bases his causal explanation of miscegenation on the sexual attractiveness of the *morena* in Brazilian culture, which goes back in turn to the idealization of the "enchanted Moorish woman" in Portuguese culture.[24] Though this cultural element is undoubtedly present in Brazil, it hardly accounts for the generality of miscegenation.

Another main line of argument is that of economic motive. White slaveowners were eager to produce half-breed slaves because the latter were of higher monetary value.[25] This factor was undoubtedly operative, but it hides a more general cause, and it does not account for miscegenation in cases where there was no chattel slavery, as, for example, in the Mexican hacienda system with peon labor. The question then becomes: why were mulatto slaves worth more than Negro slaves?

The answer is that in the white scale of evaluation they were closer to the dominant whites both racially and culturally. In other words, the *status* of the mulatto was higher than that of the Negro. The emergence of a mulatto or mixed-breed middle class in many of these societies was common. To date, the Coloureds in South Africa enjoy a somewhat higher status than the full-blooded "Natives." In Brazil the amount of Negroid or Mongoloid traits is an inverse function of status. Within the American Negro group, the lighter the skin, the higher the status, other factors remaining constant.[26]

Interracial hypergenation, then, was a method whereby a woman of full color could raise the status of her offspring and, accessorily, her own status through preferential treatment.[27] As long as interracial concubinage was widely institutionalized, the white man, on his side, did not suffer a loss of status by having connections with colored women. The hypothesis of maximization of status is, then, supported.

Up to this point we have taken examples of miscegenation from the past. But this same kind of institutionalized hypergenation of colored women with white men continues to take place in modern African colonies. Data on intermarriage in modern Brazil are scanty, but available studies suggest that marriage between persons of widely different color is both rare and disapproved of. On the other hand, there is still much extramarital miscegenation between lower-class mulatto and Negro women and middle- and upper-class men.[28]

In South Africa and the United States, however, this type of hypergenation through concubinage has all but disappeared since both societies have moved from a paternalistic to a competitive type of race relations.[29] Concubinage of whites with colored women has been illegal in South Africa since 1927 and highly disapproved in both South Africa and the United States—in the latter country by both whites and Negroes. Interracial marriage has been prohibited in South Africa since 1949, as it has been in the majority of the American states until recent years.[30]

The virtual disappearance of hypergenous concubinage lends indirect support to our hypothesis of maximization of status. In the United States and South Africa the attitudes of whites against miscegenation became so strong that a white man could lose status by keeping a colored mistress. Conversely, among American Negroes, marriage to a Negro became preferable to being the concubine of a white man. Indeed being a white man's mistress often came to mean loss of respectability for a Negro woman in the Negro community. This form of hypergenation declined, then, as it ceased to entail maximization of status.

In South Africa, even before the ban on interracial marriages, whites constituted for all practical purposes an endogamous caste. Between 1925 and 1946, mariages of whites to nonwhites constituted less than 1 per cent of the total number of marriages involving whites, with a tendency to decline from 0.9 per cent in 1925 to 0.3 per cent in 1946. Of these interracial marriages, between 1940 and 1945, approximately 84 per cent involved white males to nonwhite females;[31] that is, the great majority of these marriages were hypergamous from the point of view of caste.

Similarly, in the United States, whites and Negroes constitute almost completely endogamous castes. In Los Angeles County, the percentage of Negro-white marriages to total marriages in 1948–1949 was less than 0.2 per cent. Of all marriages involving whites in Boston between 1914 and 1938, Negro-white marriages constituted bewteen 0.18 per cent and 0.10 per cent. Interracial marriages in the same city and period amounted to between 3.1 per cent and 5.2 per cent of all marriages involving Negroes. Similar findings hold for New York State.[32]

The few cases of interracial marriages that do occur, however, seem to contradict the hypergamy principle. In contrast to South Africa, most American interracial marriages (from 75 per cent to 93 per cent of all interracial marriages in the Wirth and Goldhamer samples) involve white females and Negro males. That is, from the point of view of *caste* they are *hypo*gamous. There is strong evidence, however, that a *class* factor is operative here. The female white partners tend to be lower-class and of immigrant stock, whereas the male Negro partners tend to be of upper- and middle-class status.[33] Merton has suggested that such marriages involved an exchange of high caste status on the part of the white women for high class status on the part of the Negro men.[34]

From the point of view of class these marriages tend to be hypergamous, thereby substantiating the general principle. A further confirmation of the class hypergamy hypothesis is that, whereas Negro grooms in interracial unions are of generally high socioeconomic status, Negro brides fail to show an occupational superiority.[35]

Marriages within the American Negro caste offer further

evidence of class hypergamy. Within the Negro caste, color is one of several criteria of class status. In consequence there is a tendency for Negroes to desire a "light" marriage partner.[36] It seems, however, that in most marriages where skin color between the spouses is noticeably different, the male is darker, although his general social-class status within the Negro caste is higher than that of the lighter-skinned female partner.[37] Again, the woman trades her lighter skin for the high social status of the man, and the marriage is hypergamous from the viewpoint of class.

Obviously, the evidence reviewed in this chapter is very selective and anything but conclusive. The hypothesis of maximization of status is only very tentatively supported by the evidence. Should the hypothesis be proven invalid on further testing, however, the *fact* of the widespread occurrence of hypergenation would still remain and would still have to be accounted for.

Summary

This chapter suggests the widespread occurrence of hypergamy, or more broadly hypergenation, in stratified societies. Some structural conditions for and consequences of hypergenation are drawn. The hypothesis of maximization of status is advanced to account for the phenomenon. The cases of India, China, Japan, the United States, and western Europe are briefly reviewed and found to lend tentative support to the hypothesis. Miscegenation in Brazil, the United States, and South Africa is examined as a special case of hypergenation and also found, in general, to confirm the hypothesis.

NOTES

1. Robert E. Park, *Race and Culture* (Glencoe: The Free Press, 1950), pp. 133–135.
2. Kingsley Davis, "Intermarriage in Caste Societies," *American Anthropologist* 43 (1941): 376–395.
3. Among other factors, Professor Davis suggests gain of status as

a condition favoring hypergamy. Our debt to him on this point will become clear later in this chapter. Insofar as Davis makes a sharp distinction between marital and extramarital unions, however, our views diverge on the interpretation of miscegenation. Helpful suggestions, criticisms, and germinal ideas were also contributed by Dr. E. Kathleen Gough and by Professors Claude Lévi-Strauss and Talcott Parsons, but the responsibility for the views herein expressed is entirely our own.

4. We are not suggesting that extramarital relations are functionally equivalent to marital ones in every respect, but rather that the line of legitimacy is not always clear-cut. Even where the distinction is unambiguous, extramarital relations, such as stable, institutionalized concubinage, overlap greatly in function with legal marriage. For our present purposes, the distinction between marriage and concubinage is one of degree of legitimacy and institutionalization.

5. We realize, of course, that the sex ratio can vary within statistical limits, and that it can be altered by such practices as war, female infanticide, capture of women, and so on. We do not feel, however, that these conditions invalidate our general demographic assumption.

6. An important distinction should be made between two types of concubinage. The variety where the male has high status is found mostly in conjunction with monogamy, as in classical China and in Europe, or with polygamy, as in Islamic countries. It is a source of prestige (although in Christian countries it is the source of much religious ambivalence) and is almost always hypergenous. On the other hand, the lower-class variety of loose, irregular sex unions of relatively short duration is a substitute for formal marriage. Partners of both sexes in such unions are of low status.

7. See E. A. H. Blunt, *The Caste System of Northern India* (London: Oxford University Press, 1931), pp. 1–9, 36–38, 43, 46–47; I. Karvé, *Kinship Organization in India* (Poona: Deccan College, 1953), pp. 59, 65, 116, 141–142, 144, 157; M. Opler and R. D. Singh, "The Division of Labor in an Indian Village," in C. S. Coon, ed., *A Reader in General Anthropology* (New York: Holt, 1948), pp. 464–496; M. N. Srinivas, *Religion and Society among the Coorgs of South India* (Oxford: Clarendon Press, 1952), p. 30.

8. Karvé, *op. cit.,* p. 269.

9. See D. H. Kulp, *Country Life in South China* (New York: Teachers College, Columbia, 1925), pp. 151, 174–175; Olga Lang, *Chinese Family and Society* (New Haven: Yale University Press, 1946), p. 221.

10. See W. L. Warner and P. S. Hunt, *The Social Life of a Modern Community* (New Haven: Yale University Press, 1941), pp. 101–102; J. A. Kahl, *The American Class Structure* (New York: Rinehart, 1957), p. 136; A. B. Hollingshead, "Cultural Factors in the Selection of Marriage Mates," *American Sociological Review* 15 (1950): 619–627; M. L. Barron, *People Who Intermarry* (New York: Syracuse University Press, 1946); R. Centers, "Marital Selection and Occupational Strata," *American Journal of Sociology* 54 (1948): 533–534. Many factors are involved in class hypergamy in the United States. Among them is the physical attractiveness that women can "trade" for lower-class status much more readily than can men. Another factor is education. More girls than boys complete high school and thereby secure jobs in the lower white-collar ranks as secretaries, nurses, and the like. Through their work they come into contact with professional men and increase their chances of hypergamy. Such opportunities for marrying "up" are not available to men.

11. E. O. Reischauer, *Japan, Past and Present* (New York: Knopf, 1956), p. 97.

12. Alice M. Bacon, *Japanese Girls and Women* (Boston and New York: Houghton Mifflin, 1892), p. 113.

13. *Ibid.,* p. 288.

14. *Ibid.,* pp. 103–106; Naomi Tamura, *The Japanese Bride* (New York: Harper, 1893), p. 7; R. N. Bellah, *Tokugawa Religion* (Glencoe: The Free Press, 1957), p. 47.

15. Park, *op. cit.,* pp. 133–135.

16. G. Freyre, *The Masters and the Slaves* (New York: Knopf, 1956), pp. xi–xii, xiv; E. B. Reuter, *Race Mixture* (New York: McGraw-Hill, 1931), pp. 33–35; H. Koster, *Travels in Brazil* (London: Longmans, 1816), pp. 385–394; S. A. Lowrie, "Racial and National Intermarriage in a Brazilian City," *American Journal of Sociology* 44 (1939): 685; C. Wagley and M. Harris, *Minorities in the New World* (New York: Columbia University Press, 1958), pp. 51, 106.

17. M. J. Herskovits, *The American Negro* (New York: Knopf, 1928), p. 9.

18. M. H. Alsop, *The Population of Natal* (Cape Town, London,

and New York: Oxford University Press, 1952), p. 10; J. S. Marais, *The Cape Coloured People, 1652–1937* (London: Longmans, Green, 1939), p. 283.

19. Pierre L. van den Berghe, "The Dynamics of Racial Prejudice: An Ideal-Type Dichotomy," *Social Forces* 37 (December 1958): 138–141. See also Chapter 1 in this volume.

20. Freyre, *op. cit.,* pp. xxiii-xxiv.

21. See Wagley and Harris, *op. cit.,* pp. 59, 100.

22. See Reuter, *op. cit.,* pp. 40–41; C. F. Marden, *Minorities in American Society* (New York: American Book, 1952); L. Wirth and H. Goldhamer, "The Hybrid and the Problem of Miscegenation," in O. Klineberg, ed., *Characteristics of the American Negro* (New York: Harper, 1944), pp. 253–369; I. D. MacCrone, *Race Attitudes in South Africa* (London: Oxford University Press, 1937), p. 69.

23. Wirth and Goldhamer, *op. cit.,* p. 263.

24. Freyre, *op cit.,* pp. 12–14.

25. Wirth and Goldhamer, *op. cit.,* p. 265.

26. D. Pierson, *Negroes in Brazil* (Chicago: University of Chicago Press, 1942), pp. 155, 159–160; Reuter, *op. cit.,* pp. 162, 189; Wagley and Harris, *op. cit.,* p. 117; Marais, *op. cit.,* p. 281; Muriel Horrell, *South Africa's Non-White Workers* (Johannesburg: Institute of Race Relations, 1956), pp. 87–90; C. Wagley, *Amazon Town* (New York: Macmillan, 1953), p. 128; Lowrie, *op. cit.*

27. Wirth and Goldhamer, *op. cit.,* p. 264.

28. Lowrie, *op. cit.,* p. 696; see also Chapter 6 in this volume.

29. Van den Berghe, *op. cit.,* pp. 138–141.

30. Muriel Horrell, *Non-European Policies in the Union and the Measure of Their Success* (Johannesburg: Institute of Race Relations, 1954), p. 30; Gunnar Myrdal, *An American Dilemma* (New York: Harper, 1944), pp. 62–63; Reuter, *op. cit.,* pp. 39, 82.

31. H. Sonnabend and C. Sofer, *South Africa's Step-Children* (Johannesburg: South African Affairs Pamphlets, n.d.), p. 26; Ellen Hellman, ed., *Handbook of Race Relations in South Africa* (Cape Town, London, and New York: Oxford University Press, 1949), p. 12.

32. R. J. R. Kennedy, "Single or Triple Melting-Pot?" *American Journal of Sociology* 47 (1944): 331–339; R. Risdon, "A Study

of Interracial Marriages," *Sociology and Social Research* 39 (1954): 93, 95.

33. *Ibid.*, p. 93; Reuter, *op. cit.*, p. 40; Wirth and Goldhamer, *op. cit.*, pp. 281–282, 289–292; St. C. Drake and H. Cayton, *Black Metropolis* (New York: Harcourt, Brace, 1945), pp. 137, 139, 140, 144–145; Barron, *op. cit.*, pp. 116–117.

34. R. K. Merton, "Intermarriage and the Social Structure: Fact and Theory," *Psychiatry* 4 (1941): 372.

35. Wirth and Goldhamer, *op. cit.*, p. 292.

36. Marden, *op. cit.*, p. 20.

37. M. J. Herskovits, *Cultural Anthropology* (New York: Knopf, 1955), p. 83; Reuter, *op. cit.*, p. 160.

4

Racialism and Assimilation in Africa and the Americas

The aim of this chapter is to refute a common misconception regarding the relationship between acculturation and miscegenation, on the one hand, and the presence or absence of racial prejudice and discrimination, on the other. Historical evidence from America and Africa makes untenable the notion that cultural assimilation and miscegenation are symptoms or consequences of a tolerant, nonracial ethos among the colonizers; it suggests, rather, that these factors are independently variable. We shall briefly examine the facts, refute partly or wholly several outwardly plausible explanations, and present an alternative thesis.

In outline, the facts are as follows. The Americas emerged from colonialism with a predominantly European culture, except for some of the remoter areas of the northern Andean region, the Amazon Basin, Paraguay, and Guatemala (not to mention smaller Indian pockets in southeastern Mexico, southwestern United States, and elsewhere). This remains true in spite of the fact that appreciable Indian and African influences are readily traceable in the modern national cultures of the Western Hemisphere and that unassimilated Indian minorities persist in most countries. A large

Reprinted from *Southwestern Journal of Anthropology* 19, no. 4 (Winter 1963): 424–432.

mestizo or mulatto population arose, except for the nontropical parts of the continent where the whites supplanted and almost completely exterminated the indigenous population without replacing it with Negro slaves. Furthermore, this dual process of cultural assimilation and genetic amalgamation was quite rapid, being already far advanced within fifty years of the conquest or of the importation of Negro slaves. In Africa, on the other hand, the European impact was considerably weaker, both culturally and "racially," except for South Africa, and more particularly the Cape Province. While all Africans were affected to some extent by colonialism, only a tiny educated elite became profoundly westernized, and there was comparatively little racial intermixture. Broadly speaking, the Americas are a cultural extension of Europe, and Africa is not.

Much has been made of the difference between the racialist, Protestant, Anglo-Saxon or Germanic countries and the tolerant, Catholic, Latin countries.[1] Undeniably, there is an important difference in the racial ethos of these two European subcultures, and this difference has influenced the development of race relations in the respective areas. Our argument is that the attitudes and policies of the colonizing power toward race and assimilation are not directly related to the degree of acculturation or miscegenation.

The thesis that the tolerance of the Spaniards and Portuguese facilitated miscegenation and westernization in Latin America is unconvincing for several reasons. Miscegenation, which took almost invariably the form of concubinage between white men and women of other races, is obviously not an expression of tolerance, but one of sexual exploitation of women, as Roger Bastide, Gilberto Freyre, and others rightly remarked.[2] Freyre, whose outlook is strongly psychoanalytic, interprets Brazilian miscegenation as an expression of sadism on the part of a decadent planter aristocracy toward Negro slaves. Others have stressed the economic motivation for the slaveowner to impregnate his female slaves, all the more so as mulatto slaves were generally more valuable than those of pure African descent. Some have pointed out that, by becoming a white man's mistress, a woman of color could improve her own status and that of her children. Finally, some authors have stressed that strongly ambivalent attitudes toward miscegenation have resulted from its "forbidden fruit" character. Whatever factors one chooses to emphasize, the incidence of miscegenation proves the biological unity of the human species, but not the absence of prejudice. Interracial concubinage is clearly an unequal and exploitative relationship, albeit an intimate one.

Similarly, a policy of cultural assimilation is a proof, not of liberalism, but rather of ethnocentrism and cultural (though *not* of racial) arrogance. The assimilationist policy of the Latin colonizers (France, Portugal, and Spain), whether in its early form of forced conversion to Catholicism or in its later secular version, has sometimes seemed liberal relative to British or Dutch attitudes. Even when only small elites of *évolués* or *assimilados* became absorbed into the dominant white group, the colonial policy of France and Portugal in Africa, for example, sometimes seemed progressive and tolerant by comparison with the rigid racial apartheid in South Africa. However, an assimilation policy simply reflects an unquestioning belief in one's cultural superiority coupled with the logical corollary that other people ought to be made to resemble one and to be valued to the extent that they do so. Such an attitude is more flexible than one which adheres to a theory of immutable racial inferiority, but assimilation and racialism are basically two different expressions of arrogance on the part of the dominant group.

Most importantly, the thesis does not accord with historical evidence, which indicates that in both America and Africa the actual amount of miscegenation and westernization has been largely unrelated to the racial outlook or the official policies of the colonial power. South Africa, the most westernized part of the continent, has followed a strongly racialist and antiassimilationist policy. Conversely, Angola and Mozambique are among the least Europeanized parts of Africa, in spite of the assimilationist and nonracial policies of Portugal. France, Portugal, and Spain have succeeded in assimilating their American colonies, but have failed to do so in Africa. British colonies of the Western Hemisphere are as westernized as those of the Latin powers, and, in Africa, Britain, like Portugal and France, failed to acculturate more than a small intelligentsia.

Why then is not Angola a second Brazil, or Nigeria a second Canada? Several factors suggest themselves as plausible explanations. The West met no cultural competitor in the New World comparable to Islam in the Old. However, the Western impact was not markedly stronger in the non-Muslim parts of Africa than in the Islamic countries (including the Sudan belt). To be sure, Christian missionaries made many fewer converts in Muslim than in "pagan" areas; and, as Western education in Africa was largely in the hands of the missions, particularly in the British colonies, certain Muslim areas (like northern Nigeria) are much less westernized and more traditionalist than neighboring non-Muslim regions (such as southern Nigeria). On the other hand, the predominantly Muslim country of Senegal is by far the most gallicized of the former French territories in Africa south of the Sahara.

European colonization of the New World lasted, on the whole, much longer than in Africa. Nevertheless, the Congo kingdom, which has been colonized in depth by Portugal for as long as Brazil,[3] is no more Portuguese than Nigeria is British; and, conversely, the most recently colonized parts of the New World (western North America) are, if anything, more predominantly European in culture than some of the oldest areas of European conquest (for example, Peru). European cultural dominance was established very quickly in the New World, typically within two generations of conquest, that is, within a period comparable to the duration of late European colonialism in Africa.

Yet another line of argument to explain differences is in terms of the culture of the conquered peoples. Although nomads and pastoralists have, on the whole, shown a greater resilience to Western influence than agriculturalists, this factor helps to account for some of the differences *within* the two continents, but not between them. On both continents the Europeans met a wide variety of cultures from unstratified and politically undifferentiated nomadic societies to large, urbanized, and stratified states.

If anything, the latter type of society was probably more widespread in precolonial Africa than in pre-Columbian America.

One may finally argue that the proportion of European settlers in the New World was much greater than it ever was in Africa. Taking the Western Hemisphere as a whole, the statement is true. However, massive European immigration to the Americas was largely a post-1840 phenomenon and was mostly confined to nontropical America. Most whites came to America long after it had become culturally Western, and, in tropical America where whites were in a small minority, they have nevertheless imposed their culture to a much greater extent than anywhere in Africa, except perhaps in the Cape Province of South Africa. This was true in spite of the fact that, from the late seventeenth to the mid-nineteenth century, the slave trade brought a steady flow of involuntary African immigrants to the New World. Even the most heavily Negro areas of the West Indies (Jamaica, Haiti, Guadeloupe, Martinique), where "pure" whites were small minorities, have been much more Western than the oldest Portuguese colonies in Africa.

The various factors mentioned above (and indeed many other factors) may have played some role in determining the extent of westernization. But even taken jointly, they leave a large factual residue unaccounted for. What alternative explanation can we suggest?

In America, the colonizers encountered basically two types of situation. Where they met low-density, nomadic societies (notably in Canada, Alaska, the United States, Argentina, and Brazil), the indigenous culture was quickly obliterated, its carriers being practically exterminated through disease, starvation, or war. A similar development took place in the West Indies. Where smallpox epidemics did not wipe out the indigenous population (as happened in much of the Caribbean), the expansion of the European settlements in the nineteenth century took a heavy toll, both directly through frontier warfare and indirectly through the annexation or destruction of means of subsistence (land, buffaloes) and the importation of firearms, horses, and liquor with all their destructive consequences.

In the southern United States, the West Indies, and Brazil, large numbers of Negro slaves replaced the native population as a servile labor force. There has probably never been as ruthlessly efficient an agency of cultural assimilation as European chattel slavery. Given the circumstances of the slave trade and of plantation life, the survival of *any* African cultural traits in America is more surprising than the paucity thereof. By the time an African slave reached the New World, he had already undergone an abrupt and traumatic separation from his family and, in most cases, from his countrymen, followed by several months of confinement and travel under conditions of extraordinary hardship. Random distribution on plantations and mines prevented linguistic regroupings, except fortuitously and on a small scale. The institution of slavery also prevented the reorganization of any stable family life, so that the "atomized" individual had no option but to adopt the culture of his master. Furthermore, slave women, due to a number of factors already mentioned, interbred extensively with white men and gave rise within one or two generations to a westernized mulatto population. Slavery was thus not only a cultural but also a genetic melting pot. This was about as true in "tolerant" Brazil, where the Catholic church encouraged the baptism and assimilation of slaves, as in the "racialist" English colonies, with their harsh slave laws and largely unproselyting Protestant denominations. If anything, there are more survivals of African culture in Brazil than in the southern United States.

The only part of Africa where a similar situation led to similar results was in the Cape Province at the southern tip of the continent.[4] The sparse nomadic population of Hottentots and Bushmen was decimated by smallpox, exterminated by Boer commandos in frontier warfare, pushed back to the most inhospitable parts of the Kalahari, or reduced to serfdom by the pastoral Boers. In the settled districts around Cape Town, a slave population from Madagascar, the Dutch East Indies, and Mozambique replaced the native nonwhites and furnished the necessary servile labor for the white farmers. Extensive miscegenation and westernization resulted in the formation of a relatively homogeneous population of Cape Coloureds who today number 1.8 millions. The Cape Province of South Africa stands in sharp contrast to the other three provinces of the Republic where miscegenation was much less common and where the Western cultural impact on the African population was much more restricted, although more profound than almost anywhere in tropical Africa.

The second type of European conquest in the New World is exemplified in the Mesoamerican and Andean area where the Spaniards met large agricultural societies with complex political organizations. The pattern there was a devastatingly quick and brutal conquest, followed by wholesale and deliberate destruction of the indigenous culture, a shattering of the traditional politico-religious ruling class, and forced Christianization. After these societies had been "beheaded" of their cultural superstructure, the peasantry was reduced to peonage under the encomienda system. As in the case of Negro slavery, there was extensive miscegenation and relatively rapid acculturation, giving rise to large populations of hispanicized mestizos.

Compared to plantation slavery, the encomienda system was less disruptive of traditional institutions, however. In some instances, as in the drafting of mine workers, the exploitation of Indian labor by the Spaniards was extremely ruthless, but in many cases the lot of the peasantry was not drastically changed from what it had been in pre-Columbian times. Kinship ties and family organization could, on the whole, be maintained. The Catholic church was typically content with formal allegiance through baptism, and it tolerated syncretism with traditional beliefs and practices. Westernization was consequently less rapid than under the system of Negro slavery. Indeed, Indian elements are far from negligible in the national cultures of such countries as Mexico, Guatemala, Peru, or Bolivia. In some of the more isolated areas of these republics, Indian peasant communities have succeeded in retaining an impoverished version of their traditional cultures, in spite of their formal adherence to Christianity.[5] Generally, however, the rapidity with which Spain destroyed the large Indian states, effectively occupied enormous territories, and imposed its religion, language, and customs is astonishing and quite unparalleled in the European conquest of Africa. Within fifty years of Cortez's and Pizarro's arrival, much of America was already strongly hispanicized.

In Africa, the pattern of European conquest was completely different, except for South Africa. Until the second half of the nineteenth century, Africa largely consisted, as far as Europe was concerned, of an inhospitable coastline where slaves could be captured or purchased for the American colonies and where ships on their way to the East Indies might replenish their supplies. The scramble for Africa, which characterized the last quarter of the nineteenth century, was, of course, anything but orderly and peaceful; but, on the whole, it was not accompanied by wholesale extermination or by forced acculturation. The whites in Africa (except in South Africa and Algeria and to a lesser extent in Southern Rhodesia, Angola, and Kenya) remained mostly an expatriate and transient ruling minority, which neither assimilated the African majority culturally nor interbred extensively with it. As to the traditional legal and political structures, they were retained in modified form to suit the needs of the colonial administration.

After the conquest, Africa was economically exploited and politically oppressed by the colonial powers, but there did not develop a stable system of plantation slavery or peonage as in America. Instead, the dominant source of labor was through more or less forced conscription or "recruitment" of temporary, migrant workers, serving limited terms away from their families (in prison, in the army, in road gangs, in mines, on plantations, and so on), and returning home periodically. Whether the official policy was assimilation or indirect rule, apartheid or partnership, made remarkably little practical difference.

Throughout sub-Saharan Africa, the colonial countries stripped traditional chiefs of much of the substance of power; at the same time, they recognized in chiefs an element of stability and utilized them, to a greater or lesser extent, in the lower echelons of administration. "Indirect rule" was largely an elaborate rationalization for administrative economy, and it was practiced to nearly the same extent in the Portuguese and French territories as in the

English colonies, at least at the local level. Nowhere, except in the Cape, did miscegenation lead to large groups of people of "mixed blood." Christian missionaries were more successful in some areas than others, but nowhere did they succeed in getting even the nominal allegiance of the overwhelming majority of the population. Only in Ethiopia and South Africa does Christianity have strong roots, in the former case because it has been indigenous since the fourth century, and in the latter case because of factors already discussed.

Throughout tropical Africa, vast numbers of men were forced by such devices as capitation taxes and labor conscription to enter the European money economy, and, consequently, few if any Africans have been left completely unaffected by European contact. At the same time, the vast majority of the people, due to the lack of Western educational opportunities, color discrimination, and the resilience of many African societies to Western influence, has remained culturally more African than European. Everywhere, the white minority established itself as an "albinocracy," which kept itself socially isolated from the natives. All colonial powers, except Belgium, created an African intellectual elite which became culturally assimilated but politically alienated because it almost invariably met with racial discrimination and humiliation. In Sierra Leone, Liberia, and other smaller "creole" settlements of West Africa, the Europeanized element is somewhat larger, but these settlements grew out of colonies of liberated slaves. Throughout the French and Portuguese empires in Africa, assimilation has remained an empty slogan devoid of any reality to all but a tiny privileged intelligentsia. Even if one accepts the notion that assimilation has been at some time a realistic possibility, neither France nor Portugal was ever prepared to accept the logical consequence of it, namely the political Africanization of the "mother country."

In summary, our argument is that irrespective of the colonial policy or racial attitudes of the various powers, European colonialism in the Americas has been characterized by rapid and extensive miscegenation and westernization. These developments were not a result of racial tolerance. After having shattered non-Western cultures or exterminated native populations by conquest and the importation of epidemic diseases, the colonial powers introduced a fairly stable system of plantation slavery or peonage which favored both miscegenation and westernization. In Africa, the European impact has been much milder, both genetically and culturally, because the circumstances of conquest were less devasting, because migratory labor rather than slavery or peonage followed conquest, because Christianization was largely on a voluntary rather than forced basis, and because traditional structures were retained largely for administrative convenience rather than deliberately destroyed as in America. The Cape Province is the exception that proves the rule. There, the American pattern was applied—virtual extermination of the local population followed by plantation slavery. The results were, as in America, extensive miscegenation and acculturation, in spite of strong color prejudice and antiassimilationist policies on the part of the dominant whites. Slavery and what Gilberto Freyre called "latifundiary monoculture" have been the major agencies of westernization and miscegenation in colonial history, not racial tolerance.

In more theoretical terms, this chapter stresses the importance of structural determinism in cultural assimilation and miscegenation. Structural differences between the colonial societies established by the European powers in America and in Africa determined the differences of cultural history to a much greater extent than racial ideology or colonial policy in the various countries.

NOTES

1. See, for example, Frank Tannenbaum, *Slave and Citizen, the Negro in the Americas* (New York: Knopf, 1947).
2. Roger Bastide, "Dusky Venus, Black Apollo," *Race* 3, no. 1 (1961): 10–18; Gilberto Freyre, *The Masters and the Slaves* (New York: Knopf, 1956).
3. On early Portuguese colonization of northwestern Angola, see

James Duffy, *Portuguese Africa* (Cambridge: Harvard University Press, 1959).

4. For accounts of culture contact and miscegenation in the Cape, see I. D. MacCrone, *Race Attitudes in South Africa* (London: Oxford University Press, 1937); J. S. Marais, *The Cape Coloured People, 1652–1937* (London: Longmans, Green, 1939); Sheila Patterson, *Colour and Culture in South Africa* (London: Routledge and Kegan Paul, 1953).

5. Among many studies of Indian-mestizo contact in Mesoamerica, see Melvin M. Tumin, *Caste in a Peasant Society* (Princeton: Princeton University Press, 1952); John Gillin, *The Culture of Security in San Carlos,* Middle American Research Institute Publication no. 16 (New Orleans: Tulane University, 1951); also Chapter 7 in this volume.

5

Toward a Sociology
of Africa

In borrowing the phrase "Sociology of Africa" from Georges Balandier,[1] I do not imply that Africa, because of its idiosyncracies, requires the development of a special brand of sociology. Rather, like Balandier, Gluckman, Mitchell, Kuper, Godfrey and Monica Wilson, and others,[2] I should like to suggest that African societies, through their pluralism and rapid rate of change, challenge much of conventional structural and functional anthropology and sociology and call for a more adequate approach. Elsewhere, I indicated some limitations of functionalism and the possibility of reaching a more satisfactory synthesis by combining elements of functionalism and of the Hegelian-Marxian dialectic.[3]

Here, I shall illustrate some theoretical conclusions and suggestions with special reference to South Africa. Although South Africa is anything but typical of the continent, much of the following analysis is more broadly applicable.

Two sets of problems will be dealt with in turn: first, pluralism, and second, change. The term "plural society" was given currency by Furnivall, who identified it with tropical societies, and is now being used so freely as to cover any group which is not culturally and socially homogeneous.[4] Smith reacts against this

Reprinted from *Social Forces* 43 (1964): 11–18.

loose usage of pluralism, restricts the term to societies that contain incompatible institutions, and criticizes its application to societies which are simply stratified racially or socially or exhibit several variants of a common culture. Furthermore, he reserves the use of the term to countries where a cultural minority is dominant.[5] Braithwaite defines cultural pluralism in terms of diversity of values, but tends to regard racial or class heterogeneity as a form of pluralism.[6] Boeke applies the concept to economics in dealing with the Western and non-Western sectors of the Indonesian economy.[7] Kuper suggests three levels of analysis in dealing with pluralism: the units of cleavage (ethnic or racial), the cultural diversity in basic patterns of behavior associated with the cleavages, and social pluralism or separation in social organization.[8] A similar distinction between social and cultural pluralism is made by Padilla.[9] While a detailed theoretical discussion of the concept of pluralism would be out of place here, a brief statement of my own position is nevertheless necessary. Little seems to be gained by restricting the concept as Smith does. Clearly, pluralism is best conceived as a matter of degree rather than as an all-or-none phenomenon. A society is pluralistic to the extent that it is structurally segmented and culturally diverse. In more operational terms, pluralism is characterized by the relative absence of value consensus; the relative rigidity and clarity of group definition; the relative presence of conflict, or, at least, of lack of integration and complementarity between various parts of the social system; the segmentary and specific character of relationships, and the relative existence of sheer institutional duplication (as opposed to functional differentiation or specialization) between the various segments of the society. Institutions do not have to be incompatible for a society to be pluralistic, but a degree of structural and functional duplication has to be present. In other words, a society is pluralistic insofar as it is compartmentalized into quasi-independent subsystems, each of which has a set of homologous institutions and only specific points of contact with the others (for example, common participation in a money economy, and subjection to a common body politic). A pluralistic society is one in which one cannot, to use Marcel Mauss's phrase, take a "total social phenomenon" and trace its ramifications in the entire society.[10]

Clearly, South Africa is one of the world's most pluralistic societies. Structurally, the deepest cleavage is the racial one which divides the population into four main antagonistic and hierarchized color castes. The economy consists of two largely unrelated sectors: a high-productivity money economy and a subsubsistence one. Governmental pluralism expresses itself in the coexistence of what, until a decade ago, was a parliamentary democracy for the whites and an arbitrary colonial administration for the Africans. This dual political structure is reflected, among other things, in the simultaneous operation of widely different legal systems with overlapping and often conflicting jurisdiction. Besides these various aspects of structural pluralism, South Africa is also culturally pluralistic. The cultural lines of cleavage overlap only partly with the "racial" ones, and they are much more numerous, fluid, and ill defined, though nearly as important. It is interesting to note, as does Kuper, that one of the main sources of strain in South African society arises not only from pluralism as such but also from the increasing lack of overlap between cultural and racial lines of cleavage.[11] Not only is apartheid a pluralistic ideology but it strives to reestablish an identity of cultural and structural cleavages and it ignores the existing discrepancies.

What are the implications of this multidimensional pluralism? Much of the functionalist theory has been based on a monistic model of society. In its most extreme form, functionalism assumes an almost complete cultural homogeneity in a society, whereas more sophisticated functionalists, such as Parsons, and Clyde and Florence Kluckhohn, speak of "dominant" as opposed to "deviant" or "variant" subcultures.[12] This is not to say that functionalism advances an undifferentiated model of society. On the contrary, differentiation and specialization of function and structure between complementary and interdependent parts are cornerstones of functionalism. But neither the concept of differentiation nor that of deviance (or variance) is adequate to deal with plural societies. South Africa is partly differentiated into complementary parts, but it is also split into noncomplementary, nonfunctional, and often conflicting segments. The whites are dominant in terms of power, wealth, religion, and language, but the other groups, with the possible exception of the Coloureds, cannot be called "variants" of the dominant group.

Pluralism raises the question of social integration. The two terms seem antithetical: the more a society is segmented into heterogeneous and noncomplementary parts, the less integrated it is. In Durkheimian terms, a pluralistic society is low on both "mechanical" and "organic" solidarity, insofar as it is composed neither of similar units joined by a strong collective consciousness nor of interdependent units.[13] Whereas most African countries in the face of pluralism endeavor to foster integration, the South African government wants to perpetuate racial, political, and cultural pluralism by deepening existing cleavages and counteracting the integrative forces of acculturation, urbanization, and industrialization. Nevertheless, South African society is integrated in some ways; otherwise one would not be able to speak of it as a society.[14]

Again the functionalist model of integration is inadequate in several ways. Merton and other sophisticated functionalists have successfully repudiated the extreme Malinowskian views that a society is a perfectly integrated whole in which every part has a function and is indispensable.[15] But even the more cautious proposition that integration or equilibrium is a limit toward which societies tend is very questionable. South Africa has been moving toward increasing malintegration for half a century and, in its present form, seems inevitably headed for disintegration.

The functionalist notion of integration is inadequate on another count, namely in its answer to the question: *What* makes a society hang together? The mainstream of functionalism, from Comte to Parsons via Durkheim, has answered "common beliefs" or, to use Parsons' term, "value consensus."[16] According to Parsons, not only is it necessary to the existence of a society that most members thereof agree cognitively on basic values but they must also internalize these values during the process of socialization. Unless one deals with such universals as taboos on incest or on in-group aggression, it is clear that members of the various ethnic groups in South Africa share no common system of values. This is true in at least two ways. First, as each culture has its own ethos, it follows that a pluralistic society consisting of un-related ethnic groups cannot share a common value system. Second, dissension arises, paradoxically, from the westernization of nonwhites, because of a basic contradiction in the value system of the dominant whites. On the one hand, most whites adhere to a particularistic, ascribed, racialistic ethos in order to rationalize their domination; but on the other hand they have introduced, largely through mission education and later through the mass communication media, a universalistic, Christian, liberal ethos which has been seized upon by Western-educated Africans to challenge white supremacy.

Lest the extent of value consensus be underrated in South Africa, however, it should be noted that related African ethnic groups, such as the Xhosa, Zulu, Swazi, and Ndebele, share a good many values in common. The same applies, of course, to the various European and Asian groups. Therefore, from the point of view of value consensus, it is probably more meaningful to speak of three main cultural traditions (or four, if one includes Islam), each with several variants, rather than a score of separate linguistic groups.

Of course, value consensus, when it exists, is an important basis of solidarity and integration, and, conversely, its absence does create strains. The South African case simply shows the untena-bility of the assumption that consensus is a necessary condition to the existence of a society. What are, then, some of the alterna-tive bases of social integration? Coercion, which plays an increas-ingly dominant role in South Africa, is obviously an alternative, though a notoriously unstable one, leading to the eternal vicious circle of tyranny. However, to reduce the problem of integration to a consent-coercion dichotomy, or to varying blends of these two elements, is still far from adequate.

More important than coercion as an alternative to consensus is economic interdependence. Clearly, participation of disparate ethnic groups in a common system of production is a crucial integrative factor in all African countries and is one of the major factors which have held such a conflict-ridden society as South Africa together for so long. The utter dependence (at a starvation or near-starvation level) of the African masses on the white economy in South Africa has been one of the main inhibiting factors to such mass protest actions as general strikes. There is, of course, a reverse side to economic integration in South Africa. The more economic interdependence there is, the less feasible apartheid becomes. Two major elements of the social structure, namely the polity and the economy, pull in opposite directions, thereby creating rapidly mounting strains.

Finally, there often exists *compliance* in the absence of value consensus. One can "play the game" while differing on aims. This can be a result of coercion, but behavioral conformity to norms of another group is also often the result of free choice for the sake of status, convenience, or monetary gain, for example. Or, to phrase the proposition differently, there can be consensus at the level of instrumental norms coupled with dissension concerning fundamental values. In the absence of value consensus, agreement about a set of specific norms (such as arbitration procedures or legal decisions) can become institutionalized as a mechanism to regulate conflicts and dissension. Internationally, for example, punctilious adherence to arbitrary and often trivial norms combined with conflict of basic interests and disagreement about basic aims takes an extreme form in diplomacy. Similarly, Philip Mayer, Clyde Mitchell, and other anthropologists familiar with urban African conditions have observed how migrant workers can adjust to town life, so that, while in town, they appear quite westernized, only to become very traditional again at home in the rural areas.[17] That is to say, for the sake of expediency, the migrant worker temporarily adjusts to certain norms (like rules of racial etiquette, style of dress, punctuality) without changing his basic outlook.

To phrase the remarks above in more general form, plural societies are compartmentalized into autonomous subsystems. The notion of autonomy is, of course, not incompatible with a functionalist viewpoint. Indeed, interdependence of functionally differentiated parts of a system implies the mirror-image concept of relative autonomy. But the kind of autonomy dealt with here is different. We are concerned neither with "organic solidarity" of complementary parts nor with "mechanical solidarity" of self-sufficient parts united by adherence to a common system of values and norms. Plural societies are characterized in part by the coexistence of autonomous but noncomplementary subsocieties which do not share common values, but individual members of which interact in highly segmental, though crucial, relationships. Rather than consensus and interdependence of parts, what holds such societies together is thus partially a network of segmental ties between individual members of ethnic or racial groups, some of whom may indeed "shuttle" or "commute" between cultural subsystems.

This last formulation introduces a new dimension in the analysis of acculturation or cultural contact. Much of the work done in that field has suffered from at least two shortcomings. First, acculturation or "detribalization" (to use a word dear to Africanists) has generally been conceived as a continuum on which individuals could be placed and where movement is overwhelmingly away from "traditionalism" and toward "westernization." While such a conception provides a reasonably approximate description of the over-all tendency, it breaks down if one endeavors to apply it to individuals because it grossly underrates the individual's adaptive flexibility and his capacity to shuttle between two cultures. In practice, it is often difficult to determine how detribalized an individual is, because he may continually oscillate between two systems rather than move steadily toward one and away from another. Indeed, the applicability of a unidimensional continuum to as complex a process as culture change through contact is highly problematic, but a discussion of this point would take us too far.

Second, studies of culture contact have overemphasized "borrowing" of cultural items as the major process of change through contact. Naturally, acculturation theory is not based on a simplistic and mechanistic model wherein traits are exchanged like bananas or groundnuts on a cultural market place. All anthropologists are aware of the complicating factors of selectivity and reinterpretation of items or traits, and, indeed, many avoid altogether such atomistic concepts as "item" or "trait." Nevertheless, the fact that cultures almost invariably *adjust to* and *react against* as well as *borrow from* one another has, I think, been underemphasized. White colonial society is different from white society in Europe, not so much because it borrowed from African culture, but because it adapted its values, its eating, drinking, and sleeping habits, its architecture, and so on to African and colonial conditions. African societies similarly adapted themselves to the conquerors in terms of their own internal dynamics. When, for example, an urban woman in South Africa earns her own lobola (or bridewealth) in order to hasten her marriage, she is obviously not becoming westernized; she finds a radically new solution to a new situation, but in terms of a traditional institution. Or, to use another illustration, most messianistic religious sects do contain elements borrowed from Christianity, but, at the same time, they constitute a reaction against European domination, as Sundkler shows in the case of South Africa.[18] In short, societies in contact do not only undergo a process of cultural osmosis, however complex, but also generate change from within, in terms of both adaptation to, and conflict against, other societies. We shall return to that point presently.

So far we have considered cultural pluralism in its most obvious form: the coexistence of different ethnic groups. This pluralism is gradually reduced by acculturation which has created a westernized (or, in the case of the Sudan belt, an Islamized) elite that often transcends ethnic particularism. Conversely, however, acculturation has introduced another form of pluralism and increased cultural heterogeneity. Nowhere in Africa did European culture come close to eradicating indigenous traditions, except in the Western Cape Province of South Africa. Consequently, by differentially permeating various layers or segments of ethnic groups that were originally homogeneous, westernization added a new dimension to cultural pluralism. Philip Mayer, for example, documents in detail the profound and enduring rift between the "red" and the "school" people among the Xhosa of the Eastern

Cape.[19] While, elsewhere, acculturation has typically not given rise to a sharp dichotomous cleavage in the indigenous population, it invariably introduced a new dimension of heterogeneity.

In South Africa, pluralism is related to westernization in yet another way. Obviously, westernization reduces the overlap between ethnic and racial membership. Coser, Dahrendorf, and others have suggested that a complex crisscrossing of lines of cleavage increases social integration.[20] This, however, is not the case in South Africa, where acculturation combined with a rigid color bar makes for even more acute tension and conflict. The Boers, and now the Nationalist government, have always been aware of the threat to their domination of educating and Christianizing Africans. They have thus been the only group of European colonizers in Africa consistently and logically to follow an antiassimilation policy (unsuccessful though that policy has been) and not to believe in its "civilizing mission." At the root of much conflict in South Africa are the failure of the Afrikaner antiassimilationist policy and the stubborn determination of the Nationalist government to pursue such a policy without any likelihood of success.

Let us now turn to the second major focus of this chapter, namely the analysis of change. I do not wish to repeat the unfair criticism that functionalism is a static approach. Though Radcliffe-Brown and Malinowski have, each in his own way, introduced an ahistorical bias in much African anthropology, functionalism as such allows for at least three sources of social change: individual invention and discovery; adaptation to external change; and a gradual, orderly process of growth in size and complexity through functional and structural differentiation. However, this approach to change is only a partial one and must be complemented by a Hegelian-Marxian view of change as an internally generated process of conflict and contradiction between opposites. Much change is abrupt, qualitative, and revolutionary; and pluralism often fosters acute conflict. Whether one adopts a positivist view of the Hegelian dialectic as inherent in the reality studied, or a nominalist one, considering it simply as a useful analytical tool, need not concern us here. Nor does one have to adopt

Hegelian idealism or Marxian materialism, or any other dogmatic application of the dialectic based on one-factor determinism. My argument is simply that the dialectic method complements the functionalist approach to change. This point has already been expanded elsewhere;[21] here, I shall confine myself to illustrating very sketchily the usefulness of a dialectic approach in dealing with South Africa, though several of my remarks are applicable, *mutatis mutandis,* to the rest of the continent.

A society as ridden with tension as South Africa offers almost too facile an application of the Hegelian dialectic. Let us concentrate on the major source of conflict, namely the syndrome of white domination, and show how it called forth its opposite and sowed the seeds of its own destruction. At the level of values and ideology, the European settlers developed an elaborate racial mythology to rationalize their rule, but at the same time they brought with them a libertarian and egalitarian tradition which they applied to themselves and which they wittingly or unwittingly spread among Africans through missionary education and other forms of culture contact. This ideological contradiction takes both a political and a religious aspect. While the fundamental Calvinism of the Boers has been reinterpreted to defend racialism, the English missionaries generally taught a more universalistic gospel of brotherhood and human dignity. Politically, the *"Herrenvolk* egalitarianism" of the Boer Republics, and later of the Union of South Africa, coexisted with arbitrary and despotic colonial government for the Africans. Western-educated Africans eventually adopted much of the universalistic, liberal, and Christian ethos, became aware of the contradictions in the value system of the local whites, and used Christianity and liberalism to challenge the legitimacy of white domination. At the same time, white racialism called forth its antithesis, namely the black racialism represented in the local brand of Pan-Africanism and in some religious sects of the Zionist variety. Similarly, Afrikaner nationalism and African nationalism developed side by side with, but in opposition to, each other. To the cry of white unity against the "black peril," there arose in response the call for nonwhite unity against white oppression. Ever since Union in 1910, there has been a steady polarization of political opinion along color lines.[22]

Apartheid is a tissue of contradictions between its ideology and aims, on the one hand, and the results of its implementation, on the other hand. Afrikaner Nationalists claim that cultural and racial pluralism ("separate development") is a sine qua non of group survival. Yet, to the extent that economic interdependence has fostered a measure of integration in South Africa, the implementation of territorial apartheid would bring about the disintegration of South African society. At one level, the apologists of "ideal" apartheid claim that partition into several ethnically and racially homogeneous nation-states is the government's objective; however, the same government endeavors to prevent the breakup of the existing body politic by the use of coercion. Total territorial apartheid assuming that the South African government ever seriously considered its implementation, would surely threaten white South Africa by creating hostile African states in its midst and disrupting the economy. "Practical" apartheid (white domination with "microsegregation," but no real intention of large-scale territorial partition) will just as surely lead to the overthrow of the existing regime.

White supremacy is busily digging its own grave in many ways other than ideological. Economically, the exploitation of South African resources became a large-scale venture only with the development of diamond and gold mining in the second half of the nineteenth century. This led to rapid urbanization and industrialization with its host of familiar consequences: the breakdown of geographical isolation; the spread of mass media of communication, elementary education, literacy, European languages, and industrial skills among Africans; the mass migration of millions of workers suddenly cut off from their rural environment and thrown in the great ethnic melting pot of mining compounds; the decay and prostitution of traditional authority; the undermining of family life; the rise of individualism, and so forth. Certainly, all these developments contributed, at least as much as ideology, to the breakdown of ethnic particularism among Africans and to the rise of militant, politically conscious, urban masses.

In erecting a rigid color bar, the dominant whites succeeded in maintaining a monopoly of leading positions in government, commerce, industry, finance, farming, education, and religion. By the same token, they prevented the rise of a class of Africans with a stake in the status quo. For all practical purposes, there is no African landed peasantry or bourgeoisie (in the Marxian sense of owners of means of production). Conversely, the whites created an exploited urban proletariat, a "middle class" of underpaid clerks and other petty white-collar workers, and a tiny elite of professionals and semiprofessionals who are strongly discriminated against. All these strata share a common interest in radical change. The African intelligentsia furnishes the leadership of the liberatory movements; the white-collar workers, many of the local organizers; and the proletariat, the mass support. As to the traditional African framework of authority, the government rightly viewed it as a conservative force and tried to preserve it, if only for administrative economy and convenience; but at the same time the government undermined the traditional system by misunderstanding its nature, transforming it for its own ends, and subjecting it to the onslaughts of urbanization. In short, then, the ruling white group, as in much of the rest of the continent, inevitably undermined what it sought to preserve and brought into being what it tried to prevent. It so completely monopolized wealth and power, and so rigidly identified itself with the status quo, that any change must be against it.

All the illustrations above are too obvious to need further elaboration. South Africa, and, more generally, pluralistic societies call for a model of change which gives conflict, contradiction, revolution, and malintegration a prominent place. If functionalism be called the thesis, and the Hegelian-Marxian dialectic the antithesis, African societies, because of their pluralism and their extraordinary dynamism, offer us a unique opportunity to reach a new synthesis in sociological theory.

NOTES

1. Cf. Georges Balandier, *Sociologie Actuelle de l'Afrique Noire* (Paris: Presses Universitaires de France, 1955); *Sociologie des Brazzavilles Noires* (Paris: Colin, 1955); *Afrique Ambigüe*

(Paris: 1957); "La Situation Coloniale: Approche Théorique," *Cahiers Internationaux de Sociologie* 11 (1951); "Social Changes and Problems in Negro Africa," in Calvin W. Stillman, ed., *Africa in the Modern World* (Chicago: University of Chicago Press, 1955). I am also grateful to Leo Kuper, who has read and criticized an earlier version of this chapter, and to my colleagues at the State University of New York at Buffalo.

2. Georges Balandier, "Sociologie Dynamique et Histoire à Partir de Faits Africains," *Cahiers Internationaux de Sociologie* 34 (1963): 3–11; Max Gluckman, "Anthropological Problems Arising from the African Industrial Revolution," in Aidan Southall, ed., *Social Change in Modern Africa* (London: Oxford University Press, 1961); *Order and Rebellion in Tribal Africa* (New York: Free Press, 1963); and *Custom and Conflict in Africa* (Oxford: Blackwell, 1955); Clyde Mitchell, *Tribalism and the Plural Society* (London: Oxford University Press, 1960); Leo Kuper, "Some Aspects of Urban Plural Societies in Africa," unpublished paper; Godfrey and Monica Wilson, *The Analysis of Social Change* (Cambridge: Cambridge University Press, 1954).

3. Cf. Pierre L. van den Berghe, "Dialectic and Functionalism: Toward a Theoretical Synthesis," *American Sociological Review* 28 (October 1963).

4. J. S. Furnivall, *Colonial Policy and Practice* (Cambridge: Cambridge University Press, 1948). Clearly I am not using the term "pluralism" in the older and more restricted sense in which de Tocqueville and American political scientists used it in reference to the multiplicity of partly overlapping political interest groups in the United States. The Tocquevillian tradition sees "pluralism" as conducive to democracy, whereas the pluralism with which we are concerned here bears no relationship to democracy.

5. M. G. Smith, "Social and Cultural Pluralism," *Annals of the New York Academy of Sciences* 83 (1959–1960): 763–777.

6. Lloyd Braithwaite, "Social Stratification and Cultural Pluralism," Annals of the New York Academy of Sciences 83 (1959–1960): 816–831.

7. J. H. Boeke, *Economics and Economic Policy of Dual Societies* (New York: Institute of Pacific Relations, 1953).

8. Kuper, *op. cit.*

9. Elena Padilla, "Peasants, Plantations and Pluralism," *Annals of*

the New York Academy of Sciences 83 (1959–1960): 837–842.

10. Marcel Mauss, *Sociologie et Anthropologie* (Paris: Presses Universitaires de France, 1950).

11. Kuper, *op. cit.*

12. Talcott Parsons, *The Social System* (Glencoe: The Free Press, 1951); Clyde Kluckhohn, *Culture and Behavior* (Glencoe: The Free Press, 1962), see Bibliography, pp. 373–398; Florence Kluckhohn and Fred L. Strodtbeck, *Variations in Value Orientations* (Evanston: Row, Peterson, 1961).

13. Emile Durkheim, *De la Division du Travail Social* (Paris: Alcan, 1893).

14. This point is stressed by Gluckman in his analysis of African-white relations in Zululand which he views as a system of counterbalancing conflict and cooperation, cleavage and integration. Cf. Max Gluckman, *Analysis of a Social Situation in Modern Zululand* (Manchester: Manchester University Press, 1958), pp. 26, 46, 68, 70. See also his *Order and Rebellion in Tribal Africa*, pp. 214–217.

15. Robert Merton, *Social Theory and Social Structure* (Glencoe: The Free Press, 1957), pp. 30–37; B. Malinowski, "Anthropology," *Encyclopedia Britannica*, First Supplementary Volume (London, 1926), pp. 132–136. Gluckman gives a devastating critique of Malinowski's inability to deal with pluralistic societies and with problems of conflict. See his *Order and Rebellion in Tribal Africa*, pp. 207–234, and B. Malinowski, *The Dynamics of Culture Change, An Inquiry into Race Relations in Africa* (New Haven: Yale University Press, 1946).

16. Emile Durkheim, *Les Formes Elémentaires de la Vie Religieuse* (Paris: Alcan, 1912); Talcott Parsons, *op. cit.*, pp. 36–67, 326, 350–351; *Structure and Process in Modern Societies* (Glencoe: The Free Press, 1960), pp. 172–176; and Max Black, ed., *The Social Theories of Talcott Parsons* (Englewood Cliffs: Prentice-Hall, 1961), pp. 342–343. Durkheim's conception of the importance of consensus is less sweeping than that of Parsons. In an "organic" type of society, interdependence of parts increases as collective consciousness recedes.

17. Philip Mayer, *Townsmen or Tribesmen* (Cape Town: Oxford University Press, 1961); Mitchell, *op. cit.*

18. B. G. T. Sundkler, *Bantu Prophets in South Africa* (London: Oxford University Press, 1961).

19. Mayer, *op. cit.*
20. Lewis A. Coser, *The Functions of Social Conflict* (Glencoe: The Free Press, 1956); Ralf Dahrendorf, *Class and Class Conflict in Industrial Society* (Stanford: Stanford University Press, 1959).
21. Van den Berghe, *op. cit.*
22. Actually, the intermediate position of the Coloured and the Indians complicates the situation. In recent years, there is probably an increasing tendency for Africans to reject Coloureds and Indians as political allies. Much as most leaders from these two groups have, in recent years, tried to join the band wagon of African nationalism and much as they do in fact sympathize with African demands, the mass of the Indians are afraid of future African domination, and most Coloureds still harbor feelings of racial superiority vis-à-vis the Africans. Whereas the Africans tend to view the dichotomy as separating Africans from non-Africans, the whites view it in terms of whites versus nonwhites. This leaves both Coloureds and Indians in a politically marginal position.

Part II

THE AMERICAS

6

Stereotypes, Norms, and Interracial Behavior in São Paulo, Brazil

with Roger Bastide

Although the racial situation in Brazil differs markedly from the situation in the United States, there is nevertheless a racial problem in Brazil.[1] Large-scale industrialization and urbanization in the great metropolises of the South such as Rio de Janeiro and São Paulo have brought about changes in the traditional attitudes and behavior between the various ethnic and racial groups.[2]

Lucila Hermann, from the Faculty of Economics of the University of São Paulo, devised a questionnaire to determine the patterns of race relations in the white middle class of São Paulo.[3] The questionnaire includes four parts:

1. A list of 41 stereotypes derived from the list of Johnson[4] for comparative purposes with the United States, from a content analysis of Brazilian literature, and from oral folklore. For each listed trait (foresight, suggestibility, self-control, intelligence, and so on) the subject was asked whether he considered, first Negroes, then mulattoes, as inferior, equal, or superior to whites.

From *American Sociological Review* 22, no. 6 (December 1957): 689–694.

2. A series of 27 questions on social norms of behavior. For example, should white and Negro children play together? Should whites and Negroes exchange courtesy visits? Should they intermarry?

3. A series of 16 questions on actual behavior of the subjects, similar in content to some questions of part 2.

4. A series of 16 questions on hypothetical personal behavior put in the conditional form: Would you marry (fall in love with, go out with) a Negro? A light-skinned mulatto? and so forth.

The sample is neither random nor proportional. It consists of 580 "white" students from five different teachers' colleges in São Paulo. We have good reason to believe that the questionnaire was applied to whole classes of students in a "captive" classroom situation. The percentage of refusals is unknown, but we think it was very low. We had to reject only one almost blank questionnaire. Most schedules were very conscientiously and completely filled out. The age distribution varies from 15 to 44, but it leans on the young side with a mean age of 19.9 years; 483 subjects are women, and 97 are men. Socioeconomic data on parents of the subjects are incomplete, but they indicate a predominantly lower middle- and upper middle-class background. Seventy-five per cent of the fathers have nonmanual occupations. For the 296 subjects who answered the question on family income, the mean is 7,000 cruzeiros a month. As concerns ethnic origin of parents, 384 subjects are children of Brazilians, 102 have one foreign parent, 85 have both parents foreign. Of the 384 children of nationals, 232 have at least one foreign grandparent. This ethnic situation seems representative of the middle class of São Paulo where third-generation Brazilians dominate only in the upper and in the lower class.[5] The results of this study hold only for the white middle class of São Paulo.

Analysis of the Data

The questionnaire was subjected to a twofold analysis. First, each question was treated as an entity and the answers of all subjects to each separate question were added together and reduced to percentages. Behind this procedure lies, of course, the assumption that the same answer has the same meaning for all subjects. Although some errors have undoubtedly been introduced, in particular by certain questions intended as "traps," we do not think that the conclusions have been altered.

The second part of the analysis is logically independent of the first and permits a corroboration of the conclusions. Each of the 580 subjects was treated as an entity. An arbitrary score was assigned to each subject for the various parts of the questionnaire, by simple unweighted addition of responses. The two underlying postulates behind this procedure are (1) that qualitative answers may be quantified and (2) that the same score means the same thing for different subjects. From these two postulates there is derived a classification of subjects on six scales treated as unidimensional variables. Four of these variables corresponding to each part of the questionnaire are treated as components of a general prejudice-tolerance continuum. Variable *a* is a measure of acceptance or rejection of stereotypes. Variable *b* measures tolerance or prejudice in social norms. Variable *c* measures actual interracial behavior as reported by the subjects. Variable *d* measures willingness to enter into specific personal relationships with Negroes or mulattoes. The other two variables are secondary variables on part 1 of the questionnaire. The higher the score on each of the four main variables, the more tolerant is the subject. For the sake of brevity, the great mass of descriptive statistics has been eliminated. The tabular material has likewise been reduced to the bare minimum. Only the salient conclusions have been retained.

Stereotypes against Negroes and mulattoes are widespread. Seventy-five per cent of the sample accept 23 or more stereotypes against Negroes. No one rejects all stereotypes against Negroes. For mulattoes the over-all picture is somewhat more favorable, though very similar. Mulattoes are judged inferior or superior to whites on the same traits as Negroes, but with somewhat lower percentages. The most widely accepted stereotypes are lack of hygiene (accepted by 91 per cent for Negroes), physical unattractiveness (87 per cent), superstition (80 per cent), lack of financial foresight (77 per cent), lack of morality (76 per cent), aggressiveness (73 per cent), laziness (72 per cent), lack of persistence at work (62 per cent), sexual "perversity" (51 per cent), and exhibitionism (50 per cent).

Fifty-five per cent of the sample think that Negroes are intellectually equal to whites (only 43 per cent consider Negroes less intelligent than whites), and only 22 per cent of the sample accept Negroes as musically gifted. The similarities with the North American stereotypes are more numerous than the differences, particularly as concerns the association of racial prejudice with sexuality.

Going back to the comparison between stereotypes against Negroes and stereotypes against mulattoes, one very important difference appears behind the over-all similarity. Two hundred sixty-nine subjects judge Negroes as they do mulattoes; 268 subjects are more favorable to mulattoes than to Negroes; finally, a small group of 43 subjects is more favorable to Negroes than to mulattoes. We compared this last group with the 45 subjects having the most extreme differences in the second group of 268. This comparison between the two extreme groups reveals no statistically significant differences for age, sex, nationality of the parents, or family income. But significant differences appear on the means of variables *b, c,* and *d* (p<.05 for each of the three variables). Those differences are further confirmed by the answers to the questions on intermarriage (p<.05).

The group more unfavorable to mulattoes shows much more prejudice against *both* Negroes and mulattoes in social norms, in behavior, and in willingness to intermarry than the group more unfavorable to Negroes.

We may hypothesize that there are two contrasting "schools of thought" in the sample. These two schools share a belief in the superiority of the white race. But the group more favorable to mulattoes considers the latter superior to Negroes because mulattoes are nearer to whites. It is thus less opposed to miscegenation and in general more tolerant. The group more favorable to Negroes expresses a much more virulent form of racism. It judges Negroes superior to mulattoes because the former are a "pure race." Any miscegenation is rejected, and the other manifestations of prejudice are likewise stronger. If our hypothesis is correct, there is in Brazil, at least among part of the population, an extreme form of racial prejudice rather than a milder aesthetic prejudice of "physical appearance," which has been propounded by certain students of Brazilian racial relations.[6] There is no indication from our data that this extreme form of racial prejudice where people think in terms of "pure races" has been introduced in Brazil by European immigrants, as some maintain. A research done in Rio de Janeiro also points to more prejudice against mulattoes than against Negroes, thereby giving partial confirmation to our findings.[7]

The question remains entirely open whether the genesis of such extreme racial prejudice goes back to slavery or to the dynamics of social mobility and of the labor market, where mulattoes might be considered more dangerous competitors than Negroes. Further research on this problem would be highly desirable.

Stereotypes, Norms, and Behavior

The ideal norms of behavior contrast in their relative tolerance with the wide acceptance of stereotypes. A theoretical equality of opportunities for whites and Negroes is accepted by 92 per cent in accordance with the Brazilian democratic ethos. Over 60 per cent accept casual relations between whites and Negroes. The color line is found at the level of closer emotional relationships: 62 per cent are opposed to a degree of intimacy with Negroes beyond that of simple comradeship; 77 per cent are opposed to miscegenation with Negroes, 55 per cent to miscegenation with mulattoes.

In actual behavior as reported, and in hypothetical relationships, the sample leans heavily on the segregation side (although lack of actual contact does not necessarily mean prejudice). One hundred four subjects report no contact with either Negroes or mulattoes. Ninety-five per cent of the sample would not marry a Negro; 87 per cent would not marry a light-skinned mulatto.

The linear correlation coefficients (Pearsonian r) between the four main variables are all positive, which vindicates at least

TABLE 6-1   Intercorrelations

Variable *a* Stereotypes	Var. *b* Norms	Var. *c* Behavior	Var. *d* Hyp. Rel.	
	+.60	+.25	+.37	Variable *a* Stereotypes
+.60		+.51	+.68	Variable *b* Norms
+.25	+.51		+.49	Variable *c* Actual Behavior
+.37	+.68	+.49		Variable *d* Hypothetical Relationships

partially our statistical treatment. Particularly noteworthy is the low correlation between stereotypes and actual behavior (+.25).

A paradox appears in comparing these four variables or dimensions of prejudice. On the one hand, we find a wide adherence to democratic norms, and, on the other hand, a high degree of stereotypy, a great amount of segregation at the intimate personal level, and a practically complete endogamy. This ambivalence constitutes a real "Brazilian Dilemma," different though it may be from the "American Dilemma."[8]

Differences by Sex, Socioeconomic Status, and Ethnic Origin

Manifest differences appear between men and women in our sample. Men accept more stereotypes than women, but are much more tolerant for the three other variables. The differences between the means are significant at the level $p<.01$. These differences appear for practically all questions taken separately, but particularly for the question on intermarriage. Men are much more ready to marry light-skinned mulattoes than women. This finding is in agreement with the study of Pierson in Bahia[9] and with Brazilian folklore, which emphasizes the erotic appeal of the *morena*. Several hypotheses to be tested empirically may account for these differences. Women are certainly less free in their associations than men. The penalty put on interracial mingling may be greater for women than for men. There may be a sub-conscious fear of sexual aggression by Negroes on the part of some women as indicated by the question on "sensuality": 40 per cent of the women think that Negroes are more sensual than whites as opposed to 4 per cent for men ($p<.01$). On the other hand, as women enter less in economic competition with Negroes than men, there may be less need for women to develop the racial superiority myth as a defense mechanism.

The most tenable hypothesis is perhaps to be found in the Brazilian racial education which rests on two opposite founda-tions: on the one hand, opposition to miscegenation; on the other hand, avoidance of racial tensions and of open expression of prejudice.[10] As women remain longer than men under the family influence, they absorb more of this racial indoctrination. From the rejection of miscegenation results the greater intolerance of women; from the etiquette of racial "good manners" results the greater self-censorship on the verbal expression of stereotypes.

The criterion of income alone gives a very poor index of socio-economic status. Our conclusions on this point are very tentative. In comparing the two extreme groups on the income distribution (incomes under 4,500 cruzeiros and over 14,500 cruzeiros), the high-income group accepts more stereotypes than the low-income group, but is more tolerant in its social norms and actual behavior. Only the first finding on stereotypes is significant at the level $p<.05$.

No definite assertions can be deduced from such uncertain results. The upper-income group is perhaps more "traditional" and paternalistic. In the low-income group there may be develop-ing a more acute "competitive" type of discrimination and seg-regation comparable to that of the "poor white" in the post-bellum South in the United States. These historical-dynamic considerations are beyond the scope of our study. In any case, our findings invalidate for São Paulo two conclusions of Pierson in his Bahia study:[11]

1. That prejudice in Brazil is more a class prejudice than a

racial prejudice. Although we have not been able to isolate the effects of class and racial prejudice, and although the two are certainly linked together, we can definitely assert that, after having eliminated the effects of class prejudice against colored people, there would remain an important residue of properly racial prejudice. The latent subjective relationship between sexuality and prejudice would among other facts be incomprehensible if there were only a class prejudice.

2. That prejudice against Negroes is directly proportional to socioeconomic status. Our study fails to confirm this statement for the middle class of São Paulo. The relationship between status and prejudice is certainly not as simple and direct as Pierson formulated it.

When the group of first-generation Brazilians as a whole is compared with the group of older-stock Brazilians, no significant differences appear. However, mutually canceling differences are found when the various ethnic groups are separated. The group of Japanese descent is much less prejudiced against Negroes than the general sample, perhaps because it suffers itself from some discrimination. The group of descendants of Syrians and Lebanese is much more prejudiced for reasons explained elsewhere.[12] The Italian group responds like the low-income group in the general sample, which is in accordance with the socioeconomic level of a majority of its members. The Portuguese group shows the same patterns as the high-income group. This fact may be explained by the common cultural heritage of Portuguese and Brazilians. The "high-income" type of response may come from the more traditional and paternalistic heritage of the past. All these ethnic-group differences cancel each other and are obscured when the descendants of immigrants are lumped together.

Summary and Conclusion

The existence of racial prejudice against Negroes and mulattoes has been established. Opinions vary greatly from relative tolerance to relative intolerance; freedom of attitudes and, to a lesser degree, of behavior is relatively great: social norms are directive rather than compulsive. Equality of opportunities is largely accepted, casual relations are widely tolerated, but intimate relationships with colored people are frowned upon. Mulattoes are generally less discriminated against than Negroes, but a small minority "prefers" Negroes to mulattoes. This small minority exhibits a much more virulent form of prejudice against both Negroes and mulattoes than does the general sample. Sex is an important determinant of prejudice. So is socioeconomic status, although our data are too uncertain and incomplete to determine the exact relationship. Ethnic origin of the parents likewise plays an important role.

The weaknesses of our study are many and obvious. As we have pointed out, the sample is not random nor proportional; the postulates underlying the analysis are debatable; and so on. Our conclusions must be accepted with all caution, and we have raised more problems than we have solved. Although our findings largely confirm previous studies, certain revisions of the literature seem in order. Should our study only stimulate criticism, further research, and a few working hypotheses, we should be highly satisfied.

NOTES

1. For our purposes a "race" is a human grouping socially and subjectively defined in a given society. This grouping considers itself different from other groupings similarly defined by virtue of innate and visible physical characteristics, or, in the extreme case, defined, rightly or wrongly, as biologically separate subgroups.

   The same terms such as "Negro" and "white" may, in different societies, cover objectively dissimilar groupings as exemplified by Brazil and the United States. In this research, we shall use the Brazilian definition. "Racial prejudice" is the totality of reciprocal relations of stereotypy, discrimination, and segregation existing between human groupings that consider themselves and each other as "races."

2. On Brazilian racial problems, see Gilberto Freyre, *Casa Grande*

e Senzala (Rio de Janeiro, 1934); Gilberto Freyre, *Sobrados e Mucambos* (São Paulo, 1936); Donald Pierson, *Negroes in Brazil* (Carbondale, Ill.: Southern Illinois University Press, 1966); Charles Wagely, ed., *Race and Class in Rural Brazil* (UNESCO, 1952); Thales de Azevedo, *Les Élites de Couleur dans une Ville Brésilienne* (UNESCO, 1953); L. A. Da Costa Pinto, *O Negro no Rio de Janeiro* (São Paulo, 1953); R. Bastide *et al., Relações Raciais entre Negroes e Brancos em São Paulo* (1955); René Ribeiro, *Religião e Relações Raciais* (Rio de Janeiro, 1956).

3. The present study was undertaken under the auspices of the UNESCO, but was not included in the final report because of the death of Lucila Hermann. We received the filled-out questionnaires in Paris a few years later.

4. Guy B. Johnson, "The Stereotype of the American Negro," in O. Klineberg, ed., *Characteristics of the American Negro* (New York: Harper, 1944), pp. 1–22. For the complete questionnaire, see R. Bastide, "Stéréotypes et préjugés de couleur," *Sociologia* 18 (May 1955).

5. Samuel H. Lowrie, "Origem da População de São Paulo e Diferenciação das Classes Sociais," *Revista do Arquivo Municipal* 42 (São Paulo), pp. 195–212.

6. Oracy Nogueira, "Preconceito Racial de Marca e Preconceito Racial de Origem," *Anais do XXXI Congresso International de Americanistas* (São Paulo, 1955), pp. 409–434.

7. Costa Pinto, *op. cit.,* pp. 203–208.

8. G. Myrdal, *An American Dilemma* (New York: Harper, 1944), pp. 21, 39, 84–89, 460, 614, 899.

9. Pierson, *op. cit.,* pp. 136–137.

10. Bastide *et al., op. cit.,* p. 126.

11. Pierson, *op. cit.,* pp. 348–349; and D. Pierson, *Bulletin International des Sciences Sociales* 4, no. 2 (UNESCO, no date): 488. For statements more in agreement with our conclusions, see de Azevedo, *op. cit.,* pp. 34–45; Wagley, *op. cit.,* pp. 147, 150, 159; Bastide *et al., op. cit.,* pp. 11, 123–124, 133–139.

12. *Ibid.,* pp. 128–129.

7

Ethnic Relations
in Southeastern Mexico

with Benjamin N. Colby

Although Spanish colonization of the highlands of Chiapas dates from the early sixteenth century, the region still constitutes one of the major Indian enclaves in Mexico. The state of Chiapas in southeastern Mexico is located southwest of the Yucatan Peninsula and west of Guatemala. The town of San Cristobal de Las Casas, founded in 1528, is the major center of Spanish culture in the highlands of the state. Located at 7,000 feet of elevation along the Pan-American Highway, San Cristobal had a population of 17,473 at the time of the 1950 census.[1] The climate is tropical as far as the alternation of rainy and dry seasons is concerned, but quite cool due to the elevation.

Town dwellers are almost all hispanicized to the extent of speaking only Spanish and dressing much as in the rest of Mexico. The inhabitants of San Cristobal call themselves Ladinos.[2] Genetically they range from pure or almost pure Spanish stock to pure American Indian stock. While the upper class (called *clase alta, gente bien, la crema,* or *los blancos*) is mostly white, the middle

Reproduced by permission of the American Anthropological Association from the *American Anthropologist* 63 (1961): 772–792.

class (*clàse media*) is mostly light mestizo (mixed blood), and the lower (*gente humilde*) is in majority dark mestizo or Indian-looking. Though an occasional lower-class person is Caucasoid-looking, and some upper-class persons are somewhat mestizoized, the genetic continuum overlaps greatly with the social-class continuum. This is not to say, however, that genetic characteristics are the primary criteria of social status in San Cristobal. While the town is rigidly stratified, and its inhabitants strongly class-conscious, wealth (as indexed by dress, landownership, type of house, number of servants, and the like) and education (as shown by literacy, correctness of speech, university degree, manners, and so on) are more important than physical appearance in determining one's status. An educated person of Indian appearance may be the object of mild ostracism from the old upper-class families but is accepted among the middle class. Conversely, a white skin will not exempt a poor, illiterate person from membership in the lower class.

The social-class system is reflected in the ecology of San Cristobal: the social status of houses is inversely proportional to the distance from the central town square. As one walks from the center of the town to its outskirts, houses change from bricks or stones and tile roofs to whitewashed adobe and tiles, to raw adobe and tiles, to straw-thatched huts with lattice walls. Street condition deteriorates from concrete to irregular cobblestones, to unimproved mudholes, with the exception of one main arterial street that crosses the city from east to west. The arrangement of the San Cristobal cemetery, located southwest of town, likewise reflects the social status of the defunct inhabitants. While the central path is bordered on both sides by elaborate chapellike family vaults, the fringes of the cemetery consist of unkept, weed-invaded earthen mounds with decayed wooden crosses. Small stone monuments and fenced-in wrought-iron crosses occupy the intermediate zone between the center and the periphery.

Surrounding the Ladino town for a depth of some forty miles in all directions is a rural hinterland, inhabited by an estimated 125,000 Indians belonging to two major linguistic groups (Tzotzil and Tzeltal, both of which belong to the Mayan family) and subdivided into several smaller ethnic groups (Chamulas, Zina-cantecos, Huistecos, Tenejapanecos, and so on).[3] While small Ladino nuclei live in the countryside, the overwhelming majority of the rural population is Indian. A number of Indians live in the lower-class outskirts of San Cristobal, but in most cases they become rapidly ladinoized. The same is true of Indian girls serving as maids to Ladino families in the town. In general, Indians are rural and Ladinos are urban. Indians outnumber all Ladinos (that is, rural and urban together) by about six or seven to one. This compares with an Indian minority of around 15 per cent for Mexico as a whole. Ever since the Spanish conquest in the six-teenth century, these Indians (called *indios, indígenas,* or more frequently in the diminutive form *inditos,* by the Ladinos) have been subjugated to, and living on the margin of, the dominant Hispanic society. To this date, the Indians have remained, in quasi-totality, small-scale peasants subsisting on a maize-and-beans diet. They have retained their own cultures, wear distinct costumes, are overwhelmingly illiterate, and speak little, if any, Spanish. The 1950 census lists several Indian districts as having less than 5 per cent of their population literate. In the majority of the Indian districts the percentage was under 20 per cent. In 1954, the Instituto Nacional Indigenista lists only 4,588 Indians as literate in the region; that is, some 4 per cent of the total Indian population.[4] At the time of the 1950 census, in 7 of the 15 Indian *municipios* over 80 per cent did not speak any Spanish, and in 12 of 15 municipios there were over 60 per cent non-Spanish-speaking people. In the 1940 census, of 79,849 Indians over 5 years of age, 56,523 are classified as non-Spanish-speaking.[5]

In contrast to Ladino society, the various Indian ethnic groups show relatively little internal stratification, but the Ladinos rank the several Indian groups in a definite hierarchy with the Zinacan-tecos on top, the Tenejapanecos and Huistecos at the bottom, and Chamulas and other groups in an intermediate position. To some extent this hierarchy is also recognized by the Indians themselves, at least by the Zinacantecos.[6]

The superiority of the Ladino group over all Indian groups is taken completely for granted by the Ladinos, even the most liberal ones, but the rationalization of that superiority is almost always cultural. Besides strictly cultural differences between Ladinos and Indians, economic and educational differences also contribute to the devaluation of the Indians. On the whole, Indians are poorer and less educated (in the Western sense of the word) than the Ladinos, though not always so compared with some lower-class Ladinos. Racialism, in the form found in South Africa or the United States, is either completely absent or present in such an attenuated form as to be unrecognizable. The distinction between Ladinos and Indians is cultural rather than racial. After four centuries of subjugation, the Indians, on their side, seem to have accepted, and even internalized, the Ladino scale of cultural evaluation, though not without ambivalence.

Since the Ladinos and the Indians belong to widely different cultures, it is clear that the basic values of the two groups have a bearing both on each group's self-image and on their mutual relationships. While Ladino culture is vertically structured and stresses competition and command-and-obey relations, Indian culture is basically horizontal.[7] In spite of the importance of age and of rigid etiquette based on relative age of the participants, Indian culture deemphasizes social hierarchy. Authority is exercised through persuasion and influence rather than through commands. The holding of *cargo* (religious office) in Indian groups is more of a leveling force than one making for hierarchy; for, while cargo confers prestige, it also entails the spending of large sums of money for entertainment, thereby preventing the concentration of wealth.[8] Witchcraft and the fear of witchcraft also act as powerful leveling forces in the Indian cultures. Ladino society, on the contrary, is highly status-conscious and strongly stratified along class lines. Command-and-obey relations are stressed in the family, the school, the political framework, and the work situation. This basic difference in values may account, in part, for the unquestioned assumption of cultural superiority on the part of the Ladinos, who view the cultural differences in clearly hierarchical terms. On the other hand, the horizontal stress of the Indian cultures militates against the acquisition by individual Indians of the necessary skills and resources to "pass" as Ladinos.

Another important aspect in which Indian and Ladino values are at odds concerns the attitude toward manual labor. Whereas Ladinos of all classes deprecate manual labor and go to great length to avoid it (even though lower-class Ladinos are often unsuccessful in their attempt to do so), Indians value manual work and skills as the most worthy of esteem. A "good" man is one who is skilled in the planting of maize. A "good" woman is one who is a proficient weaver and housewife. As the Indians do, in fact, most of the manual labor (at least in agriculture)[9] and Ladinos have a quasi-monopoly of nonmanual labor, it is clear that such values tend to reinforce the existent division of labor, to lower the Ladinos' estimate of the Indians, and to discourage the Indians from rising to nonmanual occupations (since doing so might involve a loss of esteem on the part of other Indians).

Though both groups are nominally Catholic, Indian religion is actually a syncretism of Mayan and Christian beliefs, whereas the Ladinos practice a more orthodox Roman Catholicism. The elaborate cargo system that plays such an important role in Indian culture is nonexistent among Ladinos. Under the cover of the Catholic saints, the Indian view of the divine is definitely polytheistic, whereas Ladino Catholicism is more monotheistic. The Indian conception of the soul is much more complex and pluralistic than the Ladino one.[10] Whereas, in their relation to the divine, Ladinos seek to maintain or restore what they consider to be the proper personal relation between themselves and God, the Indian emphasis is on maintaining harmony and integrity with a pluralistic and unpredictable universe. The Indian practice of religious curing ceremonies and *curanderos* has no counterpart in Ladino religion. The revivalistic cult of the "talking saints" is almost exclusively limited to the Indians.[11] Ladino spiritualists engage in unorthodox medical practices, but in quite different form from the Indian curanderos. A talking saint in Soyalo is owned and visited by Ladinos, but in general the practice is confined to Indians. Such differences in religious values, beliefs, and practices affect interethnic relations insofar as the Ladinos view the Indians as pagan practitioners of an idolatrous, superstitious, and corrupt form of Catholicism. However, over and above these differences, the formal structure of the Catholic church is one of the main integrating forces between the two ethnic groups, as we shall see presently.

These value differences between Ladino and Indian (more specifically, Zinacanteco) culture, as well as other value differences not so directly related to ethnic relations between the two groups, are summarized in Table 7–1.

Before proceeding to a more detailed description of the system of ethnic relations in the highlands of Chiapas, and after stressing cultural differences between Indians and Ladinos, we must raise the question of social integration. What unites the two groups into something that can be described as a system of social relations? We think that the three main foci of interethnic integration are (1) religious, (2) political, and (3) economic.

1. The Catholic church is definitely one of the major integrative factors between Indians and Ladinos. This is true in spite of the differences in religious beliefs, practices, and values between the two groups that we have mentioned before. It is not so much, then, the *ethos* of Catholicism as the *formal structure* of the church which Ladinos and Indians share. Ever since the pro-Indian stand of Fray Bartolomé de las Casas (after whom San Cristobal de las Casas was named), the Catholic church has defended a universalistic and equalitarian position on racial and ethnic issues. Today, posters pleading for "priests of all races to build a universal Church" are displayed at the entrance of most churches in San Cristobal. Though there are no Indian priests, common membership of Ladinos and Indians in the church has undoubtedly been a major integrative influence in Chiapas. Perhaps the most important interethnic religious cement is the complex of ritual kinship known in the Spanish world as *compadrazgo*. Many Ladinos are godparents of Indian children and, hence, by extension, *compadres* and *comadres* of the Indian parents of those children. More will be said about interethnic ritual kinship later.

2. The local government in Chiapas is organized on the basis of municipios or counties. The government of San Cristobal, the main municipio in the Chiapas highlands, is, of course, entirely a

monopoly of the Ladinos. In the rural municipios of the hinterland, Indians have sometimes considerable control over their local affairs, although, in other cases, a Ladino secretary (oftentimes the only literate official) is the real power in the Indian municipios.[13] At the local level, then, the governmental structure, insofar as it reflects the urban-rural division, tends to maintain the existing Indian-Ladino division.[14] The federal government of Mexico, however, has been firmly committed since the revolution of 1910–1917 to an equalitarian ideology. Since 1948 that ideology has been implemented through the action of the Instituto Nacional Indigenista (National Indian Institute, hereafter INI), a federal government organization devoted to the improvement of social and economic conditions among Indian groups in Mexico. The work of INI is directed by anthropologists from its central offices in Mexico City. Branches called "coordinating centers" are located in several of the major Indian areas of Mexico, including one at San Cristobal for the Tzotzil and Tzeltal Indians. By building rural roads, schools, and clinics and introducing cooperative stores and modern agricultural methods, INI is breaking down the isolation of the Indian municipios, improving their living standards, and slowly incorporating them into the cultural life of the Mexican nation. The backbone of the Tzotzil-Tzeltal program is the Indian promoter system. Indians are brought in to the coordinating center in San Cristobal from outlying areas and trained as teachers, nurses, and agricultural experts. Once trained, these Indians are called promoters (*promotores*) and are returned to their villages or hamlets to teach what they have learned, to implement the INI improvement programs, and to communicate to INI the Indian response to these new programs. The fact that most progress toward INI objectives has occurred in some of the more remote areas accessible only on foot or horseback has clearly demonstrated the efficacy of the promoter system, for only the promoters and the INI school inspectors have been to these villages. It is significant that INI success in Indian areas immediately surrounding San Cristobal has apparently not been as great as in some of the more distant areas. One reason may be that proximity to Ladino society has developed mechanisms of

TABLE 7-1. Basic Zinacantan and San Cristobal[a] Orientations

	Zinacantan	San Cristobal
Religious orientations	More pluralistic view of religion and universe. Belief in both Catholic and pagan deities.	More dualistic view of religion and universe. Roman Catholicism of the Spanish variant.
	Little secularization. Wide adult participation in religion through cargo and curing activities.	Considerable secularization. Specialization of religious functions in hands of professional clergy.
	Multiple soul concepts: a spiritual soul of thirteen parts and two types of animal souls.	Single soul concept.
	Need to maintain health and complete possession of souls in the face of an unpredictable supernatural universe and an evil social environment. Bargaining and exchanging with the gods. Curing ceremonies for restoring or keeping harmony with the supernatural forces and maintaining the integrity of the soul.	Belief in foreordained destiny, changeable only through supplication of God and the saints. Confession and sacraments for restoring personal relationship to God.
Relations to society	Ambivalence, uncertainty, and anxiety about relations with others.	Relatively little anxiety about relations with others.
	Rigid and intricate pattern of etiquette functions to reduce anxiety about social relations.	Etiquette not rigid or complicated and functions more to distinguish social class than reduce anxiety about social interaction.
	Hierarchy of position in ceremony and of age-deference in etiquette patterns, but hierarchization of command is relatively weak. Men are to be influenced and persuaded. Adjustment and harmony are crucial social goals.	Strong hierarchization. Men to be commanded, dominated, exploited; patrón complex.
	No social classes. Leveling forces of cargo, witchcraft, and envy prevent stratification.	Rigid social classes. Wealth and education generally inherited. (However, recent tendency toward open class system.)

TABLE 7-1 (continued)

	Zinacantan	San Cristobal
Relations to society (continued)	Open competition avoided.	Open competition encouraged.
	Status gained by engaging in ceremonial or curing activity and spending for ceremonial entertainment.	Status gained by attention-attracting activities, show, wealth, and by being a patrón.
	Traditional emphasis. A man's role or office is emphasized rather than his personal qualities.	Slightly charismatic emphasis. A man's personal qualities are emphasized rather than his role or office.
Relations to family	Competition and conflict within the nuclear family are usually intense. Aggression often physical. Little attempt made to hide family conflict from public knowledge.	Intrafamilial competition not so violent. Aggression mostly verbal. Close ties between brother-sister, mother-son, and father-daughter. Concern for family honor and desire to avoid public knowledge of family conflict.
	Both men and women condemned for adultery. Women sexually aggressive.	Women condemned, men condoned for adultery. Women sexually reserved.
	Both castration and ascension elements exist in dream interpretations and folklore.	Ascension complex (the desire to be placed above others, to receive admiration) rather than castration complex predominant.
Work and economic orientations	Routine and manual labor valued.	Routine and manual labor avoided and devalued.
	Land valued as a source of subsistence. *Milpa*-making most worthy activity for men.	Land valued for ownership as a sign of status but agricultural work considered debasing.
	Play and leisure censured.	Play and leisure valued.
Cultural range in space and time.	Local orientation limited to areas in work and trade orbit.	National orientation; Mexico City the center of "culture" for upper and middle classes.
	Vague and shallow perception of historical past.	Strong historical awareness of the Conquest and the 1910-1917 revolution.

[a]For purposes of comparison with San Luis Jilotepeque, Guatemala, we followed in part Gillin's scheme (see note 12). The contrasting view we present is valid only for one culture relative to the other, not by absolute standards or by the standards of a third culture.

stronger reactive resistance in the nearer Indian cultures. In spite of a much greater effort by INI in these closer areas—including the installation of lighting and public address systems, the building of roads, clinics, a cement basketball court, and a Ladino-style plaza and the frequent visits of INI administrative officials from the coordinating center—they continue to maintain greater psychological and cultural resistance than the more remote areas. Some change is occurring, however, even in the resistant communities, and in coming years as more funds are allocated to the INI program and as more promoters are trained greater changes will undoubtedly ensue.

3. Economically, San Cristobal and its environs constitute a unit. The Indians produce the food surplus from which San Cristobal lives. San Cristobal with its daily market, on the other hand, is the major distribution and consumption center for agricultural products in the region. The town is also a major productive and distributive center of manufactured products (such as textiles and metal goods), a producer of services (such as hospitals, prisons, barbershops), and an important labor market. It is clear that if Indians and Ladinos ceased to have trade relations, neither group could subsist in its present state. It is also true that a majority of the daily contacts between Ladinos and Indians involve an exchange of goods and services. Every morning, including Sundays, thousands of Indian men and women stream into San Cristobal carrying heavy loads, mostly of wood and food. These goods are either sold by the Indians themselves in town or bought from them at the outskirts of town by Ladino women who, in turn, resell the goods at a profit in town. These Ladino merchants, known as *atajadores* (literally "those who intercept") or *esperadoras* ("the waiting ones"), wait in groups for the Indian peasants, descend upon the Indians when they appear, bully them into selling at prices considerably below the market price, and share the profits. This form of trade has been described by Bonilla Dominguez as "purchase by assault."[15] When the Indians sell directly to customers in town they either peddle their goods from door to door or sell them on the market place. All regular stands in the market are rented by Ladinos, however, so that Indian mer-

chants are left with the less desirable locations. Indians sit and spread their goods on the ground. Bargaining is a part of most transactions. Excepting the Indian food, pottery, and wood merchants, all the trade of San Cristobal is in the hands of Ladinos. Indians, therefore, have to buy all their durable and manufactured products from Ladino merchants. As customers, Indians are often treated curtly by Ladino merchants and cheated on weights and prices. In the words of one informant, "For an Indian, a kilo is 700 grams." The Indians are aware of being cheated, but accept it as an inevitable part of commercial transactions with Ladinos.[16] Diseased meat has been known to be set aside for sale to the Indians.[17] Conversely, Indian merchants are sometimes bullied by Ladino customers into selling at prices lower than those commanded by Ladino merchants. In commercial transactions, the term "marchante" is used as a reciprocal term of address by both merchants and customers, whether among Ladinos or between Ladinos and Indians. Whether as merchant or as customer, however, the Indian is always in the subordinate position when trading with Ladinos.

Indians and Ladinos also exchange services. In the great majority of cases the Indians are employed by Ladinos rather than the other way around. The Indian girls work as servants in Ladino households. Indian men do odd jobs in Ladino houses, work on highway construction, or are hired as common laborers on coffee plantations. San Cristobal streets are swept by Indian male prisoners in the town jail.[18] The common features of all the work done by Indians are its menial nature and its low rate of pay (between 4 and 8 pesos a day for common laborers; up to 2 pesos a day for a maid; 1 peso = U.S. $.08). Lower-class Ladinos do comparable work for comparable pay, however, except for agricultural work, which is considered to be strictly Indian work.[19]

In the rural areas, Indian-Ladino relations have gone through several stages. After the Conquest, the Spanish Crown established the encomienda system. This feudal system, under which Spanish colonists were granted large land tracts and the right to exact labor and tribute from the Indians, was evolved to reward the Spanish colonists and keep the Indians under the control of the Spanish Crown. Later, when the encomienda system was abolished, large landowners had a tighter, more absolute control over their Indian labor. Exploitation of Indian labor under conditions of peonage and debt slavery persisted until the revolution of 1910–1917. Until that time, landless Indians known as *baldíos* were forced by need to offer their lifetime services to Ladino plantation (*finca*) owners in exchange for a small plot to cultivate for themselves and their families. Following the revolution, the baldíos were emancipated, many of the Ladino fincas were expropriated, much of the land was returned to the Indians, and labor laws protected agricultural workers. The coffee plantations, which were expanding in Chiapas during this time, resorted to a form of labor contracting opprobriously called the *enganche* ("hooking") system. Under this system, an estimated 15,000 Indians a year are now being recruited on a seasonal basis by finca representatives known as *habilitadores*. Indian workers are often recruited when drunk and encouraged to contract debts to the finca owners so that they can be kept in a quasi-servile condition. As the coffee fincas are located in "hot country" in the lowlands of the state, many Indian men spend several months of each year far from their homes in the highlands. Through continued government and INI intervention, the more glaring abuses of the enganche system are slowly being eliminated, however.

One of the few instances where an Indian hires the services of a Ladino occurs when an Indian wants a haircut. By custom, Indians enter only some of the poorer barbershops in town, and when they do they are given distinctively inferior service. They are made to sit on a kitchen chair (although the shop has a regular barber chair reserved for Ladino customers) and given a rough five-minute haircut. However, they pay only 1 peso instead of the regular 3 to 4 pesos.

Whether as customers or as merchants, as employees or as employers, then, the Indians are almost invariably in the subordinate role when dealing with Ladinos.

Besides the obvious subsistence functions of Indian-Ladino

economic exchanges, these exchanges make for daily interethnic contacts that otherwise would not take place. Through frequent trips into town, the Indians gradually gain some command (if only rudimentary) of Spanish and learn about the dominant Ladino culture. At the same time, Ladinos having most frequent associations with Indians learn words and phrases of Tzotzil (and less often, of Tzeltal, whose speakers live at a greater distance and visit San Cristobal less often) that are useful in bargaining. The various forms of economic exchange between Ladinos and Indians account for a large proportion of daily interethnic contacts and are definitely one of the major foci integrating Ladino and Indian cultures.

We may now turn to a more systematic characterization of the Ladino-Indian system of ethnic relations. Generally, ethnic relations in the Chiapas highlands are of a type that one of the authors has called elsewhere "paternalistic."[20] Ladinos treat Indians condescendingly, but often with a touch of affection. Indians are considered primitive, uncultured, ignorant, unreliable, irresponsible, and childish. They are referred to by Ladinos as *inditos* (literally, "little Indians") or *muchachos* (children) regardless of age. The titles of Don and Señor are not normally extended to Indians, although in constant use among Ladinos. Ladinos invariably address Indians in the familiar "tu" form, the same form in which Ladino adults address Ladino children up to adolescence. Indians, on the other hand, when addressing Ladinos use titles of respect such as Don, Señor, and patrón. Indians are also expected to use the polite "usted" form when speaking to Ladinos, but they frequently use the familiar "tu" form, due to their imperfect knowledge of Spanish.

Ladino children can often be observed making fun of Indian adults and playing practical jokes on them in the streets or in the market place. We have never observed Indians reacting verbally to these taunts, much less retaliating, though they are often visibly annoyed.

Up until a generation ago, Indians were expected to walk on the street, the sidewalk being reserved for Ladinos, but this custom has now disappeared. However, in crowded places such as the open market, Ladinos are constantly seen pushing Indians aside. Until recently, Indians were not allowed to ride on horseback in the Oxchuc area. They also were previously required to fold their arms and bow in a submissive position when speaking to a Ladino patrón. While Ladino customers in the market are spoken to courteously by Ladino shopkeepers, Indians are addressed curtly, though not necessarily in an unfriendly manner. When Ladino and Indian customers wait together to be helped, Ladinos are generally served first. This rule applies even when the Ladino shopkeeper has already started serving an Indian customer.

Formal segregation has been observed only in barbershops as described above, and, even here, the price differential in haircuts may account in part for the custom. However, when a Ladino barber was asked why Indians sit on separate chairs, he answered that the Indians were dirty and that his Ladino customers might not like to sit on the same chair where an Indian had just sat. Most Indians are, of course, debarred by distance of residence and poverty from participating in much of the San Cristobal life. Students in the San Cristobal secondary school are all Ladinos, for example, but there exists no formal barrier to the entry of a qualified Indian into those schools.[21] Similarly, few Indians can afford to go to the town's movie theater, but they are not refused admittance, and some do, in fact, go. At the great annual fiesta of the town's patron saint, a number of Indians attend. Many of them wear Ladino clothing which makes them indistinguishable from lower-class Ladinos, except for the language they speak. These *indios revestidos* (literally "reclothed Indians") tend to be onlookers on the fringe of events rather than participants in the merrymaking.[22]

Few Indians worship in the San Cristobal churches, but, when they do, they sit anywhere they want. In some of the rural churches, however, such as in Tenejapa, Indians and Ladinos each have their own saints facing each other on opposite sides of the church, and the religious fiestas of each group take place on different days with either all-Ladino or all-Indian participation.[23]

Whenever Indians and Ladinos are seen walking or talking

together in town, they are engaged in a commercial transaction, or the Indian is the servant of the Ladino (as when an Indian maid accompanies her mistress to the market to carry the baskets). We have never observed purely social contacts of an equal nature between Ladinos and Indians, except at the INI. The Indians use the central town square quite freely and sit on benches, but Ladinos tend to avoid sitting on the same benches as Indians. Commensality between Ladinos and Indians is rare, and we have never observed a case. Indians enter Ladino houses quite frequently, but as servants or peddlers, not as equals. When an Indian from the countryside stays in town overnight, he sleeps in the hallways of the house of his Ladino patrón. The custom is known as *posada,* and though it leads to long-term and often amicable relationships between patrón and Indian, the relationship is anything but equalitarian.

Among the most important relationships that cross the ethnic line are the ties of ritual kinship. Anyone familiar with Hispanic culture knows the importance of the compadrazgo complex.[24] At baptism, confirmation, and marriage a person is given one godparent of each sex who is responsible for the person's spiritual development. The godparents and the biological parents of the child term each other "compadre" and "comadre." In all cases, the biological parents of the child seek out the godparents, never the other way around. Godparents may, in fact, be relatives of the child, but more often than not they are biologically unrelated. A good Catholic, when called upon to serve as godparent, cannot, in conscience, evade the responsibility. The tendency is generally for the parents to seek persons of influence and wealth as godparents of their children so that the number of one's godchildren is always a sure index of social status.[25] It follows that Ladinos are often sought by Indians as godparents, *but never, or virtually never, the other way around.*[26] Many influential Ladinos have so many Indian godchildren that they do not know their actual number, which may run up to one hundred or more. Indian parents and Ladino godparents call each other comadre and compadre, but the term, although reciprocal, does not imply equality. The Ladinos derive prestige from having Indian godchildren. The Indians, on the other hand, get protection and a measure of economic help from the Ladino compadres (who may be asked for loans of money and other minor favors).

The complex of ritual kinship, then, makes for lasting and friendly ties between Ladinos and Indians without threatening to subvert the subordination-superordination relationship between the two groups. Compadre relations across ethnic lines are definitely unidirectional and not equalitarian.[27]

Sexual relations across the ethnic line are relatively frequent. The most frequent form they take is concubinage between Indian girls and Ladino men. Indian servant girls, both in town and on the coffee plantations, are reputed to have frequent affairs with their Ladino masters.[28] Intermarriage between Ladino men and Indian women is also common, but generally confined to the Ladino lower class. Cases of intermarriage between Ladino women and Indian men are much rarer and also confined to the Ladino lower class. When it happens, the Indian men are strongly ladinoized. The town's prostitutes, who are all more or less ladinoized, are visited both by Ladinos and by Indian men in Ladino clothes.

We have already emphasized that the definition of the various groups in Chiapas is cultural rather than physical. The Ladino group is characterized by its possession of the local variant of Spanish culture, not by any "racial" traits. Indeed, while the Indians are genetically homogeneous, the Ladinos range from white to Indian in phenotype. If an Indian acquires a fluent knowledge of Spanish, dresses in Ladino clothing, and adopts Ladino customs, he can pass the ethnic line.[29] During his own lifetime his origins may be remembered and he may still be called an Indian, but he will be treated as a Ladino for most everyday purposes. His children will definitely be considered to be Ladinos. The change of status from Indian to Ladino is thus difficult, but not impossible.[30] When an Indian passes, however, he always enters the Ladino class structure at the very botton. The fact that the great majority of lower-class Ladinos is phenotypically indistinguishable from Indians is evidence enough that passing is frequent.

In no sense, then, can the Ladino-Indian system of stratification be described as a caste system, since the ethnic groups are neither closed nor strictly endogamous. Once an Indian has entered the Ladino lower class, however, his physical appearance handicaps seriously his ascension in the middle or upper class. This is true in spite of the fact that racial prejudice *as such* is minimal and that wealth and education are more important than physical traits in determining class status. Rather, the difficulty of *class* mobility has kept the Ladino upper and middle classes predominantly white or light mestizo, so that the presumption of lower-class status is always strong in the presence of an obviously darker person. At a meeting of an upper and upper middle-class men's civic club, for example, of the eighteen members present, sixteen looked white, only two appeared somewhat mestizoized, and none was distinctly Indian-looking.

Although downward class mobility within Ladino society is possible, downward mobility from Ladino to Indian culture is unknown, except by marginally ladinoized Indian servant girls who subsequently return to their village and marry Indians. The ethnic line, then, is open almost exclusively in the "upward" direction.

Ladinos, even the most liberal, accept the postulate of their cultural superiority as self-evident, while at the same time rejecting, for the greater part, any notion of racial superiority. The difference between liberal and prejudiced Ladinos is that the former view the ladinoization of Indians with favor, whereas the latter view it with hostility, or, at best, with ambivalence. Both liberal and prejudiced Ladinos, however, view Spanish culture as unquestionably superior.[31] Even the INI has as its official policy the integration of Indian minorities into the Mexican nation via hispanization. The Ladino assumption of cultural superiority is, thus, unwittingly supported and reinforced by the official ideology of the present liberal Mexican government.

The Indians seem, for the most part, to have accepted Ladino superiority as an inescapable fact of life.[32] Their attitudes toward Ladinos are, however, laden with ambivalence. Indian folk tales, such as that of Petul—an Indian culture hero who outwits and plays dirty tricks on Ladinos—reveal aggressive feelings toward Ladinos. One Indian myth attributes the "mean" (bravo) character of the Ladinos to their origin as the offspring of a woman and a dog. Although hostility toward the Ladinos is generally repressed, several large-scale rebellions have taken place. Shortly after the Conquest, some Indians rebelled against the Spanish in 1524 and 1526. However, it seems that the presence of the Spaniards acted principally as a catalyst for previously existing rivalries between Indian groups. Some Indian groups fought as allies of the Spanish in these two revolts. A period of enthusiastic culture change, Christianization, and hispanization of the Indians followed the early revolts.[33] In 1712, a messianistic rebellion of the Tzeltal groups broke out, and in 1869 the Chamulas attacked and nearly entered San Cristobal. The 1869 rebellion was likewise messianistic in character.[34] On Good Friday, 1868, an Indian youth was crucified so that the Indians would have their own Christ. The cult of the "talking saints," which has enjoyed a recent revival, originated during the Chamula upheaval.[35] Threats of revolts appeared in the early part of the twentieth century, and in 1935 fighting in Cancuc resulted in a substantial death toll for both sides.[36] Although the era of tribal unrest seems to be over, the recent false rumor of a Chamula revolt led to a panic in San Cristobal.

Since the Mexican Revolution, a number of factors have contributed to changing Indian-Ladino relations in Chiapas. Land reform has jeopardized the position of many Ladino upper-class families, and labor legislation has emancipated Indian agricultural workers. More recently, INI has introduced a widespread program of sanitation and education among the Indians and has generally protected the Indians against many forms of exploitation and discrimination on the part of the Ladinos. The appearance, within the past few years, of Indian-operated stores in the Zinacantan center and in outlying hamlets, of an INI-sponsored cooperative store in Zinacantan, indicates a significant change in economic relations between Indians and Ladinos. The recently completed Pan-American Highway and the INI-built rural roads make the region easily accessible to the rest of Mexico, foster the urban development of San Cristobal, and facilitate Ladino-Indian contacts. Younger Indian men tend to be most widely traveled, to speak more Spanish, and to become increasingly ladinoized.[37]

All these trends combine to undermine the traditional paternalistic type of Indian-Ladino relations and to bring about the gradual hispanization of the Indians. San Cristobal, as the largest Ladino town in the highlands of Chiapas, is the major focus of these changes.

We may now attempt to summarize the Chiapas ethnic situation. A superordinate minority of Ladinos concentrated in San Cristobal lives among a subordinate majority of Indians dispersed in the rural hinterland. As the differences between the groups are cultural rather than racial, Indians do become ladinoized, although the process is neither easy nor rapid. Interethnic concubinage is frequent, and intermarriage occurs, though not commonly. Ritual kinship ties growing out of common membership in the Catholic church are frequent but unequal and unidirectional. The ethnic division of labor is clear-cut and complementary with the Indians as peasants, unskilled laborers, or servants and the Ladinos as merchants, artisans, clerks, and professionals. Ladinos generally treat Indians with the condescending kindness accorded to a backward child. Indians, though latently ambivalent and sometimes hostile to the Ladinos, are outwardly accommodated to their subservient status. Rigid rules of etiquette maintain the social distance between Indians and Ladinos, but physical distance in the shape of formal segregation is minimal. Contacts between Indians and Ladinos are frequent, particularly in the sphere of economic exchanges, but only exceptionally are such contacts of an equalitarian nature. Since postrevolutionary days, governmental action, economic transformations, and improvement in means of communication have combined to remove gradually the handicaps under which Indians have traditionally found themselves.

Ethnic Relations in Chiapas and in Guatemala: A Comparison

Indian-Ladino relationships in Guatemala have been well documented in a number of studies.[38] From these studies and from the present study, many similarities emerge between the ethnic situations in Guatemala and Chiapas. The geographical proximity of the two areas, their close political ties until the early nineteenth century, and the cultural similarity between Ladino and Indian groups in the two regions all contribute to the resemblance in patterns of ethnic relations on both sides of the Mexican-Guatemalan border.

In both areas, a minority of Spanish-speaking Ladinos lives among a majority of non-Spanish-speaking Indians belonging to a variety of Maya-speaking groups. On both sides of the border, the line of cleavage between Indians and Ladinos is cultural rather than racial, and Ladinos are strongly mestizoized. Indians are mostly maize-growing peasants, and Ladinos are concentrated in urban centers in Guatemala as well as in Chiapas. Similar hierarchical relations between Ladinos and Indians prevail in the two areas, with many resemblances in rules of etiquette, division of labor, interethnic compadrazgo, and so on. Our earlier discussion of Ladino as contrasted to Indian values in Chiapas coincides largely with the contrasting schema given by Gillin[39] and with observations made by Tumin.[40] Ladinos in both areas look down on manual labor and are stringently stratified into classes, and in both cases interethnic compadrazgo is frequent but unidirectional.[41]

Our own findings that Ladinos express more social distance toward the Indians than the Indians do toward the Ladinos agree with Tumin's findings in San Luis Jilotepeque, Guatemala.[42] Objective differences between Indians and Ladinos in dress, language, division of labor, education, type of housing, and the like are likewise very similar in the San Cristobal and the San Luis areas.[43] Patterns of intergroup etiquette such as the Ladino avoidance of the title of Señor when talking to an Indian are found in both areas.[44] Interethnic concubinage between Indian women and Ladino men occurs in San Luis as well as in San Cristobal.[45] In both areas, Indians are resigned to their lower status and do not express overtly their aggression against the Ladinos.[46]

This list of specific similarities across the Mexican-Guatemalan border could be extended. In view of the common or closely related historical and cultural heritage of the two areas, these similarities are not surprising. Indeed, *differences* between the two areas, to which we shall now turn, are more problematical than similarities.

The most apparent difference between the Chiapas situation and the Guatemalan one is the greater rigidity of the Ladino-Indian line in Guatemala. Both Gillin[47] and Tumin[48] describe the San Luis ethnic barrier in terms of "castes." Whereas in San Cristobal interethnic marriage occurs and passing is relatively frequent, in San Luis acquisition by an Indian of Hispanic culture does not make him a Ladino unless he moves to another community where his origins are unknown, and intermarriage between the two groups is not practiced.[49] Furthermore, Ladinos in San Luis seem to be much more conscious of physical differences between Indians and themselves than the San Cristobal Ladinos.[50] Tax[51] and Redfield,[52] on the other hand, report a less rigid situation more akin to the Chiapas one in their studies in western Guatemala. Tumin suggests that such differences as are reported by the various investigators in Guatemala are the result not so much of divergences in interpretation as of actual differences in the local situations. He contends that caste divisions are more rigid in eastern Guatemala (where his own community of San Luis Jilotepeque is located) than in western Guatemala (where Redfield and Tax made their studies).[53]

As the studies above were made in small towns, it is interesting to compare Quezaltenango, Guatemala's second largest city with a population of 27,700 in 1950, to San Cristobal in Chiapas. The two towns are of comparable size; yet the ethnic situation is quite different. As in many other towns of Guatemala, many Quezaltenango Indians live in town and the Indian group is itself stratified into socioeconomic classes. Neither of these conditions prevails in San Cristobal. While most of the Quezaltenango Indians know Spanish, most of them continue to speak their language, and the women still wear Indian clothes. Some of these urban Indians are quite well to do. Roughly 20 per cent of the artisans are Indians, and most of the bakeries are owned and operated by Indians. One Indian who recently died is reputed to have had a half-million dollars, and another owns a large hotel and other business. Indeed, Indians may be seen in almost any occupation from bank clerk to auto mechanic.

Indian students from Quezaltenango attend high schools and universities. One has studied English at a university in the United States, and a wealthy Indian sent his sons for training in Germany. An estimated 10 per cent of the registered members of the Lincoln Library (established by the United States government) are Indians. Before the recent conservative revolution, a number of Quezaltenango Indians held political posts both in Guatemala and abroad.

Wealthy, educated Indians in Quezaltenango are the object of mixed feeling on the part of the Ladinos. While Ladinos do not address them in the familiar form, and some Indians may even be addressed with the title of Don, there is resentment about their competitive economic position. Indians are sometimes said to be "taking over the town plaza," or central business district. One informant has heard a noted Ladino advocate the machine gun as the best Indian policy, though this was an unusual instance. Although we could determine no cases of segregation, an informant once heard Ladinos complain about wealthy Indians sitting in the higher-priced section of the movie theater.

Upper-class Indians appear quite culture-conscious. Recently, an academy of the Maya-Quiché language was formed to study, purify, and preserve Mayan languages and to create a special alphabet for the Quiché language. This Indian group also makes excursions to Indian towns and ruins.

Marriage is a major barrier between upper-class Indians and upper-class Ladinos in Quezaltenango. A Ladino will say that a prospective suitor for his daughter is intelligent, educated, and hard-working, but conclude with the remark that his being an Indian prohibits the marriage.

We believe that the striking differences between ethnic relations in San Cristobal and in Quezaltenango derive, in great part, from a difference in the flexibility in the ethnic line. Quezaltenango, like San Luis Jilotepeque and other Guatemalan towns, has a more rigid ethnic line than San Cristobal. Both in San Cristobal and in Quezaltenango, Indians settle in town, but in San Cristobal they pass into the Ladino group upon acquiring Ladino culture and language, whereas in Quezaltenango they rarely do so. In Quezaltenango the urban Indians remain a separate group and, though some may have lost the ability to speak Quiché or Cakchikel, their identity as Indians is maintained, with the women continuing to wear Indian costume. Insofar as Indians rise in education and wealth, the Indian group becomes internally stratified. Prevented as he is from entering the Ladino group, the Quezaltenango Indian resorts to the defensive mechanism of preserving his own cultural integrity and glorifying his own culture, much as United States Negroes resort to "race pride."[54] In San Cristobal, economic and educational mobility are accompanied by passing into the Ladino group and by entering the Ladino class structure. Hence, upwardly mobile Indians in the Chiapas situation are continuously drained out of the Indian group, which remains rural and unstratified.

Two complementary hypotheses may be advanced to account for the generally greater rigidity of Guatemalan ethnic relations as compared to the situations in Chiapas and even more so in Mexico as a whole:

1. Until the democratic revolution of 1944, the Ladino population of Guatemala held a monopoly of political power. Only since 1944 has the Guatemalan government introduced a program of social reforms and been committed to an ideology of cultural assimilation of the Indians.[55] Mexico, on the other hand, underwent its great social revolution in 1910–1917, and its government has introduced a series of agrarian and social reforms since that date. Since the period of government intervention in favor of the Indians has been longer in Mexico than in Guatemala, it can reasonably be assumed to have affected ethnic relations in Chiapas more profoundly than in Guatemala and in the direction of greater flexibility.

2. In Guatemala, the Indians constitute a majority (53.5 per cent) of the total population.[56] In Mexico as a whole, on the other hand, the Indian population consists of a number of small minority groups relegated to the most isolated parts of the country.

Even in regions where the Ladinos are the minority, as in San Cristobal, the Ladino middle and upper classes identify with the national community and, like most Mexicans, view the country's population as consisting basically of a culturally homogeneous group of hispanicized mestizos. In Guatemala, the near ubiquity of the Indians and the high visibility of cultural and linguistic differences leads, on the part of the Ladinos, to a much greater consciousness of ethnic differences, and to a dichotomous view of the national community.

The dimension of flexibility of ethnic line has some important consequences in the development of ethnic relations through time. One of the authors has presented elsewhere a dichotomous ideal-type model of race and ethnic relations.[57] The paternalistic type of group relations is typically found in preindustrial societies with little social or geographical mobility, a clear-cut division of labor along group lines, and a wide gap in wealth, education, and/or culture between dominant and subjugated groups. Inter-group relations are of the master-servant variety with benevolent despotism on the part of the dominant group and submissive accommodation on the part of the subjugated group. Such relations are generally intimate, but inequality of status is strictly enforced. Urbanization and industrialization undermine this paternalistic system, which then tends to evolve toward the competitive type of group relations *if the racial or ethnic line remains rigid*. The economic and social rise of the subjugated group is then perceived as a threat by the dominant group. The lower group ceases to be accommodated and is viewed by the dominant group as "uppity," aggressive, pushy, and dangerous rather than as childish, immature, inferior but lovable so long as it remains "in its place."[58] Whenever the ethnic or racial line becomes fluid, however, the competitive stage may be by-passed to the extent that group distinctions become obliterated through acculturation and miscegenation.

To return to our Chiapas-Guatemala comparison, we view both regions as having inherited from colonial times a paternalistic system of Ladino-Indian relations. In San Cristobal and in much of Guatemala the present system is still predominantly paternalistic, but rapidly changing. The direction of future change in both areas is going to be determined in part by the degree of ethnic-line rigidity prevailing in each local setting. In Chiapas, the relative flexibility of the line (as indexed by the amount of passing and the assimilative ideology of the upper- and middle-class Ladinos toward the Indians) is reflected in the virtual absence of competitive elements, with most exceptions among the lower classes. As Indians become acculturated and rise in education and wealth, they enter the urban Ladino class structure. Although the total assimilation of the Indians in Chiapas is far from completed, the long-range prospect for an integrated, mestizo-Hispanic society in Chiapas is good. For Mexico as a whole, this assimilative process is already very advanced.

In contrast, the Quezaltenango situation with its competitive elements shows the direction of change from a rural, folk, paternalistic system of ethnic relations to an urban one where the ethnic line remains rigid. Of course, the virtual absence in Guatemala of racism on North American or South African lines makes is very unlikely that a virulent form of competitive prejudice will ever develop in Guatemala. Cultural pluralism accompanied by invidious group distinctions, however, may be expected to persist longer in Guatemala than in Mexico.

NOTES

NOTE: Among the many people who helped us at various stages of our study we should like to mention G. W. Allport and E. Z. Vogt, of Harvard University, J. de la Fuente, A. Villa Rojas, and F. Montes Sanchez, of the Instituto Nacional Indigenista, L. Velasco Robles, P. Moscoso Pastrana, J. Baroco, F. Blom, J. M. Duran Aldana, and our many Zinacantan and San Cristobal informants who were at all times most kind and helpful. This study is part of the Mexican Cultural Change Project supported by the National Institute of Mental Health and directed by Professor E. Z. Vogt. The present chapter is mostly descriptive and qualitative. The quantitative results of our questionnaire and interview studies are reported in Pierre L. van den Berghe and Benjamin N. Colby, "Ladino-Indian Relations in the Highlands of Chiapas, Mexico," *Social Forces* 40, No. 1 (1961), 63–71.

1. Jorge A. Vivo Escoto, *Estudio de geografía económica y demográfica de Chiapas* (Mexico: Sociedad Mexicana de Geografía y Estadística, 1959), p. 217.
2. Originally the word "Ladino" was used to refer to the Indians who knew *the* language, that is, Spanish. By extension, Ladino came to be applied to all persons of Spanish culture as opposed to the Indians. Ladino also means literally "cunning" or "crafty." The origin of the term is thus clearly cultural, not racial. Richard N. Adams, *Encuesta sobre la cultura de los ladinos en Guatemala* (Guatemala: Editorial del Ministerio de Educación Pública, 1956), p. 18.
3. The 1950 census lists 110,233 persons in the 15 Indian municipios, but this number, even then, was probably an underestimate. Alfonso Villa Rojas, "La zona Tzeltal-Tzotzil: Su configuración social y cultural," *Acción Indigenista* 72 (1959): 4.
4. *Ibid.*, p. 2.
5. *Ibid.*, p. 4; Vivo Escoto, *op. cit.*, pp. 237–245.
6. There is some objective economic basis for placing the Zinacantecos on top of the various Indian groups. On the whole, Zinacantecos are better off than the other groups. Zinacantecos often hire other Indians, principally Chamulas, to work for them on their cornfields. Chamulas, on the other hand, seldom, if ever, hire Zinacantecos.
7. Tumin emphasizes this distinction between Ladino and Indian cultures in Guatemala and speaks of the asymmetry of the two groups' value systems. Melvin M. Tumin, "Cultura, casta y clase en Guatemala: Una nueva evaluación," in *Integración social en Guatemala* (Guatemala: Seminario de Integración Social Guatemalteca, 1956), pp. 185, 188.
8. Evon Z. Vogt, "Zinacantan Settlement Patterns and Ceremonial Organization" (Paper read at annual meeting of the American Anthropological Association, Mexico, 1959).
9. In a semiurban hamlet on the outskirts of San Cristobal, all Indian inhabitants over 15 were common laborers or domestic servants in Ladino households. Celia Bonilla Dominguez, *El proceso de cambio cultural en medicina* (Mexico: Instituto Nacional Indigenista, 1953), p. 6.

10. Evon Z. Vogt, "Ancient Maya Concepts in Contemporary Zinacantan Religion" (Paper read at the Sixth International Congress of Anthropological and Ethnological Sciences, Paris, 1960).

11. Donald E. Thompson, *Maya Paganism and Christianity* (Tulane University, Middle American Research Institute Publication No. 19, Pt. 1, 1954).

12. John Gillin, *The Culture of Security in San Carlos: A Study of a Guatemalan Community of Indians and Ladinos* (Tulane University, Middle American Research Institute Publication No. 16, 1951): 121–122.

13. Gonzalo Aguirre Beltrán, *Formas de gobierno indígena* (Mexico: Imprenta Universitaria, 1953), pp. 119–121.

14. For an analysis of differences in Indian and Mexican justice in a Chiapas Tzeltal community, see Duane Metzger, "Conflict in Chulsanto, a Village in Chiapas," *Alpha Kappa Deltan* 30 (1960), pp. 35–48.

15. Bonilla Dominguez, *op. cit.*, p. 8.

16. *Ibid.*, p. 9.

17. Villa Rojas, *op. cit.*, p. 3.

18. At the time of our visit the men's jail had 53 inmates, of whom 49 were Indians. The women's prison had 5 inmates, of whom 3 were Indians. No segregation existed in the two jails. Until recently, the San Cristobal police arrested drunken Indians and detained them for one or more days in jail so as to furnish the town with a constant supply of street sweepers. Even regular courts discriminate against the Indians, according to Aguirre Beltrán, *op. cit.*, pp. 108, 110.

19. Recently, the municipality of San Cristobal hired a Chamula Indian as policeman. We heard two Ladinos express astonishment at his getting such a "good" job. On the other hand, one Zinacanteco informant implied that being a policeman for the Ladinos would be beneath his dignity.

20. Pierre L. van den Berghe, "The Dynamics of Racial Prejudice: An Ideal-Type Dichotomy," *Social Forces* 37 (December 1958): 138–141.

21. However, up until recently, there were separate schools for Ladinos and Indians in some of the rural municipios where both ethnic groups were represented (Villa Rojas, *op. cit.*, p. 3). Recently, Indian youths being trained by INI for future teaching of children in their home areas have entered two of the previously all-Ladino schools in San Cristobal.

22. Up until a few years ago, Indians were debarred from the merry-go-round on the fiesta grounds, but this is no longer the case, due to the action of INI.

23. Aguirre Beltrán, *op. cit.*, p. 114; Villa Rojas, *op. cit.*, p. 3.

24. George M. Foster, "Compadrazgo in Spain and in Spanish America," *Southwestern Journal of Anthropology* 9 (1953): 1–28; Sidney Mintz and Eric R. Wolf, "An Analysis of Ritual Co-parenthood (Compadrazgo)," *ibid.* 6 (1950): 341–368; Edward H. Spicer, *Potam, a Yaqui Village in Sonora* (American Anthropological Association Memoir No. 77, 1954).

25. Foster, *op. cit.*

26. Van den Berghe and Colby, *op. cit.*

27. On this point we disagree with Tumin, who states in his San Luis study that ritual kinship between Ladinos and Indians makes for more equalitarian relations between the two groups. Tumin's own description of a baptismal fiesta for the Ladino godparents of an Indian child is clear evidence of inequality in the relationship. Melvin M. Tumin, *Caste in a Peasant Society* (Princeton: Princeton University Press, 1952), pp. 131–132. We are more in agreement with Gillin's interpretation of inter-ethnic compadrazgo (*op. cit.*, p. 61).

28. Villa Rojas, *op. cit.*, p. 3.

29. In some areas more distant from San Cristobal, such as Oxchuc, Indians wear Ladino clothing at all times; thus clothing is not always a distinguishing characteristic.

30. Minor variations in the degree of Ladino receptivity to changing Indians exist in smaller Chiapas communities. For brief descriptions of some of these, see Julio de la Fuente, "Relaciones etnicas en los altos de Chiapas," mimeographed (no date), and for a detailed account of Indian change in a Huistecan community, see Frank C. Miller, "The Influence of Decision-Making on the Process of Change: The Case of Yalcuc," *Alpha Kappa Deltan* 30 (1960): 29–34.

31. Aguirre Beltrán, *op. cit.*, p. 113.

32. *Ibid.*, p. 116.

33. Oliver La Farge, "Maya Ethnology: The Sequence of Cultures," in *The Maya and Their Neighbors* (New York: Appleton-Century, 1940); Ralph L. Beals, "The History of Acculturation in Mexico," in Juan Comas *et al.*, eds., *Homenaje a Alfonso Caso* (Mexico: 1951), p. 228.

34. Aguirre Beltrán, *op. cit.*, pp. 119, 141.
35. Thompson, *op. cit.*, pp. 19–21.
36. Aguirre Beltrán, *op. cit.*, p. 117.
37. Van den Berghe and Colby, *op. cit.*
38. Adams, *op. cit.;* Gillin, *op. cit.;* John Gillin, "Race Relations without Conflict: A Guatemalan Town," *American Journal of Sociology* 53 (1948): 337–343; Robert Redfield, "The Relations between Indians and Ladinos in Agua Escondida, Guatemala," *America Indígena* 16 (1956): 253–276; Sol Tax, "Ethnic Relations in Guatemala," *ibid.*, 2 (1942): 43–48; Tumin, *Caste in a Peasant Society*, and "Cultura, casta y clase"; Charles Wisdom, *The Chorti Indians of Guatemala* (Chicago: University of Chicago Press, 1940); Charles Wagley, *The Social and Religious Life of a Guatemalan Village* (American Anthropological Association Memoir No. 71, 1949).
39. Gillin, *The Culture of Security*, pp. 121–122.
40. Tumin, *Caste in a Peasant Society*, p. 117, and "Cultura, casta y clase," p. 184.
41. Gillin, *The Culture of Security*, p. 61; Tumin, *Caste in a Peasant Society*, p. 131.
42. *Ibid.*, pp. 133–135, 239–241.
43. *Ibid.*, pp. 25–37, 71–121; Gillin, "Race Relations without Conflict," p. 339.
44. *Ibid.;* Tumin, *Caste in a Peasant Society*, pp. 184–186.
45. Gillin, "Race Relations without Conflict," p. 338.
46. *Ibid.*, pp. 340–343; Tumin, *Caste in a Peasant Society*, p. 170.
47. Gillin, "Race Relations without Conflict," and *The Culture of Security*.
48. Tumin, *Caste in a Peasant Society*.
49. *Ibid.*, pp. 207, 215; Gillin, "Race Relations without Conflict," p. 338, and *The Culture of Security*, p. 53.
50. Tumin, *Caste in a Peasant Society*, pp. 63–64.
51. Tax, *op. cit.*
52. Redfield, *op. cit.*
53. Tumin, "Cultura, casta y clase," pp. 174–175.
54. Gordon W. Allport, *The Nature of Prejudice* (Cambridge: Addison-Wesley, 1954), p. 230.
55. Gillin, "Race Relations without Conflict," p. 339, and *The Culture of Security*, p. 51.
56. Of course, the high proportion of Indians in Guatemala can be

considered both a cause and an effect of the rigidity of the ethnic line.

57. Van den Berghe, *op. cit.*

58. The paternalistic-competitive distinction overlaps, of course, with Redfield's folk-urban continuum and Tönnies' *Gemeinschaft-Gesellschaft* types. Examples of paternalistic situations are the ante-bellum southern United States, the plantation regimes of the West Indies, Latin America, and Brazil, and most colonial regimes in their early phase. The modern United States and South African situations and anti-Semitism in much of the Western World are examples of competitive group relations.

8

Ethnic Membership and Cultural Change in Guatemala

Guatemala, a country of 4.2 million (1964 census), is one of the least westernized countries of the hemisphere. Its population is divided into a dominant group of Spanish-speaking Ladinos (who constituted 56.7 per cent of the total in 1964) and various subordinate Indian groups speaking related Maya languages. Four of these, Quiché, Mam, Cakchiquel, and Quecchi, include over 100,000 people each. The Indian population is heavily concentrated in the western and central highlands of the country, where the elevation is highest and the soil among the poorest and most difficult to cultivate. The coastal zones, the Petén, and the east, including the capital city, are predominantly Ladino.

Ethnic relations in Guatemala have been the object of considerable study, mostly by North American anthropologists.[1] Most studies have been of small local communities, and few attempts have been made to incorporate ethnic relations in the study of the whole of Guatemala as a complex plural society. Within the relatively small area of Guatemala, local ethnic situations vary greatly in such factors as demographic ratios, local dominance

Reprinted from *Social Forces* 46, no. 4 (June 1968): 514–522.

of Ladino versus Indians, and degree of conflict between the two groups. Such comparisons as have been made have seldom gone beyond stating differences in ethnic situations between local communities and suggesting *ad hoc* "explanations" for the differences.

Demographic Changes in Ethnic Composition

The purpose of this chapter is to account for two seemingly paradoxical sets of facts concerning ethnic membership in Guatemala:

1. While several community studies stress the rigidity of ethnic boundaries and while some authors go so far as to describe the Ladino-Indian distinction as a caste system,[2] there has been a steady decline in the relative size of the Indian group (Table 8-1). This decline, as we shall see, must be attributed mostly to "passing."

TABLE 8-1   Ethnic Composition of Guatemalan
Population (1774-1964)

Year	Per Cent Indian	Per Cent Ladino
1774	78.4	21.6
1880	64.7	35.3
1921	64.8	35.2
1940	55.7	44.3
1950	53.6	46.4
1964	43.3	56.7

2. Although the Ladino-Indian distinction has been described as largely cultural rather than racial, actual hispanization and ladinoization by Indians does not seem to affect the rigidity of the ethnic line at the local level. A number of "social Indians" are in fact strongly hispanicized.

The decline in the relative proportion of the Indian population could, of course, be due to several factors besides cultural assimilation, notably foreign immigration, a change in the definition of ethnicity in the census, and differential rates of net reproduction. In the last censuses, "ethnic group" has been consistently defined in terms of "social estimation in which a person is held in the place where the census is taken." Migration to and from Guatemala is on much too small a scale to account for a significant proportion of the change in ethnic ratio.

This leaves differential net reproduction rate as a possible determinant of the ethnic change. This factor, however, is also minor. There are no good vital statistics by ethnicity. It might be expected that both infant and adult mortality are somewhat higher for Indians than for Ladinos because of the latter group's better economic position. On the other hand, the disproportionate concentration of Ladinos in the low-altitude regions with malaria, intestinal parasites, and other tropical diseases may cancel out the Ladinos' slight economic advantage. The birth rate is quite high for both groups, leading to a 3.1 per cent annual population growth between the 1950 and the 1964 censuses. Statistics by *departamento* (or province) indicate that the net reproduction rate for Indians and Ladinos is nearly equal. There is no clear relationship between the rank order of Guatemala's 22 *departamentos* in the percentage of their Ladino population and in their rate of population increase (Table 8–2). The Spearman rank correlation is +.19. If one excludes the five *departamentos* which increased at rates considerably above the national average because of high rates of in-migration from other *departamentos,* the rank correlation becomes −.18.

The relative decline in the Indian population is thus largely a result of gradual cultural and social assimilation to the dominant Ladino group. On the average, some 15,000 to 20,000 Indians probably pass as Ladinos each year. In fact, the rate of ethnic mobility at the national level is probably comparable to that of class mobility within the Ladino group. Can one then speak of Guatemalan ethnic relations as constituting a caste system? The answer is clearly "no" at the national level; but in many local communities with a predominantly Indian population, the two ethnic groups closely approximate the three basic criteria

TABLE 8-2   Population Increase and Ethnicity

	Per Cent Yearly Population Increase 1950-1964	Rank Order in Rate of Population Increase	Per Cent Ladino 1964	Rank Order in Per Cent Ladinos
Izabal	5.3	1	88.5	7
Escuintla	5.1	2	92.9	4
Guatemala	4.2	3	89.7	5
Petén	4.0	4	75.1	8
Retalhuleu	3.8	5	66.1	9
Quetzaltenango	2.7	8.5	46.0	14.5
Suchitepéquez	2.7	8.5	46.0	14.5
Quiché	2.7	8.5	15.3	19
Baja Verapaz	2.7	8.5	47.7	13
Santa Rosa	2.7	8.5	99.1	3
Totonicapán	2.7	8.5	4.6	22
San Marcos	2.5	12.5	39.5	16
Huehuetenango	2.5	12.5	32.5	17
Alta Verapaz	2.4	14	8.1	20
Progreso	2.3	15	99.6	1.5
Zacapa	2.2	16.5	88.6	6
Jutiapa	2.1	16.5	99.6	1.5
Chimaltenango	2.0	18	23.9	18
Sacatepéquez	2.0	20	54.4	11
Sololá	2.0	20	7.3	21
Jalapa	2.0	20	57.4	10
Chiquimula	1.8	22	50.4	12
Total Guatemala	3.1	—	56.7	

of Kroeber's definition of caste, namely endogamy (accompanied by extensive interethnic concubinage), hierarchy, and ascribed membership by birth and for life. Methodologically, this discrepancy highlights the danger of extrapolating from the local microcosm to the larger society.

Assuming that changes in ethnic ratios reflect mostly cultural assimilation, an examination of statistics by *departamento* reveals wide regional differences in rates of assimilation (Table 8–3). Two main factors seem to affect the situation. The first one is relative size of Indian population. In all the heavily (75 to 95 per cent in 1964) Indian *departamentos* (Totonicapán, Sololá,

Alta Verapaz, Chimaltenango, and Quiché), the ethnic ratio remained quite stable. In all five *departamentos,* there was a large absolute increase in the Indian population, and in Quiché there was even a slight relative increase of 0.6 per cent between 1950 and 1964. The other four *departamentos* showed a relative decline of only 1.1 to 1.5 per cent. With the exception of Chimaltenango, these *departamentos* were also remarkably stable between 1940 and 1950. In short, there has been little change in ethnic composition of the heavily Indian western and central highlands for the last quarter-century.

TABLE 8-3   Changes in Ethnic Composition by *departamento* (1940-1964)

Departamento	Per Cent Indian			Change in Per Cent Indian		Rank Order of Change in Indian Population	
	1940	1950	1964	1940-1950	1950-1964	1940-1950	1950-1964
Izabal	19.0	17.2	11.5	−1.8	−5.7	13	16
Escuintla	18.9	15.9	7.1	−3.0	−8.8	8	8
Guatemala	19.5	18.1	10.3	−1.4	−7.8	14	11.5
Petén	32.3	27.9	24.9	−4.4	−3.0	4.5	17
Retalhuleu	56.3	51.9	33.9	−4.4	−18.0	4.5	2
Quetzaltenango	69.8	67.6	54.0	−2.2	−13.6	10.5	4
Suchitepéquez	66.9	67.7	54.0	−2.2	−13.7	10.5	3
Quiché	84.8	84.1	84.7	−0.7	+0.6	17	22
Baja Verapaz	60.4	58.5	52.3	−1.9	−6.2	12	13
Santa Rosa	10.5	9.4	0.9	−1.1	−8.5	16	9
Totonicapán	96.1	96.8	95.4	+0.7	−1.4	20	20
San Marcos	73.8	72.5	60.5	−1.3	−12.0	15	6
Huehuetenango	76.5	73.3	67.5	−3.2	−5.8	6.5	15
Alta Verapaz	93.9	93.4	91.9	−0.5	−1.5	18	18.5
Progreso	16.1	9.4	0.4	−6.7	−9.0	3	7
Zacapa	30.9	19.2	11.4	−11.7	−7.8	1	11.5
Jutiapa	22.2	19.6	0.4	−2.6	−19.2	9	1
Chimaltenango	86.6	77.6	76.1	−9.0	−1.5	2	18.5
Sacatepéquez	54.8	51.6	45.6	−3.2	−6.0	6.5	14
Sololá	93.3	93.8	92.7	+0.5	−1.1	19	21
Jalapa	49.5	50.5	42.6	+1.0	−7.9	22	10
Chiquimula	61.0	61.9	49.6	+0.9	−12.3	21	5

On the other hand, in four of the seven *departamentos* where Indians numbered only 10 to 20 per cent of the population in 1950, the decline has been rapid. In Jutiapa, the percentage of

Indians declined from 19.6 to 0.4, and absolute members went from 27,249 to 840; in Progreso, from 9.4 to 0.4 and from 4,482 to 240; in Santa Rosa, from 9.4 to 0.9 and from 10,294 to 1,460. Escuintla experienced an absolute decrease from 19,600 to 17,880 and a relative one from 15.9 to 7.1 per cent. Of the seven *departamentos* with Indian populations of less than 20 per cent in 1950, only Izabal, Zacapa, and Guatemala retained Indian minorities in excess of 10 per cent. Where Indians are in minority, especially in the eastern part of the country, they are becoming rapidly absorbed into the Ladino group. Ethnic ratios by *departamento* account for approximately 32 per cent of the variance in rate of assimilation. The Spearman rank correlation between Indian percentage in 1964 and relative decline of Indian population between 1950 and 1964 is −.54.

There are, however, five *departamentos* which had Indian majorities of 52 to 73 per cent in 1950 and nevertheless experienced large declines of between 18 and 12 per cent between 1950 and 1964. With the exception of Chiquimula, those *departamentos* are located in the southwestern zone of large-scale coffee, sugar-cane, and cotton plantations. San Marcos, Quetzaltenango, Retalhuleu, and Suchitepéquez are all rapidly growing due to the steady influx of agricultural laborers. It might be thought that the Indian population declines relatively (despite a slow rate of absolute growth) because of Ladino in-migration. Such is not the case, however, because much of the in-migration consists of Indians coming from the adjacent western highlands. If it were not for assimilation, the Indian proportion should rise rather than decline as a consequence of in-migration into that zone. The region of large-scale commercial agriculture is probably, with the capital city, the one where passing takes place most rapidly and on the largest scale. The fifth *departamento* with a relatively large but rapidly declining Indian population, Chiquimula, does not resemble the other four. Its rate of population growth is the lowest in the Republic, indicating considerable out-migration. Its location in eastern Guatemala is probably the main factor accounting for the rapid Indian decline. Chiquimula is surrounded by predominantly Ladino *departamentos* and is also relatively accessible to the capital city. A number of Indians probably emigrate to neighboring Ladino areas and become assimilated.

Factors of Sociocultural Change and Stability

What then are the conditions making for ethnic fluidity in some parts of the country and great rigidity in other parts? Passing across the ethnic line is largely a function of geographical mobility. The Indian who stays in his village or town of birth almost never passes; the one who goes to work in a larger city or on a large coffee, cotton, or sugar-cane plantation frequently becomes accepted as a Ladino after a few years. The *departamentos* where the Indian population is in greatest relative decline also tend to be those which, through in-migration, increase fastest in total population. Since most of the immigrants are Indians from the western highlands, this Indian migration is clearly accompanied by considerable ladinoization.[3]

In short, the more isolated, rural, economically stagnant parts of Guatemala with a predominantly Indian population have a stable ethnic situation; conversely, the larger urban centers, especially the capital city, and the zones of large-scale commercial agriculture which attract a mobile rural proletariat and where the Ladino population is larger are characterized by more fluid ethnic boundaries. Any comprehensive view of ethnic relations and culture contact in Guatemala or indeed anywhere must analyze the entire country as a differentiated system, rather than compare a series of small local "peasant" communities.

The second apparent paradox is that, at the local level, in the more stable part of the country, the ethnic line remains quite rigid in spite of considerable hispanization of the Indian population. Local Indians who are literate, speak fluent Spanish, dress as Ladinos, live in town, and practice nontraditional occupations are still frequently regarded as Indians by both Indians and Ladinos. Actual acculturation of Indians often seems to have no perceptible effect on the permeability of the local ethnic line. This situation appears paradoxical, of course, only if one accepts the common statement that the criteria of ethnic membership in

Guatemala are cultural. At this point we must examine more closely the definition of Guatemalan ethnic groups.

Most North American authors dealing with Latin America in general and Guatemala in particular have stressed the nonracial character of group distinctions in that part of the Western Hemisphere.[4] Some Latin-American and European authors, on the other hand, have argued that there is at least some racism in Spanish America and certainly in Brazil.[5] With the exception of a few atypical individuals, racism in Spanish America is at most a residual phenomenon. There is a clear priority of sociocultural criteria in the definition of group boundaries.

Although Guatemalan informants occasionally mention physical traits as distinguishing characteristics between Ladinos and Indians, the division is almost entirely nonracial.[6] Any attempt to divide the population phenotypically would, to be sure, overlap with ethnicity somewhat above the level expected by chance. However, most working-class Ladinos look undistinguishable from Indians, and a few Indians are genetically mestizos and phenotypically Caucasoid-looking. To most Guatemalans, physical appearance is of little significance except perhaps as a crude indicator of ethnicity. The most commonly used and most discriminating criteria of group membership are home language and clothing, especially footgear or its absence. There are a number of other cultural correlates of ethnicity such as literacy, the practice of orthodox versus syncretistic Catholicism, diet, house architecture, and standard of living; these characteristics taken individually are not completely reliable, but, used in combination, they leave little ambiguity as to a person's ethnic status.

Yet, the possession or nonpossession of certain objective cultural characteristics does not give one a complete picture of ethnic boundaries and mobility. Thus, for example, the asymmetry in the assimilation process also makes for an asymmetry in ethnic definition. In terms of objective characteristics, many Indians exhibit various degrees of biculturalism and bilingualism, whereas very few Ladinos do. Ladino status, then, is determined not only by knowledge of Spanish but also by ignorance of any indigenous tongue, while conversely biculturalism and bilingualism are associated with Indian status. This resolves the apparent paradox noted above. An Indian may acquire most of the cultural attributes of Ladinos and still be regarded as an Indian in his local community.

It might be expected that this rigidity would result from the reluctance of Ladinos to accept persons of known Indian ancestry into the superordinate group. Although some Ladinos are exclusivistic, the dominant attitudes of Ladinos (and the officially sanctioned policy of the government) are assimilationist. Most Ladinos regard indigenous cultures as backward and inferior to their own, and hence conclude that hispanization of the Indians is an improvement to be encouraged and that it contributes to national integration and progress. To the extent that ethnic attitudes are a determining factor, the rigidity of the ethnic line is probably more a function of the Indians' lack of desire or motivation to pass than of Ladino rejection. Many Indians show strong ethnic solidarity and only regard certain material and technological aspects of the dominant culture as desirable. Furthermore, Indians in some of the more remote parts of the highlands have locally retained sufficient political and economic autonomy from the larger society and from local Ladinos to make passing unattractive. The achievement of relative wealth, primary education, high political office in the municipality, and upward class mobility is often locally possible for an Indian without becoming assimilated to the Ladino group. High prestige through religious office in traditional Indian organizations such as the *cofradias* can be achieved only by remaining Indian.[7]

The Cultural Dynamics versus the Social Structure of Ethnic Relations

In practice, passing takes place overwhelmingly in three kinds of cases:

1. When Indians move outside of their home area;
2. When Indians are adopted or serve as domestic servants in Ladino households from childhood or adolescence on;

3. In cases of interethnic marriage or concubinage, when one of the spouses adopts the way of life of the other. In this last instance, there are some cases of Ladinos who become Indianized, as well as the more common reverse situation. The ethnic affiliation of mestizo children is generally determined by the dominant culture of their family of orientation, or, in the case of illegitimate children, by the ethnic affiliation of the parent who brings them up. Some local communities, however, recognize an intermediate category of mestizos.

A common feature of all three situations leading to passing is that the persons involved are partially or totally removed not only from their cultural milieu but, even more importantly, from their *socially significant groups* and from their traditional networks of interaction with kinsmen, friends, and acquaintances. Migration and adoption are, of course, facilitating factors in cultural assimilation and change, but they also mark an abrupt severance of social ties. It is useful here to distinguish between the *cultural dynamics* of ethnic situations and their *social structure* in terms of networks of relationships. Ethnicity is defined just as much by membership in a specific group which has distinct structural properties and social boundaries as by sharing of a cultural heritage and speaking a common language.

Most American anthropologists working in the Western Hemisphere have stressed the cultural aspect of ethnicity and have approached passing from the point of view of acculturation theory. European anthropologists studying similar phenomena in Africa, on the other hand, have adopted a more structural approach, focusing their analyses on social roles or on networks of interaction.[8] The Mexican anthropologist Aguirre Beltrán has adopted elements of both approaches and has thereby presented one of the most cogent analyses of culture contact and change in Mesoamerica.[9]

First, passing and acculturation are not one-way phenomena. This is true not only in the sense that members of the dominant group sometimes become assimilated to the subordinate group but also in the more interesting sense of "cultural commuting."

Acculturation and passing are not only continuous phenomena where individuals gradually move from one group and from one culture to another. A number of people exhibit various degrees of biculturalism and biethnicity and abruptly shift or commute back and forth in cultural and social space.[10]

This phenomenon is especially common among the migrant *Lumpenproletariat* in agriculture and industry. Thus, in Guatemala, the highland Indian who goes to work on the coastal plantations or takes a trip to the capital often dresses indistinguishably from Ladinos while away from home, uses Spanish as his lingua franca, and temporarily ceases to be readily identifiable as an Indian. When he returns home, he or she resumes wearing the local dress and again becomes more visibly Indian. The ladinoized Indian who is fluent in Spanish accommodates to the Ladino world for reasons of convenience and expediency, or simply to remain inconspicuous, or perhaps even to avoid discrimination. At home where he is known, he cannot pass, but in alien territory he frequently passes temporarily, shuttling back and forth between two cultural and social universes. Since many more Indians than Ladinos are bicultural, most people involved in this commuting are Indians. The nearly total absence of phenotypical differences between Ladinos and Indians makes passing in transitory, segmental, and public forms of interaction (such as the employer-employee or the merchant-customer relationship) relatively easy.

Cultural and social commuting raise, of course, the problem of what a person "really" is. A census taker using the criterion of local definition of ethnicity may classify the same person as a Ladino in one place and an Indian in another. Ethnic fluidity is a function not only of long-range, irreversible movement across the ethnic line but also of the repeated and sometimes quite rapid oscillations on both sides of it. Clearly, this commuting has both a cultural and a social dimension, and the latter is frequently the more important or relevant one.

The social structural approach to ethnicity leads us to a second phenomenon, namely asymmetry in the subjective perception of ethnic membership by the dominant and the subordinate groups.

In somewhat oversimplified terms, Ladinos tend to have a di-chotomous view of their country's ethnic structure, while Indians tend to have a more fragmented one. To most Ladinos, Guatemala consists basically of Indians and Ladinos. This does not mean, of course, that Ladinos are not aware of the existence of differences between Indians; these differences are so obvious as to strike even the most casual tourist. However, Ladinos tend to ascribe a distinctly secondary importance to ethnic distinctions between Indians, and they view the country as divided into the two significant groups. To most Indians, on the other hand, any concept of common "Indianness" is of little or no significance. The local town or *municipio* or at most the language community is the basic membership and reference group, so that most Indians will refer to themselves by locality (for example, as people of Cobán, San Cristobal, or Sacapulas) or as speakers of a given language (such as Quiché, Mam, or Cakchiquel). Other Indians are, to be sure, distinguished from Ladinos, but are typically treated as ethnic strangers and sometimes collectively referred to by a single generic term denoting any nonlocal Indian.

These two "models" of Guatemalan social structure are, of course, meaningfully related to the respective positions of Ladinos and Indians. Ladinos are indeed a culturally homogeneous group and a single-speech community. Although social-class distinctions between Ladinos are important, Ladinos are nevertheless a mean-ingful national group whose frame of reference is the State of Guatemala, and, in the case of the upper class, even Central America or the entire Spanish-speaking world. Many high-status Ladino families have kinship and friendship ties which extend over the entire country and even beyond. Nothing comparable is found among Indians who belong to localized groups without extensive outside ties and are surrounded by culturally distinct ethnic groups speaking related but frequently not mutually intel-ligible languages. Nor is there any significant political conscious-ness of common Indian status vis-à-vis Ladinos to overcome ethnic diversity, as there is for example between Zulu, Sotho, and Xhosa in South Africa.

Given the reality of ethnic differentiation among Indians, and the fragmented perception of that reality by most Indians, the close relationship between passing and geographical mobility becomes almost inevitable. Physically separated from his group of origin, the Indian finds other Indians almost as alien as Ladinos and has little or no prospect of acceptance into the local Indian group. On the other hand, to the extent that he already speaks Spanish, he will use that language almost exclusively in his dealings with both Ladinos and other Indians, unless he also happens to know the local Indian tongue. In order to be less conspicuous, he will abandon his own ethnic dress, and, if only for reasons of economy, he will dress as a Ladino rather than as a local Indian. (Hand-woven Indian clothes typically cost at least twice as much as cheap machine-made Ladino clothes.) In the absence both of strong resistance to assimilation by Ladinos and of an Indian solidary group to help maintain one's separate identity, the outcome is almost inevitably assimilation to the dominant group. Social benefits accruing from acceptance as a Ladino may not be very great in some areas, but they are sufficient to determine the main direction of assimilation, in much the same way as, for example, European immigrants to Canada predominantly assimilate to the English rather than to the French group even in Quebec where the French are a numerical majority.

Conclusion

In conclusion, an adequate understanding of the dynamics of ethnic relations requires a partial shift of focus from the conventional approach used by most North American anthropologists who worked in Mesoamerica. More specifically:

1. Local communities are not simply microcosms of the national society, nor is the national society simply a conglomerate of diverse ethnic groups. As Aguirre Beltrán, de la Fuente, and other Mexican anthropologists have noted, ethnic relations must be understood in the larger regional and national context.[11] In Guatemala, the picture which emerges from the macrocosmic view is radically different from that conveyed by the local community in the heavily Indian areas. Yet, the two perspectives complement each other, and the apparent paradoxes disappear if

one analyzes local communities in the context of the larger society.

2. The analysis of ethnic relations must not be focused exclusively or even primarily at the cultural level; ethnic relations cannot satisfactorily be accounted for simply in terms of cultural differences, culture contact, and acculturation between groups. It is important to distinguish analytically the structural elements of ethnic relations from the cultural ones. The dynamics of group membership, solidarity, and conflict, and the network of structured relationships both within and between groups, are at least as essential to an understanding of ethnic relations as the cultural dynamics of group contact. People are not only "carriers of culture"; they are also members of structured groups. Insofar as systems of ethnic relations are largely determined by structural asymmetries in wealth, prestige, and power between groups, an inventory of cultural differences gives one a very incomplete picture of group relations. Cultural differences are frequently symptoms rather than determinants of intergroup behavior, even in systems where the distinguishing criteria of group membership are predominantly cultural.

NOTES

NOTE: The field work which led to this chapter was made possible through a summer research grant of the Graduate School of Arts and Sciences, University of Washington, for which I want to express my gratitude. In the course of eight years of professional collaboration in Mesoamerican research, I have greatly profited from my exchanges with Benjamin N. and Lore Colby. I am also indebted to Ernest T. Barth and John F. Scott, of the University of Washington, who criticized an earlier draft of this chapter, and to my Mexican colleague Gonzalo Aguirre Beltrán with whom I discussed problems of culture change and ethnic relations in Mesoamerica.

1. See Richard Adams, *Political Changes in Guatemalan Indian Communities, A Symposium* (New Orleans: Tulane University, 1957); Ruth Bunzel, *Chichicastenango, A Guatemalan Village* (Locust Valley, N.Y.: Augustin, 1952); Allain X. Dessaint,

"Effects of the Hacienda and Plantation Systems on Guatemala's Indians," *Practical Anthropology* 10 (July–August 1963); John Gillin, *The Culture of Security in San Carlos,* Middle American Research Institute Publication, no. 16 (New Orleans: Tulane University, 1951); John Gillin, "Race Relations without Conflict: A Guatemalan Town," *American Journal of Sociology* 53 (1948): 337–343; Jackson Steward Lincoln, *An Ethnological Study of the Ixil Indians of the Guatemala Highlands* (Chicago: University of Chicago Microfilm, 1945); Marvin K. Mayers, ed., *Languages of Guatemala* (The Hague: Mouton, 1966); Manning Nash, *Machine Age Maya* (American Anthropological Association Memoir no. 87, 1958); Robert Redfield, "The Relations between Indians and Ladinos in Agua Escondida, Guatemala. *America Indígena* 16 (1956): 253–276; K. H. Silvert, *A Study in Government, Guatemala* (New Orleans: Tulane University, 1954); Sol Tax, "Ethnic Relations in Guatemala," *America Indígena* 2 (1942); and Melvin Tumin, *Caste in a Peasant Society* (Princeton: Princeton University Press, 1952). The principal works in Spanish are the series of publications of the Seminario de Integración Social Guatemalteca (Guatemala: Ministerio de Educatión Pública).

2. See especially Tumin, *op. cit.*
3. There is, of course, nothing unusual or surprising about the relationship between geographical mobility and a breakdown of social barriers between ascriptive groups that are not phenotypically distinguishable. The Hindu caste system is also being undermined by horizontal mobility and urbanization, but the motivation and mechanics of "passing" are quite different in India and Guatemala. The low-caste Hindu who claims higher status is deliberately trying to "cheat" in order to evade onerous disabilities. Many Hindus who went overseas as indentured laborers, for example, passed by changing their names. See Pierre L. van den Berghe, *Caneville, The Social Structure of a South African Town* (Middletown: Wesleyan University Press, 1964), p. 191. In Guatemala, on the other hand, there is relatively little opposition by Ladinos to assimilation and little desire by Indians to become assimilated. Passing there is largely a gradual consequence of interaction. In the Guatemalan context, Mario Monteforte Toledo notes the importance of internal migration for acculturation. See his *Guatemala, Monografía Sociológica* (Mexico: Universidad Nacional Autónoma de México, 1959), pp. 105, 107.

4. Cf., for example, Charles Wagley and Marvin Harris, *Minorities in the New World* (New York: Columbia University Press, 1958).

5. Monteforte Toledo, for example, claims that the Ladino-Indian distinction in Guatemala is based at least partly on a social conception of "race," *op. cit.,* p. 116. The presence of at least mild racism in Brazil is unquestionable. Cf. Chapter 6 in this volume. In Spanish America, however, there is a clear predominance of cultural criteria of group membership over phenotypical ones. Beyond the expression of mild esthetic preferences for certain physical traits, one is hard put to encounter any evidence of racism in Spanish America, although there was some anti-African prejudice in colonial days. See Pierre L. van den Berghe, *Race and Racism* (New York: Wiley, 1967).

6. For example, in a sample of 40 Ladinos in the town of Nebaj, in the *Departamento* of Quiché, where I conducted field work in the summer of 1966, 33 mentioned only cultural differences when asked what distinguished Ladinos from Indians. Six respondents mentioned both cultural and physical traits. None listed physical traits only. (One person did not reply.) Benjamin N. Colby and I have written up the results of our study in a monograph, *Ixil Country, A Plural Society in Highland Guatemala* (Berkeley: University of California Press, 1969).

7. *Cofradias* are religious brotherhoods with ranked officeholders who devote themselves to the cult of a saint. The statues are carried around in elaborate processions, and the *cofradias* are the center of much ritual in the syncretistic Maya-Catholic religion of Guatemalan Indians.

8. See, for example, Philip Mayer, *Townsmen or Tribesmen* (Cape Town: Oxford University Press, 1961); and his article, "Migrancy and the Study of Africans in Towns," *American Anthropologist* 64 (1962): 576–592.

9. See Gonzalo Aguirre Beltrán, *El Proceso de Aculturación* (Mexico: Universidad Nacional Autónoma de México, 1957).

10. For a discussion of similar problems and a critique of acculturation theory in the African context, see Pierre L. van den Berghe, ed., *Africa, Social Problems of Change and Conflict* (San Francisco: Chandler, 1965), Introduction.

11. See Aguirre Beltrán, *op. cit.,* and Julio de la Fuente, *Relaciones Interétnicas* (Mexico: Instituto Nacional Indígenista, 1965).

Part III

SOUTH AFRICA

9

Research in South Africa:
The Story of My
Experiences
with Tyranny[1]

That the social scientist (or, for that matter, any scientist) can achieve olympian detachment and objectivity is a myth which is fortunately not as widespread as it was thirty or more years ago when the behavioral sciences, except in Germany, were still largely under the sway of positivism. An increasing number of autobiographies, mainly of anthropologists, have been published, highlighting, often in moving terms, the human drama of social research.[2] Social scientists have even become characters in works of fiction, and the ambiguities of their roles have been a rewarding subject for novelists and for social scientists analyzing their own profession.[3] Here I want to relate my experiences as a sociologist working in a highly explosive situation ridden with racial conflict, namely in South Africa, during the period February 1960 to December 1961.[4] While South Africa probably represents an extreme case, many of the incidents and feelings mentioned here have, of course, been reported by other social

Reprinted from Gideon Sjoberg, ed., *Ethics, Politics, and Social Research* (Cambridge: Schenkman, 1967), pp. 183–196.

scientists, notably anthropologists doing field work in a colonial context.

South Africa was not my first exposure to tyranny. As a child, I had experienced subjugation under German military occupation in Belgium and France. As an adolescent, I learned what it meant to belong to the *Herrenvolk* when I returned to the land of my birth, the then Belgian Congo. I am ashamed to confess that I rather relished this feeling of racial superiority which, as a white colonial, I rapidly shared with my fellow Europeans. At that time, I completely failed to make a parallel between the tyranny I had suffered under in Europe and that from which I benefited in Africa. So much does one's class position blind one to social realities that superficial dissimilarities can hide profound resemblances. Only by repeating this cycle of being alternatively on the subordinate and on the dominant side of the fence did I reach my present position. A few years after my Congo interlude I found myself again in the position of the underdog, as a private in the United States Army. When I finally went to South Africa, I once more became a member of the *Herrenvolk* by virtue of my skin pigmentation, but this time it was despite my militant rejection of such a role. During my two years' stay in the country, my political opinions continued to evolve from a rather old-fashioned nineteenth-century liberalism toward a nonmaterialistic Gandhian socialism.

I should perhaps spell out my present position somewhat more fully. I have become increasingly convinced that parliamentarianism in a Western type of bourgeois democracy, even under conditions of universal adult suffrage and legal equality, is not capable of solving the most fundamental problems faced by modern societies (such as land distribution, the optimum use of human labor and leisure, medical care, city planning). The liberal laissez-faire model, which is increasingly being abandoned in "developed" countries, is even more blatantly inadequate in the Third World. At the same time, I believe that, while the work of Marx was a great contribution to sociology and to the analysis of nineteenth-century European capitalism, Marxian socialism is hardly more relevant than liberalism to the problems of the still largely agrarian countries of the twentieth century. This is particularly true of tropical Africa, where Marxian class analysis bears little relationship to social reality, a fact recognized by the proponents of African Socialism.

In addition to these and many other problems of substance, I disagree with the classical Marxian ethos on two major ideological grounds. First, I am a nonmaterialist in the dual sense that, as a pantheist, I cannot deny the existence of the "supernatural," and in that I do not accept the primacy of material over nonmaterial goals and determinants of social action. For all its wealth, I regard the United States as farther removed from the ideal society than many poorer social orders. Similarly, South Africa, the continent's richest country, also has the most ethically bankrupt social order. Nor is the problem simply one of *distribution* of wealth, for gross inequities can exist in societies with a relatively equal distribution of material rewards, a problem long recognized by Marxian and other socialists. Second, I regard physical violence against persons as morally reprehensible, and I consider Gandhian techniques of opposition to be both ethical and efficacious. Nevertheless, I regard myself as a socialist insofar as I believe that private property should be limited to consumer goods, and, in developing economies where still relevant, to small-scale land and tool ownership by self-employed farmers and artisans.

The present account is an attempt to retrace the impact of the South African brand of racial tyranny on myself as a sociologist and as a person and on my scientific methodology and findings. I shall try to deal with the problem from four main points of view: (1) relations with the government; (2) relations with private persons, both whites and nonwhites; (3) subjective feelings and attitudes; (4) problems of scientific objectivity.

Defining my relationship with the South African government seemed at first a fairly simple matter, dictated mostly by expediency. From the outset, I decided that I should have no scruples in deceiving the government and that the paramount consideration in my dealings with the state would be to minimize obstacles to my research without compromising my principles. When applying for a South African visa, I decided that it would be unwise to reveal the real purpose of my stay (namely to study race relations), and I declared that I was a social scientist interested in "the spectacular economic development of South Africa." Once in the country, however, the problem became much more difficult. Generally, my strategy was to avoid attracting the attention of the authorities without letting undue caution interfere with my research and without sacrificing my integrity. If caught in a violation of law or custom, I was determined to "play it dumb." Such a broad line of conduct, while it proved workable in most instances, nevertheless required constant decisions as new contingencies arose. I quickly became aware that, try as I might, there was no escape from the color bar and that I must, however reluctantly, comply with segregation much of the time. Inviting arrest for violation for apartheid regulations would have defeated the purpose of my stay, and besides, jails also are segregated, so that even in prison I should have enjoyed against my will countless special privileges.

Probably to save my self-respect and allay my feelings of guilt, I decided that I would engage in some symbolic protest actions, that I would refuse certain "customary" white privileges, and that I would break some laws which I considered iniquitous or which exposed my nonwhite friends to embarrassment. For example, I refused to be served before nonwhite customers in shops or in government offices; similarly, I filled in the item labeled "race" on official questionnaires with the term "human" or "American," often to see it changed surreptitiously to "white" by a state official who must have wondered at the stupidity of foreigners who do not even know that they belong to the master race. When I invited Africans to my house, I offered them alcoholic beverages, a criminal offense until 1962, and when in the company of nonwhites I always tried to avoid using segregated facilities, or, when I did, I used the nonwhite ones.

In addition, I broke other laws and regulations, not so much on grounds of principle, but because compliance with them would have jeopardized my research more than their evasion. For example, whites are required to carry special permits to enter most

African "locations" and "reserves." I entered such places count-less times without ever asking for a permit. To state candidly the purpose of my visits (either research or simply social intercourse with African friends) would have appeared both incredible and suspicious to the authorities. Violation of the law, on the other hand, made me more inconspicuous, inasmuch as I was rarely detected. When caught, my skin color ironically protected me from adverse consequences, and I always got away with a warn-ing. Most of the time I pretended to have lost my way, and the police gave me elaborate road directions, while commenting on the danger of traveling unarmed in "Native areas." Had I had a black skin, of course, I would have been repeatedly arrested and convicted for "pass" offenses. Even in my defiance of the law, I was given preferential and often deferential treatment, simply because of my lack of pigmentation.

On one occasion, however, I narrowly escaped arrest for breaking a racial taboo. When I offered a female colleague of mine a lift home in my motorcar, she accepted but suggested that my wife accompany us. As my colleague was a Muslim of Indian origin, I assumed at first that her request was motivated by rea-sons of propriety, although, emancipated as she was, I was some-what surprised. I soon discovered that her prudent foresight spared both of us arrest for "immorality." Under the Immorality Act, it is a criminal offense punishable with up to seven years of prison for whites and nonwhites of opposite sex to engage in "immoral or indecent acts." (Oddly, homosexual intercourse across the color bar is licit, perhaps because it does not lead to "bastardization" of the *Herrenvolk*.) My colleage sat next to me on the front seat of the car and my wife in the back. As we reached an intersection a policeman, shocked by the sight, was about to pursue us on his motorcycle and only desisted when he noticed my wife in the back of the car. Had my wife not accom-panied us, we would undoubtedly have been arrested and our presence alone in an automobile would have been accepted in court as incriminating evidence of intention to have "illicit carnal relations."

In one respect, at least, my role vis-à-vis the state was simpli-

fied. As a naturalized American citizen, I was debarred from taking part in any political activity in South Africa on penalty of
losing my United States passport. This proved a useful conscience-
saving device to justify my political inaction, although this reason
seemed to wear thinner as time went on.

As part of my effort to avoid attracting official attention, I had
recourse to the authorities for information only as a last resort.
While this course of action may have debarred me from certain
sources of data, I am convinced that the loss has been smaller than
the gain. On the few occasions when I did approach government
agencies for information, I encountered such secrecy and lack of
cooperation that my attempts proved fruitless.

There were many occasions, however, when my policy of in-
conspicuousness proved impracticable. These included attendance
as an observer at nonwhite political meetings and demonstrations,
participation in interracial gatherings, and delivering public
lectures. All these activities gave me insights and entrees into
groups that would otherwise have been closed to me, but they
also exposed me to observation and, on one occasion, to inter-
rogation by the secret police. However, as these actions were all
perfectly legal, I decided that the advantages outweighed the
drawbacks and that the dangers involved were minimal. In public
lectures, I was often asked to talk on some racial topic, and I
generally obliged by talking about the United States, the Congo,
Mexico, or some other foreign countries, but I never tried to
evade questions dealing specifically with South Africa.

Generally speaking, I encountered many fewer hindrances to
my research on the part of the state than I had anticipated. This
reflects, I believe, the inefficiency of South African officialdom
rather than its tolerance. I am reasonably certain that the state
was unaware of the nature of my activities. In one respect only
did racial restrictions interfere with my research. When I was
doing a community study of a sugar town, I found it impossible
to reside there, as the town had been zoned for Indians or Africans; whatever white housing existed was reserved for civil servants or sugar company employees. Except when invited overnight
by friends, I had to commute from nearby Durban. There were,

to be sure, two hotels for whites in town, but, inasmuch as I could not have received nonwhites on the premises, there would have been little point in staying at either of them; the one non-white hotel was not licensed to accept me.

As my stay in South Africa lengthened, my aversion to the entire state machinery became more intense, to the point where, like most Africans, I reacted with faint nausea at the mere sight of any police or army uniform. This seemingly hysterical reaction built up as a consequence of observing police brutality and shooting at first hand and of having many people recount their arrests, searches, beatings, and periods of imprisonment.

My relations with individual South Africans as private citizens are much more difficult to describe, for they involve several dimensions, among which the most important are skin color, political opinions, the definition of my role, and the degree of intimacy. Normal, uninhibited relationships across the color line are practically impossible in South Africa. This is true in part because the range of places and activities which can be attended or engaged in by persons of different races is extremely limited and because the legal sanctions and social pressures against breaking apartheid taboos are severe. But, more importantly, there is a climate of mutual distrust and conflict which poisons most attempts to bridge the racial chasm.

Naturally, this state of affairs substantially affects, and interferes with, data collection and raises important questions of factual validity. In my own work, the most extreme example of interference with data gathering arose from my attempt to conduct interviews among migrant agricultural workers. These nonliterate peasants belonged to the Pondo subgroup of the Xhosa and were at the time (early 1961) in open revolt against the South African government. With few exceptions, they spoke only Xhosa and Zulu. On both linguistic and political grounds I decided to train an African assistant to conduct the interviews. The latter were anonymous and quite short (taking from ten to fifteen minutes to administer). They consisted largely of nonsensitive questions on family composition, work history, and the like, with, however, two sensitive items tacked on at the end concerning attitudes toward whites and Indians. A trial run in a geographically isolated workers' compound was made, during which the African assistant conducted the interviews under my supervision. The workers responded, though slowly and sullenly, as they would have in most situations involving a white man giving orders.

The replies to the census-type questions seemed trustworthy enough, but the responses to the items concerning attitudes toward whites were highly uniform, stereotyped, and evasive. Almost invariably, the workers cautiously replied, "I have nothing against them," or "They don't bother me." Intuitively I knew better than to attribute much validity to these answers, but, as I felt reasonably satisfied with the conduct of the interviews, I left my assistant on his own. On the same day, he conducted another thirty-five interviews, and as soon as I had left the scene, answers to the attitude questions revealed, as I had expected, intensely negative feelings toward whites: "They are my worst enemies," "I hate them," "I will feel much better when I am dead than being ruled by the Europeans," and so on.

On the following day, my assistant again attempted to interview workers in three other compounds up to twelve miles away from the first one, and he met with complete failure. Overnight a noncooperation order had spread over the entire area, and my assistant returned with a none-too-common 100 per cent refusal rate. It turned out that the interview schedule was thought to be a government census. A few weeks earlier the government had conducted its decennial population census and had met with an effective boycott in Pondoland. The workers now plausibly assumed that the government was making a fresh attempt to collect the information, and they consequently boycotted my study.

To a degree, one can determine the nature of one's relationships through one's own behavior. Here the basic alternative in my case was either to behave as most white South Africans did, or to act in a "color-blind" fashion as I would in Europe or America. The first approach would have meant ignoring the most elementary rules of courtesy toward nonwhites. Not only would I have found such a role highly uncongenial, but such an approach would have seriously jeopardized my research. For a white person living permanently in South Africa, the rigid master-servant model of interracial behavior is undoubtedly the easiest to adopt, but for my purposes it would never have worked, assuming that I would have been willing to compromise my principles. The other possibility—to act in a way which made it clear that I considered race as of no consequence—was obviously the one I adopted, not as a result of long deliberation but, rather, "naturally." The simple fact of treating non-Europeans with elementary courtesy, I quickly discovered, was enough to arouse the hostility of many whites. This animosity was, however, a relatively small price to pay. Nevertheless, "color-blind" behavior, because of its highly unusual character in South Africa, entails many other complications, including frequent suspicion among nonwhites.

On both sides of the color bar, attempts were made to explain or rather reinterpret my unconventional behavior in terms of existing roles. For whites I was a Communist agitator, or more frequently an odd foreigner who had not yet learned how to "handle the Natives." Amusement at my social "ineptness" was a more common reaction than anger or even annoyance. Often whites predicted that I would soon become converted to their way of thinking and acting. It was probably on the part of westernized Indians that my role was most readily accepted at face value and that initial suspicion, amusement, or hostility was most completely absent. Among Africans distrust was common. Politically militant and educated Africans often tried to fit me into the role either of a police informer or an *agent provocateur,* or of a missionary-type "do-gooder" or paternalist. Traditional or older Africans, on the other hand, whether through caution or through inability to shed suddenly the force of habit, often continued to behave in the submissive manner that most whites expected. Needless to say, this imbalance in the relationship made for much awkwardness.

My experience thus confirms a common observation of social scientists doing field work: Due to the unusual nature of their role, they can only partially determine its definition. A note of humor might be interjected here. Lest the suspicion that I belonged to the secret police appear far-fetched, I should add that it was not entirely unfounded. I discovered, rather late in my field work, that the car I had purchased, a beige Volkswagen, happened to be the model and color used by the "Special Branch" of the police. My Afrikaans-sounding surname, a common one in South Africa, was an added liability, not only among nonwhites but also among Afrikaners who considered that our ethnic affinity made my lack of color discrimination an even more heinous crime. To make matters even worse, a high-ranking police officer was named Colonel van den Berg, another bit of "evidence" which linked me, however vicariously, with the forces of repression in the minds of Africans. In fact, I myself developed such an aversion to my surname that, when I learned that a namesake was to become my next-door neighbor, I feared the worst. Actually, he turned out to be one of the country's hundred-odd Afrikaner liberals, and we became close friends.

Except in small intellectual circles, regular association with nonwhites on the basis of equality entails nearly total ostracism from the white community. But the small avant-garde interracial cliques that form in the large cities and to whom my social contacts became gradually more restricted constitute by no means "normal," unstrained islands of sanity in a sea of racialism. They too are poisoned, however subtly, by the larger environment. Africans associating with such groups open themselves up to accusations that they are tame "mission boys" curtseying for the favor of white paternalists who condescend to "drink tea with clean Natives." Parties can be held only in private homes, usually of whites, and nonwhites are mostly in no economic position to reciprocate the hospitality. Interracial parties are frequently raided by the police, spontaneously or on the complaints of white neighbors, and African guests are subjected to humiliations such as smelling their breath to check whether they have been drinking. Recent white converts to nonracialism behave unnaturally under the strain of trying to be "natural" and remain conscious of their unconventionality—which they display with the self-complacency and titillation of one who has entered a daring, reckless bohemia. At the same time, a white person must be constantly on guard lest an innocent remark be given a racial twist, or lest he mention an activity or place from which nonwhites are debarred. Many topics of conversation, such as the cinema or the theater, thus become taboo, and consequently the only safe topic becomes, paradoxically, politics. However, as political opinions tend to be homogeneous in these small self-contained groups, disagreement is rare except on minor tactical issues, and discussions soon become dull. Once in a great while, a relationship across the color bar becomes intimate enough that one's racial caste can be forgotten or at least laughed away, but this is exceptional.

My role as a lecturer at the University of Natal, at that time still an "interracial" though internally segregated institution, was also greatly complicated by the racial situation. As with most of my colleagues, I faced the dilemma of whether I should grade the work of all my students strictly on the basis of their objective performance, or whether I should make allowances in the case of my nonwhite students. The temptation was, of course, to do the latter. To most nonwhites, the language of instruction was a foreign idiom; furthermore, as a consequence of school segregation, nonwhite students had received an inferior primary and secondary education. Even within the university they did not have equal opportunities with whites, for they were denied access to the main library, to all the best dormitories, dining halls, and lounges, to all sports grounds, to laboratories, and to many other facilities. Yet how could I justify discrimination in reverse? I adopted the attitude that my judgment was to be based solely on objective performance, while at the same time I tried to redress some of the most glaring aspects of academic inequality (such as differential access to books), but I felt quite uncomfortable about it all the same. I should add that several of my best students were Africans and Indians, though a disproportionate number of students with inadequate backgrounds also were.

As employers of African labor, my wife and I have had a completely unsuccessful experience, largely again because of the racial situation. For a short period of about three months we employed a part-time maid. The master-servant relationship quickly proved untenable, however. On the one hand, we felt unbearably guilty for being exploiters; although we paid her more than current wages we could not afford to compensate her on a scale which we would have considered equitable. On the other hand, our domestic, unused to being treated as a human being, rapidly became more of a liability than a help. As we failed to fulfill her role expectation of white bosses, she became unable to play her role of servant and neglected her most elementary duties. We decided to terminate her services, but she continued to visit us, and our relationship became a friendly one when it ceased to be on a master-and-servant basis. Henceforth, we did not employ any domestics, an almost unprecedented fact among white South Africans.

However much environmental contingencies aggravate one's difficulties in a country like South Africa, the greatest source of strain in my case and in that of most white liberals and socialists is internal, not external. To maintain one's intellectual and emotional balance becomes an extremely difficult task. Oppressed nonwhites carry a heavy burden of frustration, but white liberals carry, besides ostracism and punishment, the millstone of their own guilt for enjoying privileges which they abhor. There is no escape from apartheid, not even in suicide, for even hearses and cemeteries are segregated. One may, of course, leave South Africa, but then one feels guilty for abandoning the sinking ship. I could not escape a nagging feeling of guilt for doing the simplest things such as going to the cinema, driving my car, or swimming, all things from which my nonwhite friends were debarred by law, custom, or poverty. Even the freedom to take a leisurely stroll becomes a white caste privilege in a country where Africans have to carry passes in order to have the right to be anywhere at all.

One may seek, of course, to escape the guilt by identifying completely with Africans, assuming that those around you will let you forget your skin color. But then, one can easily become antiwhite, a danger of which my wife had to keep reminding me, oftentimes to my considerable annoyance. All things considered, the surprising fact is not that there are so few white liberals in South Africa, but rather that there should be any at all, at any rate outside psychiatric hospitals.

Fear of physical violence was never a source of strain as far as I was concerned, although in periods of particularly acute crisis many whites became panic-stricken, stocked food, and bought large quantities of firearms. If I stress this point, it is not to brag about my courage, but to dispel the myth that individual white civilians in South Africa are under constant threat of violence. Nonwhites are the victims of considerably more violence, both on the part of police and from thugs and criminals, than are whites. Even at the height of the abortive revolt of 1960 I never was personally threatened although I frequently went to African areas at night and was sometimes in the midst of crowds of African demonstrators.

So far I have dealt mostly with personal relations and attitudes. From a scientific viewpoint, the effect of these on my research is of far greater importance than my personal tribulations. Some of my writings about South Africa have been attacked as biased, and their language has been described as intemperate. Thus, a recent book of mine which was reviewed in American periodicals as "objective," "remarkably clear," and "meeting the highest standards of scholarship" was described in the Johannesburg *Sunday Express* in the following terms: "Dr. van den Berghe . . . gives a confused picture of South Africa, and his book, which is a strange mixture of the sensational and the sociological, contains several contradictions." On another occasion, one of the prominent members of the small community I studied (who was one of my main informants and was by no means a virulent racist) accused me of antiwhite and anti-South African feelings. He seemingly regarded the two charges as synonymous with each other and with a rejection of racial discrimination and segregation.

Far from denying the charge of bias, I have tried to make my ideological position explicit. I have always claimed that the attainment of objectivity is an illusion, although its approximation may be an ideal. I feel reasonably confident that the selection of my facts has not been influenced by my views and experiences.

Likewise, I think that I am familiar with every argument advanced by each of the major South African political groups to defend a given ideology. My interpretation of facts has, of course, inevitably been colored by my own position. For instance, many persons who are not racists make value judgments and use double standards in comparing different cultures. Such people often accept discrimination and segregation based on cultural differences or the standard of Western education (as distinguished from "race") as inevitable, natural, and "in the nature of things." Differential treatment is justified by the premise that some people are civilized and responsible, while others are in a state of permanent cultural infantilism and dependence. Now, I am not an extreme cultural relativist, and I accept that there is such a thing as cultural evolution from the simple to the complex (at least in material culture). However, I regard the concept of primitivism as misleading and invidious insofar as it often connotes inferiority or incapacity in the moral, intellectual, and political spheres, and I reject the postulate of cultural infantilism. Hence, I interpret invidious distinctions between people of different cultures, not as being dictated by the nature of social "reality," but rather as the product of ethnocentrism. Since very few white South Africans, including even "liberal" ones, share my premises, my interpretation of the facts must necessarily and rightly appear biased to them.

Some South African and American scholars have also taken exception to my choice of vocabulary. Terminology is, of course, highly debatable and, in last analysis, largely arbitrary. However, in a situation such as that of South Africa ordinary words become inadequate. For example, to use "conservative" as a euphemism for "reactionary" distorts reality. Terms like "oppression," "exploitation," "racialism," "tyranny," and "reaction," although they have acquired derogatory connotations, are the only appropriate ones, intemperate though they may sound to scholarly ears.

The problem of objectivity plagues all the sciences, but our present concern is with South Africa, or, more broadly, African scholarship. Much, if not most, of the African literature is accepted as "objective" because it uses the accepted vocabulary of western European academics and refrains from making *overt* value judgments. Yet, until the last few years, most publications on Africa were written from a predominantly European viewpoint and contained a great number of unstated value judgments and double standards. Until Africans regained their independence, African historiography, for example, was almost entirely the monopoly of European scholars and consequently became the historiography of colonialism, with its elaborate mythology of African primitivism and the European "civilizing mission." African nations and states became tribes; African religions were dubbed heathen or pagan; European military conquests were termed "punitive expeditions" or "pacification"; white persons traveling through areas known for centuries to the outside world became heroic explorers by virtue of their skin color; Christian missionaries were held to be selfless dispensers of all of civilization's blessings. The history of the slave trade was rewritten to make it sound like an Arab undertaking to which great humanitarians like Léopold II of Belgium (whose agents killed and maimed Congolese by the tens of thousands) put an end.

Anthropologists have generally been more sensitive to the distortions of ethnocentrism, at least during the last three or four decades; nevertheless, they often became tools of the colonial administration and tended to advocate policies which favored the status quo under the guise of not disturbing traditional African societies. Though they often served colonial regimes, many anthropologists strangely seemed to ignore the colonial situation in their descriptive monographs, thereby also slanting African reality.

All these criticisms of the old "colonial" school of African scholarship apply to much of the literature on South Africa. Even attacks against apartheid have been mostly couched in the restrained terms of an obsolete, nineteenth-century, British-style, humanitarian paternalism, and until recently the "Natives" were viewed as the passive objects of white administration. Only in the past decade is the African point of view becoming heard.

It is far from my intention to plead for a rewriting of African history from the point of view of Pan-Africanism or any other form of fashionable orthodoxy. For South Africa, I have simply tried to show that it is not a "white man's country" with a few "Native" and game reserves as a colorful backdrop, but a conflict-ridden country where a nonwhite majority is exploited and oppressed by a racialist albinocracy. I have done so in universalistic terms; that is, in terms which reject the particularistic creed of apartheid. Apartheid is not only a set of laws and regulations but also a deeply ingrained ideology shared by most whites and a frustrating, crippling way of life for its nonwhite victims. Any account of apartheid must include not only "objective" realities but also the subjective feelings of the participants in the system.

I readily confess that writing on South Africa has often had cathartic value for me; every revision of my manuscripts has raised anew the nagging problem of objectivity and has resulted in a deletion of gratuitous sarcasm or of misplaced emotionality, a toning down of adjectives, and an elimination of value judgments. If the end result still conveys a repellent picture of apartheid, could I suggest that the fault lies perhaps with the South African government rather than with my lack of objectivity? Some pictures are *not* two-sided, and an attempt to make them so does not lead to objectivity, but to distortion.

There is, of course, one facile way to escape emotional involvement—namely, to adopt an attitude of detached, urbane amusement at the insanity of apartheid. Before going to South Africa this outlook was easy to maintain, but on the spot the humor of the situation wore thin. To be sure, humor remained a useful tension-release mechanism, and particularly incongruous twists of apartheid occasionally excited a grim kind of hilarity on my part. On the whole, however, apartheid is not very funny if you are on the receiving end of it.

The one salient conclusion which the South African scene confirms is that the distinction between ethics and politics in an actual research situation is analytical rather than empirical. Once more, the South African case is extreme in that the fundamental tenets of the ideology and practice of apartheid conflict with virtually all religious or secular systems of ethics evolved over the last three thousand years of human history. In that context, the injunction to be apolitical thus becomes a precept of amorality. These remarks are not exclusive to South Africa, of course; they apply with nearly equal strength to such other places as Mississippi and Alabama, or indeed California and Ohio. The last centuries of Western history, and most especially the nineteenth, have been tainted by the nearly ubiquitous aberration of racism.

My last dealings with the South African government took place in December 1961 at the customs office of the Johannesburg airport. A bored official routinely inspected my luggage, which contained many irreplaceable and incriminating documents. I greeted his lack of zeal (to which the ungodly hour of 4 A.M. probably contributed) with a subliminal sigh of relief. I had successfully passed the last test of my *rite de passage* as an Africanist. Invaluable as my two years in South Africa had been, I knew that they would leave a profound and durable impact on me; I also knew that I would badly need the six-month European vacation ahead of me in order to regain some intellectual balance.

NOTES

1. The title of this chapter paraphrases Mahatma Gandhi, who spent two trying but highly formative decades of his life in South Africa. See Mohandas K. Gandhi, *An Autobiography: The Story of My Experiences with Truth* (Washington: Public Affairs Press, 1954).

2. See, among others, Claude Lévi-Strauss, *Tristes Tropiques* (Paris: Plon, 1955); Elenore Smith Bowen, *Return to Laughter* (New York: Harper, 1954); and J. F. Holleman, *African Interlude* (Cape Town: Nationale Boekhandel, 1959).

3. For example, a brilliantly satirized and thinly disguised Lloyd Warner appears under a pseudonym in John P. Marquand, *Point of No Return* (Boston: Little, Brown, 1949). Dennison Nash analyzes the function of field work in anthropology in "The Ethnologist as Stranger: An Essay in the Sociology of Knowledge," *Southwestern Journal of Anthropology* 19 (1963): 149–67. A number of issues germane to this chapter are discussed in three

recent collections by sociologists: Arthur J. Vidich, Joseph Bensman, and Maurice R. Stein, eds., *Reflections on Community Studies* (New York: Wiley, 1964); Phillip E. Hammond, ed., *Sociologists at Work* (New York: Basic Books, 1964); and Gideon Sjoberg, ed., *Ethics, Politics and Social Research* (Cambridge: Schenkman, 1967).

4. I have reported the bulk of my findings in a community study entitled *Caneville, The Social Structure of a South African Town* (Middletown: Wesleyan University Press, 1964), and in a more general work, *South Africa, A Study in Conflict* (Middletown: Wesleyan University Press, 1965).

10

Apartheid, Fascism, and the Golden Age

The old antithesis between "idealism" and the various brands of "realism" (such as *Realpolitik* and dialectical materialism) has plagued social science from the days of Hegel to the present via Marx, Weber, Pareto, Mosca, Parsons, and others. The safe, eclectic, compromise position inherent in the model of "multiple and reciprocal causation" has by now become one of the most common escape mechanisms to this dilemma, as indeed to most other dilemmas in social science. But unless one disentangles the amorphous causative cobweb created by the model of multiple and reciprocal causation and delimits the sphere and level of operation of the various factors, one cannot hope to proceed beyond the platitudinous statement that "it all hangs together."

The present chapter is a modest and crude attempt to disentangle the "idealist" and "realist" strains in South African Nationalist policies since 1948, with special reference to the "color policy." The latter has been interpreted with equal plausibility and onesidedness as either an honest (if misguided and impractical) attempt to solve the South African "color problem" or a deliberate, cynical plot to divide and rule. Both interpreta-

Reprinted from *Cahiers d'Etudes Africaines*, No. 8, 1962, pp. 598–608.

tions lead to the inescapable conclusion that apartheid is despotic. The first interpretation draws a somewhat more palatable picture of obsolete, paternalistic, benevolent despotism, whereas the second view evokes the spectrum of ruthless Fascism using "ideal" apartheid as an ideological smoke screen. Evidence for the two views can be found in the two recognized currents of Nationalist thought: on the one hand the "ideal" apartheid of SABRA (South African Bureau of Racial Affairs) intellectuals and the Dutch Reformed churches, and on the other hand the "practical" apartheid of the government.

Both extreme views are, in our opinion, inadequate. The "idealist" view fails to account for the instruments and methods used in implementing apartheid, for the brutally repressive aspects of the policy, and for cynical and blunt remarks made by prominent politicians. The "realist" view does not account for the purely gratuitous or the self-defeating aspects of government policy such as the antagonizing of the English-speaking whites over the Republican issue, the estrangement of the completely westernized Coloured population, the discouraging of white immigration, and the extension of African primary education.[1]

Our argument is that both the "idealist" and the "realist" strains, both the benevolent and the Fascist forms of despotism, are found in South Africa since 1948. But the apparent incompatibility between the two strains is resolved insofar as they each operate at a different level. The answer lies in the old dilemma of means versus ends that is inherent in the exercise of power. The *ideology* of Afrikaner Nationalism is a complex blend of provincialism, isolationism, xenophobia, pastoralism, egalitarianism within the *Herrenvolk,* and deeply ingrained color prejudice with a touch of condescending benevolence so long as the master-servant relationship is unthreatened.[2] The nostalgic and idealized vision of the Golden Age of the Boer Republics in the nineteenth century (which vision was the heritage of defeat in the South African War) was translated into reactionary policy when the National Party came to power in 1948. The *ends* of Nationalist policies are the restoration of the Golden Age. Nationalist ideology is despotic, obsolete, and reactionary, but *not* Fascist.[3] It does not, for example, idealize the supremacy of the state at the expense of the individual or stress the *Führer* principle with a rigid hierarchical delegation of power in the state. However, the *means* to reestablish the bygone Utopia have increasingly become those of modern Fascism. The choice of these means, given the ends of apartheid, is predetermined by internal South African conditions of advanced technology, industrialization, and urbanization, as we shall try to show later.

We must first disclaim any adherence to two extreme views. The first is that apartheid, in the restricted sense of segregation and discrimination on the basis of color, originated in 1948. The absurdity of that view is obvious. The second and opposite point of view is that the United and National parties hold basically to the same color policies. This latter statement has almost become a dictum in "liberal" circles and is incorrect or at least misleading.

Parliamentary opinion in many modern democratic systems of government is organized into parties which can be ordered in a continuum from right to left, with the center standing for gradual reform and ordered meliorism. Conservative and reactionary parties are lumped together as belonging to the right, and radical parties form the left. In South Africa, the disenfranchisement of the 80 per cent of the population most likely to vote left has restricted the parliamentary spectrum to the right. Center groups such as the Progressive, Labour, and Liberal parties have either been absorbed into the right, hardly gained any parliamentary foothold, or been in a highly precarious position. Leftist opposition has, of course, always been extraparliamentary. It is quite correct to say then, that both the United and the National parties are right-wing parties and fundamentally agree on many issues such as white supremacy, but this does not mean that the two parties play a similar role.

The United party is conservative: it stands for the status quo; whereas the National party is reactionary, standing for *change*. As is generally the case, the status quo party has been on the defensive and has lost ground, and the change party has been on the offensive and has gained ground. At the same time, the status quo party has tended to move (with a time lag) in the direction of the change party, or in other words to accept the new status quo as modified by the change party.[4] As in most parliamentary systems, the South African judiciary has played the conservative role of slowing down change, in this case re-actionary change. The South African cycle of cumulative reaction is the opposite of the more familiar western European cycle of gradual and cumulative reform, but the basic mechanisms are the same in both cases. Very simply, whether the change party is left or right of the status quo party will determine the direction of change.

Let us now turn to the first part of our central argument, namely that Nationalist policies attempt to turn the clock backward to the Golden Age of the Boer Republics. It is obvious, indeed platitudinous, to remark that ever since Malan's split from the old Nationalist Party of Hertzog, the rise of the "puri-fied" Nationalist Party has meant the increasing ascendancy of the defeated Boer Republics, the gradual elimination of the compro-mise of Union, and the ever more militant embodiment of ex-treme Afrikaner nationalism. The outward symbols of such nationalism (from national anthem to the design of stamps and of flags) are a constant reminder of this trend. Yet, as regards color policy, the argument is often heard that apartheid is merely the logical continuation and intensification of the policies of previous governments. If apartheid is defined narrowly as racial segregation and discrimination, the argument is, of course, cor-rect. It is also true that all governments since Union have unequivocally stood for perennial white supremacy. But apartheid is much more than that. It is part of a broader *Weltanschauung* which looks on the Boer Republics, or rather, on an idealized and mythical version of conditions in the Boer Republics, as the Golden Age of South Africa. In the words of the Prime Minister on May 31, 1960: "We should control the future of our State and people in the same way as it was controlled for us by our forefathers."

The relatively simple pastoral society of the Boers in the nine-teenth century saw itself threatened by two enemies. On the one hand, the Bantu tribes were a constant threat to immediate survival. On the other hand, the British Empire and all it represented (capitalism, urbanism, liberalism) challenged both the political autonomy of the Republics and all the values that the Boers considered basic to their way of life: isolationism, austere Calvinism, a deeply rooted color prejudice against all dark peoples, an idealization of the free, simple, wholesome, pastoral way of life. These threats were, and still are, too realistic for the Afrikaner fears to be called paranoid. The outside world is and has always been hostile to the Afrikaners, with the exception of the short interlude of the South African War when the Boers aroused the world's sympathy for the underdog, that same sympathy that is now turned against them. Capitalism, urbanization, the *uitlanders,* liberalism, have indeed spelled the doom of the Republics and now continue to undermine Nationalist policies.

Evidence of Nationalist xenophobia, isolationism, and attempts to revive the political structure of the Boer Republics is too clear to need elaboration. However, the extent to which Nationalist non-European policies also endeavor to reproduce prewar conditions is not so apparent. Whatever case may be made for "positive" apartheid in relation to the Africans, Nationalist policies toward the Indians have been entirely negative and repressive. To quote from a party brochure: "The Party holds the view that Indians are a foreign and outlandish element which is unassimilable. They can never become part of the country and must therefore be treated as an immigrant ·community."[5] From the Nationalist point of view, Indians symbolize everything that the Afrikaner Volk opposes. They are not only a nonwhite group, but also *uitlanders,* a city people, and, as far as the Transvaal Indian community is concerned, a trading people. They began to appear in the Transvaal only by the close of the Golden Age; hence they are an alien, superfluous, unassimilable group to be eradicated from South Africa. Since attempts at "repatriation" of the Indians to India have failed, Asians must be systematically uprooted and ruined by the discriminatory application of the Group Areas Act.

Nationalist policy toward the Coloureds has always been characterized by ambivalence. On the one hand they share for the most part, the language, religion, and culture of the *Herrenvolk*. But, at the same time, they are only a second-rate "bastardly" offshoot of Afrikanerdom and the product of a shameful process of miscegenation. They are valuable insofar as they identify with the Europeans no matter how much they are deprived of their rights in the Cape. Beyond the fact that the government intends to keep the Coloureds apart from all other groups and accord them a status somewhat higher than that of the other non-Europeans, Nationalist policy toward them is unclear; no "national home" for the Coloureds is being contemplated.

Nationalist policy toward the Africans, in contrast to Coloured policy, forms a well-integrated program of reaction. The ascendancy of its main architect to the post of Prime Minister indicates the important place that "Bantu policy" takes in the government's vision of the future (and, by the same token, of the past). The Boer Republics had to deal with basically two types of Africans: on the one hand the serfs or "apprentices" furnished the basic agricultural labor force of the Boers and live in close contact with them; and on the other hand a number of Bantu tribes surrounded the white settlement. The policy of the Trekkers was to limit the former category to the minimum necessary labor force and to push back the latter, defeat them militarily, and render them harmless.[6] By 1880 the Bantu tribes had ceased to be a military menace to the white settlers. The African population of the Republics now consisted of subservient helots in the service of the Boers or of broken, impoverished, and dispossessed tribes of "raw kaffirs." The heroic phase of the Trek was over, and the conquerors could now enjoy the fruits of victory . . . until the discovery of gold on the Rand spelled the doom of the quasi-feudal Republics.

Let us now examine the fundamentals of Nationalist Bantu policy and show that all of them attempt to reverse developments since the turn of the twentieth century and revert to the Golden Age of the Republics. The main elements of the policy are:

1. Permanent and complete denial of civic and political rights in the "European" state;
2. Permanent and complete disarmament of the Africans, and white monopoly of the use of armed force;
3. Influx control;
4. Migratory labor policy;
5. Development of tribal "Bantustans" under white control;
6. Revival and idealization of tribal institutions;
7. Segregation of Africans from other "races" and between Africans of various ethnic groups;
8. State-controlled education in the vernacular.

All these elements are related to one another in a highly coherent program. Some of those elements have been present in the African policy of previous governments, but only as disconnected and unsystematic measures to retard the development of a multiracial industrial society. Only with the present government have all these elements been combined into a grand scheme of reaction. The first element follows simply from the postulate of inherent black inferiority.[7] The principle of inequality and disenfranchisement was already clearly stated in the Constitution of the South African Republic: "The [Afrikaner] people will suffer no equality of whites and blacks either in state or in church." It is clear therefore that the franchise policy of the British liberals and missionaries at the Cape must be reversed. By now the last vestige of African representation in Parliament has disappeared.

The second element is the product of a long period of frontier warfare between Boers and Bantu. From that history the notions emerged that guns are part of the treasured heritage of "Western Civilization," that armed Africans are dangerous, and that only the British would think of arming Bantu. Any semblance of military organization among the Bantu must be smashed. Only then can the white man rule indefinitely. As a reluctant concession to the practical task of controlling the African masses, African policemen are armed with sticks, or, under the pressure of extreme necessity, with spears.

Influx control and the migratory labor policy with the whole complex machinery of pass laws are attempts at minimizing the number of permanently urbanized Africans. Ideally, there should be no city Africans at all, because the cities are "white" and because the urban African loses all the good qualities of the "raw tribal kaffir." He becomes an idler and a criminal, he absorbs all the dangerous notions put into his head by liberals, *tsotsis,* agitators, the English press, and so forth, and he loses his respect for the white *baas.* In short, he "forgets his place" as drawer of water and hewer of wood. Unfortunately, however, his labor is indispensable. As a reluctant compromise with economic realities, the minimum number of Africans is allowed to live in the white cities, but only temporarily and in menial capacities. In the words of Mr. Schoeman, Minister of Labour: "pick and shovel work is the natural work of the Native . . . the Native has a special aptitude for repetitive work."[8]

Under no circumstances must Natives be allowed to compete with whites. Job reservations must be extended to cover all fields of employment; African labor must not be permitted to strike, and African labor unions must not be recognized as bargaining instruments. The state knows what is good for the Natives and must be the sole mediator in labor disputes. Redundant Natives, idlers, *tsotsis,* agitators, and the like, must either be sent to secret labor camps or deported to rural areas and be made to work at low wages for *platteland* farmers. The Europeans must be ready to make sacrifices in dispensing with African labor wherever possible and paying the cost of developing uneconomic ventures in border areas to decentralize industry. Urban Africans must live miles away from their places of employment, in ghettos carefully prevented from contaminating the white areas by buffer zones, brick walls, barbed wire, rows of trees, and so on. To make cities even more unattractive to the Africans, the latter must not be allowed to own land in urban areas. Where they did, they must be deprived of their freehold rights. They must be made to carry reference books ("for their own protection," of course), to apply for permits to seek employment, and so forth. They must be forbidden to drink any alcoholic beverage except "kaffir beer" brewed by the municipality and sold to them at a profit. Since all these vexations and disabilities still fail to deter Africans from coming to towns, they must be further harassed, intimidated, and beaten by the police (again in their own interest, of course, to protect them against "*tsotsis*").

In a nutshell, cities are bad, corrupting places, particularly for "childish" people like the Bantu.[9] The fewer Africans in cities, the better, even at the cost of heavy economic sacrifices. Africans in "European" areas must remain indefinitely a transient, menial, subservient, powerless, unorganized, undemanding proletariat.

The other side of government Bantu policy is the development of the Bantustans. If Africans are discouraged from settling in the "European" areas, they must be encouraged to settle in the Native Reserves. If their urbanization is to be reversed, tribalism must be revived. The overpopulation and poverty of the Reserves make these areas inadequate to support even the 38 per cent of the Africans still living there, much less an increased population. The fact that Africans continue to migrate to the cities is evidence enough of that inadequacy. It is also clear that vastly greater sums would be required to develop the Reserves than the government has spent to date or is likely to spend in the future. But here we are concerned more with the intent of the Bantustan policy than with its practicability. The intention of the policy is to recreate a set of semiautonomous "tribal homelands" where Africans will lead a happy, idyllic rural existence sheltered from the evil influences of the cities and under the wise and benevolent guidance of the Minister for Bantu Administration and Development (who *knows* what is good for the Bantu better than the Bantu himself). In 1951, Dr. Verwoerd has allayed any fears that these tribal homelands might be independent: "Now a Senator wants to know whether the series of self-governing Native areas would be sovereign. The answer is obvious. . . . It stands to reason that White South Africa must remain their guardian."[10] Since then, the Prime Minister has outwardly reversed that position by stating that those "states" would in due course be developed toward complete self-government when they would become fit for it. One must believe, however, that the

Prime Minister had such a long period of time in mind as to make his statement meaningless.

Clearly the intent of the Bantustan policy is to recreate a set of agricultural "states" rendered perpetually harmless and under perennial white suzerainty such as existed toward the end of the Golden Age. Where tribal authorities and customs have long disappeared, they must be revived, for "the best Bantu is the raw tribal one" with an "uncontaminated" mind. The tribal way of life is idealized as "best for the Bantu" in the same way as the Great Trek and the Golden Age of the Republics is idealized. Tribal dancing and festivals are encouraged as safe and wholesome pastimes. White officials playing the role of Great White Father condescendingly pat the back of tribal puppets who gravely assure the government of their undying gratitude and servility. As each *Volk* must develop "along its own lines," each language group must be segregated from all other language groups. Children must be taught in their mother tongue in government schools where they will learn to be satisfied with their humble lot. The elite will even be granted the privilege of attending bush colleges, safely away from the cities.

It would, in our estimation, be a distortion of the facts to believe that Nationalist policy toward the Africans is *purely* a conscious, sinister, Machiavellian plot to divide and rule. The element of condescending benevolence and conviction that "we know what is good for them" cannot be disregarded. Neither can one ignore the Nationalist's projection of his own narrow provincialism onto other people who, far from struggling to preserve their ancestral culture, want to assimilate Western culture. Certain aspects of government Bantu policy even bear the stamp of paternalistic magnanimity within the rigid framework of master-servant relationships. From the point of view of material welfare, the Nationalist government has probably "done more for the Bantu" than its predecessor, partly under the interesting delusion that economic well-being (such as exists) is a substitute for political rights and for human dignity.

Kuper has lucidly shown that the present South African government is doing exactly the opposite of what social scientists have shown to improve race relations.[11] That Nationalist policies have in fact immeasurably worsened race relations in South Africa has been abundantly and tragically illustrated by recent events. This is, of course, an unwanted consequence of Nationalist policies. The government is attempting to eliminate racial frictions in a competitive industrial society which, with Nazi Germany, is the most virulently racialist that the world has seen. The absurdity of the attempt, however, lies in the fact that the formula used is not only unethical by modern Western standards but also obsolete. The government endeavors to re-create a paternalistic master-servant or suzerain-vassal relationship such as existed in the Golden Age of the pastoral Republics at a time when African Nationalism emerges victorious everywhere and when overseas hostility steadily mounts. Apart from external pressures, the reaction scheme is being forced through under internal conditions of advanced industrialization and urbanization which doom the attempt from its inception.

So far, we have been concerned with the ideology of apartheid, not with its implementation. Now we must show how internal conditions predetermined the mode of implementation. Why has South Africa evolved toward a modern Fascist totalitarian state, as Keppel-Jones so lucidly predicted?[12]

The ideology of Afrikaner Nationalism and of the Boer Republics is one of benevolent despotism rather than Fascism. Fascism is logically incompatible with the rugged individualism and the egalitarianism (within the *Herrenvolk*) of Boer frontier society. The difference between the organization of Hitler's Wehrmacht and that of the Boer Commandos of the nineteenth century, between the Nazi state and the loose patriarchical Republics, should make it clear that the spirit as well as the reality of the Golden Age was not Fascist. Yet the South African state since 1948, while still falling short of Nazi totalitarianism, is steadily moving in that direction, as even a casual reading of the Public Safety Act or the Suppression of Communism Act cannot fail to convince one.

It is our contention that any attempt to implement the *ends* of apartheid, given a modern, technological, industrial, urban

society, must use the *means* of Fascism. The control of an increasingly educated and politically conscious non-European
population of twelve millions (which are either actively or
passively opposed to apartheid) is a different matter from the
control of a few hundred thousand Bantu divided into tribal
groups on the fringes of nineteenth-century white settlement.
More than one-third of those twelve million people is concentrated in cities where it is exposed to outside news and "sub-
versive" currents of thought. Modern communication systems
make for the almost instantaneous spreading of mass resistance,
as witnessed in 1952 and 1960. The only way to repress these
movements is not by the hasty and impoverished gathering of
volunteer commandos as during the Golden Age, but by a highly
centralized (if not very efficient) machinery involving a large
bureaucracy, a secret police, a vast system of prisons and "labor
camps," a mobile military force equipped with modern weapons
from airplanes to armored cars and machine guns—in short
the arsenal of totalitarian repression.

Furthermore the executive branch of the government must be
supreme and unhindered by the judiciary or the legislative
branch. Rigging of the electoral system must ensure and perpetuate minority rule and give the government the power to
change the Constitution and pass repressive legislation while
keeping a façade of legality. If the courts rule against the government, new laws such as the Separate Amenities Act are promptly
passed to close the last remaining loopholes. Legislation en-
trenching police powers of arbitrary arrest, search without
warrant, and the like, effectively suspend the rule of law under
the specious appearance of legality. Other statutes outlaw such
forms of peaceful opposition as strikes and passive resistance.[13]
Schools, broadcasting, and the Afrikaans press are used as propaganda instruments for the ruling party. The party itself is tightly
controlled by its secret and unofficial "executive committee,"
the *Broederbond*.

In short, then, internal conditions in South Africa have predetermined the use of Fascist *means* to implement an ideology
which in itself is not Fascist. Fascism is a product of the twentieth

century, whereas Nationalist ideology is a revival of nineteenth-century paternalistic despotism. Apartheid, the youngest child of this obsolete ideology, is doomed in the near future. Even if apartheid were not an anachronistic white elephant accomplishing the opposite of its avowed aims, even if South Africa could isolate itself from world indignation, even if policies were applied in the most benevolent fashion by sincere and dedicated men, apartheid would still be an unethical monstrosity in its attempt to reduce men to the role of Aldous Huxley's Epsilons. No amount of hypocritical denial can convince one that apartheid is anything but unmitigated *baasskap*. If any doubt should remain on this point, the words of the late Prime Minister Strydom should clarify the Nationalist position once and for all: "Our policy is that the Europeans must stand their ground and must remain *baas* in South Africa."[14]

It is in the nature of tyranny that it can be maintained only by the ever increasing use of repressive force for which an ever more staggering price in money, fear, and suffering has to be paid. The only question is whether this deepening whirlpool of insanity can still be broken short of bloody revolution. In any case, Dr. Verwoerd's prediction of "hardships" facing South Africa[15] will, one may safely forecast, be remembered as one of the greatest understatements of the twentieth century.

NOTES

NOTE: Leo Kuper contributed valuable suggestions to this chapter, but the responsibility for the views herein expressed is entirely our own.

1. African education is, of course, rigidly controlled by the state since 1954, but why should the Africans be allowed to receive any education at all, if apartheid were *purely* repressive?
2. For a perceptive analysis of the Afrikaner *Weltanschauung,* see S. Patterson, *The Last Trek* (London: Routledge and Kegan Paul, 1957). See also I. D. MacCrone, "The Great Trek," *Race Relations* 5 (1938): 81–84.

3. The Ossewa-Brandwag is the only large-scale Afrikaner organization with a distinctly Nazi ideology, and it began to fade away in 1942 after a bitter struggle with the National Party under Malan from which Malan emerged victorious.

4. This is, of course, a logical evolution for a status quo party to undergo. Indeed, the evolution is inherent in the definition of a status quo party, for, if this evolution did not take place, the status quo party would become either reactionary or radical, depending on the direction of change.

5. Quoted in *Thought* (Johannesburg: S. A. Institute of Race Relations).

6. See J. A. I. Agar-Hamilton, *The Native Policy of the Voortrekkers* (Cape Town: Maskew Miller, 1928). See also the articles by Agar-Hamilton and A. H. Murray in the Voortrekker Centenary Number of *Race Relations* 5 (1938): 72–79.

7. As the cruder expressions of racialism have recently become unfashionable even in Nationalist circles, most leading Nationalists will outwardly deny any belief in inherent black inferiority and maintain that discrimination is based on cultural differences. If that were the case, the Nationalist Party and the Progressive Party should be in basic agreement.

8. Quoted by Ralph Horwitz, *Expand or Explode, Apartheid's Threat to South African Industry* (Cape Town, 1957), p. 33.

9. The same Nationalist concern applies to the *platteland* Afrikaner who "drifts" to the cities, loses his Afrikanerdom, and is in mortal danger of becoming anglicized and of voting United Party.

10. *Report of the United Nations Commission on the Racial Situation in the Union of South Africa* (New York: General Assembly, Eighth Session, Supplement No. 16, 1953), p. 153.

11. Leo Kuper, "The Heightening of Racial Tension," *Race* 2 (1960): 24–32.

12. A. Keppel-Jones, *When Smuts Goes* (Cape Town: African Bookman, 1947).

13. For analyses of the legislative aspects of repression, see G. M. Carter, *The Politics of Inequality* (New York: Praeger, 1958); Leo Kuper, "The Control of Social Change," *Social Forces* Vol. 33 (1954); Julius Lewin, "Power, Law, and Race Relations in South Africa," *Political Quarterly* (1959); as well as the

numerous publications of the South African Institute of Race Relations.

14. *Treatment of Indians in South Africa* (Washington: Government of India Information Services), p. 5.

15. Speech at Bloemfontein on June 30, 1960.

11

Race Attitudes in
Durban, South Africa

Introduction

The quantitative study of racial attitudes in South Africa is still relatively undeveloped. MacCrone's and Pettigrew's studies of university students and Malherbe's study of armed forces personnel constitute, to the best of our knowledge, the list of major publications in the field.[1] The present study overlaps in scope with both MacCrone's and Pettigrew's work and attempts to verify some of their findings.

The Questionnaire

The questionnaire, consisting partly of open, partly of closed items, comprises personal data, stereotype, social distance, and actual contact questions. It also contains three short essay questions asking the subjects to give their "solution for the South African race problem," to predict events for the next twenty years, and to assess race relations over the past twenty years. For the stereotype, social distance, and actual contact questions, the subjects are asked to react to seven groups found in the South

Reprinted from *Journal of Social Psychology* 57 (1962): 55–72.

African population: Coloureds, Indians, Jews, English-speaking whites, Afrikaans-speaking whites, city Africans, and tribal Africans. The questionnaire was administered in April–May 1960, that is, after the shooting of Sharpeville and Langa, during the state of emergency, but after the peak of the unrest. These turbulent events have probably affected answers to some extent, but racial unrest provoked by discriminatory legislation and police brutality has become so commonplace in South Africa that rioting and shootings rather than peace can be considered the "normal" state of affairs. The questionnaire was anonymous, and subjects were verbally reassured that nothing they might say could in any way be used against them. We have no reason to suspect uncandidness in the answers.

The Sample

A sample of 383 Durban students was drawn from several faculties of the University of Natal, from two technical colleges, and from a hospital nursing school.[2] The sample was not random. In all cases, entire classes were administered the questionnaire in a "captive" fashion. Nine persons refused to cooperate with the study, giving a return rate of 97.65 per cent. Of the 374 students who returned their questionnaire, 33.4 per cent are Europeans, 37.2 per cent are Indians, 26.5 per cent are Africans, and 3.0 per cent are Coloureds. These proportions closely correspond to the proportion of these four "racial" groups in the Durban population.[3] Africans are slightly underrepresented in the sample, and Europeans are slightly overrepresented. One hundred and sixty-one of the subjects are women, and 213 are men. Men range in age from 16 to 43 with a mean of 19.66 years, and women range from 15 to 37 with a mean of 21.59. The over-all mean age is 20.75 years.

With the exception of a few African nurses, all of our subjects completed high school and all have received postsecondary education. As may be expected in South Africa, the fathers of our European respondents have more education and higher occupations than the fathers of our African and Indian subjects.[4] Sixty-

seven per cent of the European fathers have nonmanual occupations, and 57 per cent completed high school. The respective
figures are 55 per cent and 22 per cent for Indians, and 57 per
cent and 42 per cent for Africans. Unlike what the percentages
above suggest, we can expect that the middle-class bias of our
sample is strongest for the Africans and smallest for the Europeans. The latter, as a politically and economically privileged
group, probably show the least class selection in the acquisition
of postsecondary education. Due to high European wages, the
vast majority of South African whites are financially able to send
their children to college, regardless of their own education or
occupation. Africans in our sample presumably show the most
class selection as they belong to the most underprivileged group,
and Indians fall somewhere in between the other two groups,
though probably closer to the Africans than to the Europeans.
Like MacCrone's and Pettigrew's respondents, the present subjects
are mostly young middle-class adults and are not representative
of the total population. Our sample can only be said to be representative of the educated urban middle class of Durban.

The Findings

Perception of Groups

The question "What different groups of people would you say
there are in South Africa?" was asked to determine the relative
salience of "racial" as opposed to other criteria of group membership. As expected, racial criteria were used by far the most
frequently. Of 346 people who answered the question, 93.1 per
cent mentioned racial groups. This salience of racial criteria is not
surprising considering that skin color is by far the most important
determinant of status and rights in South Africa. Four subjects,
two Europeans and two Indians, refused to categorize people into
groups at all, 17 (all non-Europeans) mentioned only nonracial
groups, and 160 gave both racial and other groups such as
linguistic and religious groups. Only 49 persons (29 of whom
were white) distinguished between English and Afrikaans-speaking whites. Although whites made the distinction to a greater

extent than nonwhites, only 23.2 per cent of the Europeans did
so in spite of the political importance of this linguistic split. By
far the most common single answer was in terms of the four
official racial groups recognized in the South African census and
in apartheid legislation: Africans (or Bantu or Natives), Indians
(or Asians or Asiatics), Coloureds, and Europeans (or whites).
The use of terms was itself significant. Half of the Europeans
still used the words "Bantu" or "Native" in reference to Africans
although the two terms have in recent years become anathema
to educated Africans (largely because these terms are officially
used by the government). Of the Indians, 15 per cent used the
words "Bantu" and "Native," compared to none of the Africans.[5]

Stereotypes

To elicit group stereotypes, the subjects were asked to give the
positive and negative traits that came to their minds when they
were thinking of people of the seven different groups mentioned
earlier. No list of traits was given to the subjects, whose responses
were left entirely open.

By simple addition of all stereotypes, positive and negative
given by a person, a score was arrived at. As predicted, the number of stereotypes given is directly proportional to position in
the South African racial hierarchy. Europeans give a mean of
17.27 stereotypes, Indians, 16.19, and Africans, 13.62. There
is no significant difference between the mean number of stereotypes given by men (15.82) and by women (15.91). However,
when race is held constant, European women are found to give
more stereotypes than European men. The reverse is true for
nonwhites, and the two sex differences cancel each other in the
total. We hypothesized that low-stereotype persons would tend
to accept outgroups on the social distance scale and to have high
actual contact with members of the out-groups. In fact, no significant relationship exists between number of stereotypes given and
either social distance or actual contact.

In most cases, the average number of positive stereotypes about
a given group exceeds the number of negative stereotypes. In the
case of European stereotypes toward city Africans, and of Indian

and African stereotypes toward Afrikaners and Coloureds, however, the number of negative stereotypes is greater than that of
positive ones.

Table 11–1 shows the stereotypes that the various groups hold
of one another. Several interesting conclusions emerge from the
list of traits. As in many other studies of stereotypes, antithetical
traits are attributed to the same group by the same people. For
example, Europeans consider city Africans lazy and hard-working, progressive and uncivilized; Indians consider the English
tolerant and intolerant; and so on. The data simply confirm the
alogical character of stereotypes. The similarity between stereotypes of Indians and of Jews is also striking. While Europeans
express a much stronger anti-Indian prejudice than anti-Semitic
one, the basic ingredients are common to both. Indians tend to
project onto Jews the traits that Europeans attribute to Indians.
It is a commonly heard phrase in South Africa that the Indians
are "the Jews of Africa." It would seem that merchant communities of middlemen, whether the Chinese in Malaya, the Indians of Africa, or the Jews of eastern Europe, are the object of
much the same form of prejudice. On the part of non-Europeans,
Afrikaners are the object of the strongest prejudice, as they are
identified with the apartheid policies of the Nationalist government. Non-Europeans tend to dichotomize between the imputed
blunt oppressiveness of the Afrikaner and the subtle hypocritical
snobbishness of the English. Interestingly enough, the white subjects also accuse themselves of snobbery and intolerance, a finding which seems to indicate guilt feelings over the treatment of
non-Europeans. Both Africans and Indians resent the imputed
color-consciousness of the Coloureds and their desire to be white.
There is, of course, more than a grain of truth in accusations
of color prejudice against whites and Coloureds, though Africans
and Indians are by no means devoid of it in the virulently racialist climate of South African society. Another interesting finding of the stereotypes table is the European dichotomy between
the simple, unspoilt, honest, happy, tribal African who stays "in
his place" and the insolent, rowdy, dishonest urban African who
challenges and threatens white supremacy. Though this dichotomy

is an old one, the disturbances of March–April 1960 (which were an African urban proletarian movement) may have reinforced the preexisting dichotomy. The happy and musical stereotypes toward Coloureds are largely due to "Coon Carnival" at the Cape, which is a Coloured tradition. The stereotype of Coloured alcoholism has also a "grain of truth" due to the "tot" system whereby European farmers in the Cape have traditionally given their Coloured workers a ration of cheap wine.

Social Distance

Social distance is measured by a 14-item schedule that attempts to isolate two main variables: intimacy and equality in contact. Items 1 to 7 in Table 11–4 hold intimacy constant (low in all cases) but range from subordinate to superordinate status, whereas items 8 to 14 hold equality constant (equal status in all cases) but range from casual to intimate contacts. Three sets of scores are obtained by simple addition of rejective responses. An item-by-item score (possible range from 0 to 7) shows the number of groups rejected on a given item by a given subject (Table 11–4). Each subject also receives a group-by-group score (ranging from 0 to 14) which shows the number of items on which he rejects a given group (Table 11–3). Finally, the sum of a subject's rejective answers for all groups and on all items becomes his Social Distance (SD) score ranging from a possible 0 to 98 (Table 11–2). In all these sets of scores, the higher the score, the higher the social distance.

Table 11–2 confirms the hypothesis that women show more social distance than men in all three racial groups and that social distance increases with the position of the respondent's "race" in the South African hierarchy. The sex difference confirms Petti-grew's findings.[6] In South Africa, as in many other countries, the taboos and penalties for crossing color lines are stronger for women than for men. It is interesting to note that the sex difference is greatest among Indians, the group among which women are most sheltered from outside contacts. The Indian taboo against gainful employment of women is strongest, and Indian women, both Hindu and Muslim, are still restricted to a greater

TABLE 11-1 Stereotypes Held by Ten or More Subjects of a Given Group Toward a Given Group

Group Holding the Stereotype	Group Toward Which Stereotype Is Held					
	Coloureds		Indians		Jews	
Europeans	Musical	28	Dishonest	53	Good in business	34
	Gay, happy	24	Dirty	36	United	25
	Alcoholic	19	Intelligent	31	Generous	24
	Hard-working	17	Good in business	26	Money-conscious	16
			Hard-working	21	Religious	11
			Over-reproducing	14	Intelligent	11
			Educated	11	Hard-working	11
			Religious	10		
			Helpful	10		
Total Number of European Responses		294		340		284
Indians	Color-conscious	27	Hard-working	34	Good in business	32
	Alcoholic	19	Good in business	31	Stingy	31
	Quarrelsome	18	Religious	18	Money-consc.	19
	Gay, happy	15	Selfish	17	Selfish	17
	Sociable	15	Conservative	16	Dishonest	15
	Good craftsmen	14	Politically conscious	13	Clannish	12
	Hard-working	14	Progressive	13		
	Apathetic	13	Kind	11		
	Uncultured	12	Money-conscious	11		
	Hedonistic	12	Cultured	11		
	Friendly	11	Poor	10		
	Unmannered	10	Hospitable	10		
Total Number of Indian Responses		364		438		244
Africans	Color-conscious	51	Good in business	29	Money-conscious	20
	Alcoholic	15	Dishonest	20	Good in business	14
	Gay, happy	10	Hard-working	15		
			Exploitative	14		
Total Number of African Responses		191		216		146

TABLE 11-1 (continued)

Group Toward Which Stereotype Is Held							
English		Afrikaners		City Africans		Tribal Africans	
Snobbish	31	Intolerant	38	Insolent	36	Happy	26
Tolerant	17	Hospitable	35	Violent	26	Backward	26
Apathetic	15	Provincial	31	Hard-working	24	Simple	23
Cultured	10	Fanatical	21	Progressive	18	Cruel	15
Jingoistic	10	Friendly	18	Uncivilized	15	Dirty	14
Intolerant	10	Patriotic	14	Lazy	14	Respectful	14
						Peaceful	11
		Religious	14	Dishonest	14	Hard-working	12
		Uncultured	12	Immoral	11	Honest	12
		Conservative	10	Easily led	10	Unspoiled	11
	295		323		318		323
Kind	35	Oppressive	49	Hard-working	35	Backward	64
Hypocritical	24	Intolerant	46	Violent	24	Hard-working	25
Tolerant	24	Haughty	24	Educated	23	Subservient	13
Snobbish	21	Frank	23	Uncultured	20	Traditional	12
Intolerant	21	Uncultured	21	Impolite	17	Peaceful	11
Domineering	21	Selfish	17	Progressive	15	Violent	10
Cultured	14	Good farmers	11	Politically			
Apathetic	12			conscious	14		
Fair, just	11						
	335		330		309		299
Hypocritical	30	Oppressive	30	Progressive	25	Backward	28
Cunning	20	Prejudiced	23	Violent	19	Subservient	17
Educated	11	Frank	22	Educated	13	Hospitable	13
Tolerant	10	Inhuman	21	Politically			
		Uncultured	13	conscious	10		
		Snobbish	12				
		Dogmatic	11				
	207		218		209		220

TABLE 11-2   Mean Social Distance by Race
and Sex (N = 350)

	Male	Female	Total
European	35.15	36.46	36.01
African	24.70	26.65	25.34
Indian	28.10	39.30	31.64
Total	28.46	35.27	31.41

extent than Europeans and Africans in their movements outside
the home. Concerning the racial difference in SD, Europeans
may be expected to show the most exclusiveness since their claim
to rule is based on color prejudice. Racial prejudice among the
nonwhite groups probably is in large part a reaction against
white racialism.

TABLE 11-3   Mean Number of Items (Social Distance) on Which a Given
Group Is Rejected by a Given Group (N = 350)

	Rejecting Group					
	Europeans		Africans		Indians	
Rejected Group	Male	Female	Male	Female	Male	Female
Coloured	6.68	7.09	3.38	3.19	3.54	6.53
Indians	6.95	6.66	4.38	4.13	1.15	0.91
Jews	2.29	2.46	4.02	4.77	4.74	6.14
English	0.85	0.96	2.52	2.94	2.14	3.86
Afrikaners	1.44	1.87	6.56	7.61	5.72	7.12
City of Africans	7.44	7.32	1.02	0.71	4.17	5.19
Tribal Africans	9.29	9.91	2.83	3.16	6.72	9.00
Mean of means	5.02	5.20	3.53	4.13	4.01	5.61

Table 11–3 shows that Europeans (mostly English-speaking)
reject tribal Africans most, followed by city Africans, followed by
Coloureds and Indians. This finding does not agree with the
Pettigrew and MacCrone data nor with our hypothesis that Indians would be the most highly rejected group by the Europeans
because Indians are viewed as threatening business competitors.
Possibly, the March–April 1960 protest movement that was

largely engaged in by Africans accounts for the higher European rejection of Africans as compared with Indians. Our findings confirm the Pettigrew and MacCrone ones in showing a marked dichotomy in the answers of Europeans between the three white groups which are relatively tolerated and the four nonwhite groups that are rejected.[7] Gentile white anti-Semitism is relatively mild by comparison with anti-non-European prejudice. These findings underline the strength of color prejudice among South African whites, who, while recognizing internal divisions, are eager to maintain a united front against the "black danger." Pleas for "white unity" are a recurrent theme in South African politics. These South African findings call into question the hypothesis that prejudice against one out-group will tend to generalize to all out-groups. In the light of present findings we would reframe the hypothesis that generalization of prejudice will take place only in what Allport calls "functional" or character-conditioned prejudice; that is, the prejudice that satisfies a "need" in the "Authoritarian Personality," not in what Allport calls "conformity" or socially determined prejudice.[8] In a racialist country like South Africa, the social pressure toward color prejudice is such that it will be found among people who have no personality predisposition toward it at all.

African subjects, as predicted, reject Afrikaners most, as that group is associated with Nationalist oppression. Unlike white subjects, nonwhites do not show a marked dichotomy along color lines. For example, Africans, contrary to prediction, reject English-speaking whites to a lesser extent than tribal Africans and reject Jews and Indians to nearly the same degree. Indians show the greatest distance toward tribal Africans and the second greatest toward Afrikaners. All three groups exhibit the least distance toward their in-group, but, whereas whites dichotomize between white and black, nonwhites dichotomize politically between Afrikaners and English. Indians, in their strong rejection of tribal Africans, also seem to use education or "civilization" as an important criterion of acceptance. Non-European anti-Semitism, while not so strong as anti-Afrikaner feelings, is stronger than anti-English sentiments, in spite of the fact that South African

Jews on the whole tend to be more liberal than other whites in South Africa.

Table 11–4 shows the extent of rejection of all races by item.

TABLE 11-4   Mean Number of Groups Rejected on Given Social Distance Items by People of a Given Group (N = 353)

Rejected As:	Europeans Male	Europeans Female	Africans Male	Africans Female	Indians Male	Indians Female	Mean of Means
1. Servant	2.29	3.15	2.27	2.65	2.61	3.26	2.71
2. Shop assistant	1.60	1.33	1.75	1.65	2.16	2.70	1.85
3. Business associate	2.24	1.94	2.23	1.87	2.42	3.33	2.32
4. Business superior	3.12	2.99	2.53	2.61	2.92	3.91	2.98
5. Teacher	1.62	1.83	1.02	1.26	1.62	2.07	1.58
6. Minister of religion	1.74	1.75	1.69	1.48	1.92	2.95	1.91
7. M.P. of his district	3.14	3.14	2.73	3.03	2.76	2.93	2.93
8. Casual acquaintance	1.05	1.30	0.80	0.97	1.20	1.23	1.12
9. Fellow student	1.29	1.05	0.52	0.90	0.77	1.07	0.90
10. Neighbor	2.76	2.75	1.66	1.52	1.68	2.26	2.10
11. Table guest	2.69	2.74	0.84	1.23	1.24	1.72	1.74
12. Intimate friend	3.07	3.58	1.88	2.00	1.86	2.84	2.53
13. Dance partner	3.31	3.53	1.55	1.94	1.52	3.40	2.46
14. Husband or wife	4.40	4.93	3.16	3.65	3.43	5.28	4.08
Mean of means	2.45	2.57	1.76	1.91	2.01	2.78	2.23

The relatively high rejection on item 1 is due to the fact that in South Africa the master-servant relationship so closely follows color lines. All groups tended to reject whites as servants because the situation is almost inconceivable in the local context. As expected, intermarriage (item 14) is most strongly rejected. Whites are almost unanimous in saying they would not marry nonwhites, Africans tend to reject Europeans as spouses, and Indians tend to reject both Europeans and Africans. The discrepancy between the mean scores of the three groups on item 14 is not very great, indicating that nonwhites (contrary to white racial mythology) are no more eager to marry whites than the other way round.[9] Business superiors and Members of Parliament (items 4 and 7) are second or third highest for all three groups. European rejection of non-Europeans on items 4 and 7 is probably dictated by the desire to maintain white supremacy (or, to put it in white South African terms, "white civilization"), while nonwhites reject Afrikaners in their wish to put an end to present oppression and reject tribal Africans on grounds of incompetence to hold these positions. It will be observed that in items 1 to 7, which all imply low intimacy of contact, there are no marked discrepancies between the mean scores of the three racial groups. On items 8 to 13, however, all of which imply *equality* of contact, non-Europeans, more particularly Africans, are much more tolerant than Europeans. Furthermore, European rejection of nonwhites increases much faster with *intimacy* of equal contact than it does for non-Europeans.[10] In other words, Africans, who are now at the bottom of the racial hierarchy, are most willing to have egalitarian social contacts across racial lines, short of miscegenation; Europeans, who are at the top, resist such contacts, most particularly the more intimate ones; Indians fall in between the other two groups in both position in the hierarchy and acceptance of equal contacts. These findings suggest the hypothesis that acceptance of egalitarian contact is inversely proportional to hierarchical position.

Prejudice has been found to be related to religion in many studies. Pettigrew and MacCrone found that Jews are less prejudiced than other whites.[11] Of the white subjects in the present study, Jews show by far the smallest social distance, followed by those who do not claim any religious affiliation. Members of the Dutch Reformed churches, who are almost all Afrikaners, show the highest social distance. Catholics, Anglicans, and members of other Protestant denominations occupy an intermediate position. Among Indians, Hindus show more distance than Muslims, which is contrary to expectation. One should have expected that Hinduism, with its eclectic and tolerant outlook, would lead to greater acceptance of out-groups than Islam, with its exclusivistic creed.

We predicted that, regardless of religious denomination, the amount of "religiosity" among Europeans would be related to social distance. Our hypothesis was that people who claim to be "not religious at all" and those who claim to be "very religious" would score lower than those who say that they are "slightly"

TABLE 11-5   Religiosity and Social Distance

	Mean SD Score		
	Europeans	Africans	Indians
Not religious at all	23.83	36.75	20.17
Slightly religious	40.13	27.54	27.57
Moderately religious	38.17	25.77	31.46
Very religious	27.93	20.08	41.88
Mean Score	36.85	25.35	30.93
	(N=117)	(N=95)	(N=136)

or "moderately" religious. Both extreme groups presumably react against the lukewarm institutionalized religion of South African whites which has often rationalized racialism or, at best, evaded the moral dilemma of racial inequality.[12] The data strongly support the hypothesis, as shown in Table 11–5. Among Africans, social distance decreases with religiosity, whereas the reverse is true of Indians (Table 11–5). As an ex post facto explanation for these findings, we suggest that, as all but one of the Africans claim allegiance to Christianity, and as Christianity is also the majority religion of whites and Coloureds, acceptance of these out-groups by Africans increases with the degree of religiosity. Conversely, these findings would also confirm the impressionistic observation that there is a current rejection of Christianity among radical African intellectuals who view Christianity as an instrument of white domination. Among Indians, on the other hand, 82.1 per cent of those who answered the question belong to Islam or Hinduism—religions which are hardly represented in the other "racial" groups. It can therefore be expected that the more devout Muslims and Hindus will reject out-groups on religious grounds.

Numerous studies of prejudice have shown it to be related to occupation and education. In South Africa, Pettigrew found that white subjects whose fathers are in manual occupations are more distant toward nonwhites. MacCrone, on the other hand, found that occupation was not a significant determinant of social distance.[13] In general, our own findings show no clear and simple relationship between social distance and either father's occupation or father's education. Europeans and Indian subjects whose fathers have attended university score lower than others on SD, but the difference is not found among Africans. Among Europeans, sons of farmers and businessmen score higher than the others, but there is no significant difference between manual and nonmanual occupations. Sons of manual workers score higher among Indian and African subjects, but only in the case of Indians is there a steady decline (with one minor reversal) in SD scores as one goes up the occupational scale. Of the three "racial" groups, only Indians show a clear tendency for social distance to be inversely related to both education and occupational status.

Actual Contact

A battery of ten items measures actual contact across racial lines, by asking the subjects whether they have, in fact, met persons of a given group in a given situation. Table 11–6 shows the mean number of negative answers, so that the higher the score, the lower the actual contact. European and Indian women tend to have less out-group contact and African women more contact than the men in the respective groups. As expected, the total for all subjects shows that women have less contact than men, but the difference is small. Africans associate (or claim to associate) to a greater extent with out-groups than either Europeans or Indians, and there is no significant difference between the latter two groups.

Table 11–7 shows the mean number of items on which there

TABLE 11-6 Mean Actual Contact by Race and Sex (N = 351)

	Male	Female	Total
European	33.98	35.94	35.27
African	31.22	28.94	30.50
Indian	35.00	37.36	35.73
Total	33.61	34.58	34.12

TABLE 11-7   Mean Number of Items on Which Subjects Do Not Associate
with a Given Out-Group (N = 351)

Group Not Associated With	Group Not Associating					
	Europeans		Africans		Indians	
	Male	Female	Male	Female	Male	Female
1. Coloureds	7.43	7.96	3.12	2.45	3.25	4.15
2. Indians	6.63	7.11	4.33	3.32	0.29	0.34
3. Jews	3.23	2.84	7.96	7.81	8.06	8.20
4. English	1.00	0.91	5.49	4.90	5.60	5.12
5. Afrikaners	1.63	2.01	7.43	7.48	7.42	7.41
6. City Africans	6.52	6.86	0.94	0.68	3.83	4.59
7. Tribal Africans	7.52	8.01	1.57	2.29	6.45	7.61
Mean of means	4.85	5.13	4.46	4.13	5.00	5.34

has been no association with members of a particular group. As
for social distance, whites show a sharp dichotomy between all-
white groups with which contact is relatively free and all-nonwhite
groups with which contact is restricted. Non-European respondents, on the other hand, show no sharp dichotomy along color
lines. Indians show a marked difference in contact with urban as
opposed to tribal Africans, thereby indicating a cultural rather
than a racial barrier to interaction. The relatively low contact
between non-Europeans on the one hand and Afrikaners and
Jews is probably due to the small number of these two European
groups in Natal.

Turning to Table 11–8, we see the mean number of out-groups
with whom subjects do not associate in a given situation. For
item 1, contact is limited by the fact that many of the nonwhite
subjects do not have servants and that whites in South Africa are
almost never servants. Except for that item, actual contact tends
to decrease as the intimacy and the egalitarianism of the contact
situation increases. Africans show consistently more out-group
contact than the other two groups (except on item 1 for the
simple reason that, of the three groups, Africans are the least
able to afford servants). The hypothesis may be advanced here
that a subordinate group will tend to report (though not necessarily, in fact, experience) more out-group contact with super-

TABLE 11-8   Mean Number of Out-Groups with Which Subjects Do Not Associate in Given Situations (N = 351)

Has Not Met As:	Europeans Female	Male	Africans Female	Male	Indians Female	Male	Mean of Means
1. Servant in his home	4.26	4.23	5.10	5.70	4.38	4.28	4.62
2. Shop assistant	1.49	1.20	1.71	1.76	2.98	2.82	2.05
3. Fellow student	2.88	2.78	2.35	2.28	3.36	3.49	2.93
4. Table guest	4.04	4.18	2.77	3.22	3.24	3.33	3.51
5. Visitor in his home	3.38	3.45	2.10	2.67	3.14	2.95	3.00
6. Childhood playmate	3.75	3.83	3.23	3.67	4.26	3.89	3.80
7. Sport partner	4.24	4.10	3.45	3.22	4.74	4.02	3.96
8. Casual acquaintance	2.36	1.55	1.71	2.57	2.69	2.16	2.04
9. Intimate friend	4.53	4.43	3.26	3.63	4.64	4.22	4.16
10. Neighbor	4.38	4.25	3.35	3.61	3.90	3.95	3.96
Mean of means	3.59	3.40	2.89	3.12	3.74	3.50	3.41

ordinate groups than the other way around. Outside contact enhances the status of a member of a subordinate group and hence is more likely to be reported than in the reverse situation.[14]

Social Distance and Actual Contact

The relationship between prejudice and actual contact has been the object of much experimental work in the United States. Allport has summarized these results with the proposition that equal-status contact not involving competition leads to tolerance.[15] In view of these American findings we hypothesized that actual contact would be inversely related to social distance. Table 11–9 shows that while the relationship exists, it is far from a perfect one. High social contact persons tend to be low on social distance; subjects low on social distance tend to be high on contact, and high social distance subjects tend to be low in actual contact. However, low actual contact is not a good indication of high social distance, presumably because many relatively unprejudiced persons have no opportunities for contacts across racial lines.[16] A breakdown of Table 11–9 by the three racial groups in the sample reveals that the degree of relationship between the two variables is slightly higher for Europeans than for either Africans or Indians. This could be expected from the fact

TABLE 11-9   Social Distance and Actual Contact (Frequencies)

	Social Distance			
Actual Contact	Low	Medium	High	Total
High	72	21	9	102
Medium	65	63	35	163
Low	26	18	36	80
TOTAL	163	102	80	345

that the unprejudiced white is freer to initiate out-groups contact and need not fear rebuff as the non-European would.

Political Views

The white subjects were given a choice of three alternative policy lines and asked which one they favored for each of the seven groups. The alternatives might be labeled benevolent paternalism, egalitarianism, and territorial apartheid.[17] As expected, white subjects overwhelmingly favor the egalitarian alternative for the three white groups. For Africans, the majority of Europeans are in favor of the paternalistic choice, while for Coloureds they are nearly equally divided between the paternalistic and the egalitarian choices. For Indians, opinions are almost equally divided between the apartheid and the egalitarian choice. These data further illustrate the dichotomous outlook of South African whites toward themselves on the one hand and nonwhites on the other. The minority of whites advocating an egalitarian solution for non-Europeans score significantly lower than the others on social distance and have more interracial contacts.

The last part of the questionnaire consisted of three short essays on the subject's solution for the "South African race problem," the subject's prediction of events in the next twenty years, and his assessment of the last twenty years. The "solution" essay was answered almost exclusively in political terms. We predicted that non-Europeans would be more radical than Europeans and men more radical than women. The racial difference is completely borne out by the data. Only 8.0 per cent of the whites advocate unqualified equality, and a further 23.2 per cent advo-

TABLE 11-10 Comparative Findings of Three Attitude Studies of White South African Students

	MacCrone	Pettigrew	v.d. Berghe
Afrikaners most prejudiced of the Europeans	Yes	Yes	Yes[a]
Jews least prejudiced of the Europeans	Yes	Yes	Yes[a]
Sons of farmers more prejudiced than other occupations	Yes	—	Yes
Sons of manual workers more prejudiced toward nonwhites	No	Yes	No
White women more prejudiced than men	No	Yes	Yes
Dichotomous attitudes of whites toward white and nonwhite groups	Yes	Yes	Yes
Indians most rejected by whites	Yes	Yes	No

[a]Number of cases is too small to reach statistical significance.

cate equality qualified by a "civilization" or educational test. The respective percentages for Africans are 55.6 per cent and 33.3 per cent, and for Indians, 51.1 per cent and 19.4 per cent. Only five of the non-European respondents (four of them Africans) advocate a reversal of the present situation where Europeans would be in a subordinate position. This finding should not, however, be interpreted as showing the absence of such antiwhite opinions, but rather as indicating reluctance to admit such opinions at the verbal level. The predicted sex difference is found only among Africans. Contrary to prediction, European men are politically more conservative than women. There is no sex difference among Indians.

Among Europeans, conservative political views are related to high social distance, but no such relationship exists among nonwhites. We would suggest that conservative whites want to maintain political inequality largely because of their fear of social mixing and, above all, of miscegenation. Nonwhites, on the other hand, avoid contacts with whites, irrespective of their own political views, because of fear of discrimination.

The "prediction" essay shows that nonwhites tend to be more radical than whites in their forecasts, but the discrepancy is not nearly as great as on the "solution" question. Whites and non-whites largely agree in expecting great change, but tend to disagree in their willingness to accept change. Most whites expect more change than they are prepared to accept. Among nonwhites, some anticipate less change than they hope for, though the majority expect their desire for equality to be realized. Only 12.8 per cent of the Europeans and 8.4 per cent of the nonwhites expect the status quo to last for another twenty years, whereas 15.2 per cent and 23.5 per cent respectively anticipate a black government to the exclusion of whites or of all non-Africans.

Whites and nonwhites share a nearly equal pessimism about the way change will come: 54.4 per cent of the Europeans and 58.0 per cent of the non-Europeans say that they expect large-scale violence and bloodshed. Men tend to anticipate violence more than women. While this finding is undoubtedly colored by the police shootings a few weeks previous to answering the questionnaire, such pessimism is probably realistic.

Whites and nonwhites are likewise in agreement in their assessment of the past: 81.0 per cent of the sample say that the racial situation has deteriorated in the last twenty years, and only 6.7 per cent say that it has improved. The whites who say things have improved mostly mention a rise in living standards, while the nonwhites base their optimism on the hope that the extreme reactionary policies of the Nationalist government will precipitate the struggle for liberation.

Summary

A questionnaire study was conducted on a sample of 383 urban middle-class students in Durban. One of the most striking, if not unexpected, findings is the great difference in the attitudes of European as opposed to non-European respondents. Racialism and prejudice, though not absent among Africans and Indians, is strongest among Europeans.

Social distance increases with the subject's position in the South

African racial hierarchy, being highest among Europeans and lowest among Africans. Women are more distant than men. Social distance is related to religion, but in a different way for each racial group. There is no clear relationship between social distance and either parental occupation or education. Europeans reject non-Europeans in situations implying equality more than Africans or Indians reject whites.

Actual contact findings generally resemble the social distance data. Europeans restrict their contacts along color lines to a greater extent than either Africans or Indians. Actual contact and social distance are related to each other, but low contact does not mean high distance, as opportunities for interracial contact in South Africa are limited.

Of all possible criteria of group membership, "race" is mentioned most often, a finding which accurately reflects the importance of color in South African society. Anti-Indian stereotypes are similar to anti-Semitic ones. Europeans tend to dichotomize between the "good" tribal African and the "spoiled" city African. Nonwhites distinguish between the bluntly oppressive Afrikaner and the hypocritically bigoted English-speaking white.

As expected, Africans and Indians are more radical in their political views than the Europeans who are in a privileged position. All racial groups agree in expecting considerable political change, mostly through violence, and in thinking that the racial situation has worsened in the last twenty years.

NOTES

1. I. D. MacCrone, in E. Hellman, ed., *Handbook of Race Relations in South Africa* (Cape Town: Oxford University Press, 1949), pp. 690–705; I. D. MacCrone, *Race Attitudes in South Africa* (London: Oxford University Press, 1937); E. G. Malherbe, *Race Attitudes and Education* (Johannesburg: South African Institute of Race Relations, 1946); T. F. Pettigrew, "Social Distance Attitudes of South African Students," *Social Forces* 38 (1960): 246–253. In addition, there have been some

other studies in Rhodesia and South Africa: A. S. Du Toit, "Kontak en Assosiasie van Kleurling met Bantoe in die Kaapse Skiereland" (Ph.D. diss., Stellenbosch, 1958); C. du P. Le Roux, "Vooroordele en Stereotipes in die Rassehoudings van Kleurlinge" (M.A. thesis, Stellenbosch, 1959); C. A. Rogers and C. Frantz, *Racial Themes in Southern Rhodesia* (New Haven: Yale University Press, 1962).

2. We are thankful for the help of H. R. Christopherson, H. Dickie-Clark, L. Kuper, J. Mann, H. Natrass, and A. R. Williams in planning and administering this study. The opinions expressed are entirely the author's.

3. The respective proportions in the 1960 Durban population census are 29.6 per cent, 35.3 per cent, 31.1 per cent, and 4 per cent. In South Africa as a whole the dominant Europeans (or whites) constitute 19.4 per cent of the population, the Coloureds (or people of mixed descent) 9.4 per cent, the Indians 3.0 per cent, and the Africans 68.2 per cent.

4. The small number of Coloureds (11) in the sample prevented us from including them in most of our findings. In the European group there are only 13 Jews and 6 Afrikaners, so that in most cases the white group is not subdivided by language or religion in the analysis. In that respect our study is more limited than Pettigrew's and MacCrone's, but insofar as our sample includes non-Europeans, it is more extensive than the other two studies.

5. The fact that most Europeans and many Indians do not know that the terms "Bantu" and "Native" are offensive to Africans and that they continue to use the words in complete innocence is a symptom of the communication barrier between racial groups in South Africa.

6. Pettigrew, *op. cit.*, p. 252.

7. *Ibid.*, p. 247; MacCrone, in Hellmann, *op. cit.*, p. 694.

8. G. W. Allport, *The Nature of Prejudice* (Cambridge: Addison-Wesley, 1954), pp. 68–73, 285–286; T. F. Pettigrew, "Personality and Sociocultural Factors in Intergroup Attitudes," *Journal of Conflict Resolution* 2 (1959): 29–42.

9. Miscegenation, whether marital or nonmarital, is a criminal offense in South Africa punishable with up to seven years' imprisonment.

10. The one exception is the rejection of dance partners by Indian women. This is probably due to the fact that heterosexual danc-

ing is not yet a generally accepted practice for Hindu women and is strongly condemned for Muslim women.

11. MacCrone, in Hellmann, *op. cit.,* p. 696; Pettigrew, "Social Distance Attitudes," p. 248.
12. Allport makes a distinction between "institutionalized" or "extrinsic" and "interiorized" or "intrinsic" religion. Allport, *op. cit.,* pp. 444–457; and his *Personality and Social Encounter* (Boston: Beacon, 1960), pp. 263–265. His distinction is related to our hypothesis.
13. MacCrone, in Hellmann, *op. cit.,* pp. 701–704; Pettigrew, "Social Distance Attitudes," p. 252.
14. A similar finding applies to a Mexican study: Pierre L. van den Berghe and Benjamin N. Colby, "Ladino-Indian Relations in the Highlands of Chiapas, Mexico," *Social Forces* 40, no. 1 (1961): 63–71.
15. Allport, *The Nature of Prejudice,* pp. 281–282.
16. An almost identical relation between actual contact and social distance was found in Mexico. Van den Berghe and Colby, *op. cit.*
17. The three alternatives were: (*a*) People of the X group ought to be helped and guided as a kind but just father does with his children. (*b*) People of the X group ought to be treated in the same way as people of one's own group. (*c*) People of the X group ought to be left alone in their own areas to manage for themselves.

The same question was asked of nonwhite subjects, but was found to be ambiguous or meaningless to many of them. Their answers had thus been discarded.

12

Racial Segregation in South Africa: Degrees and Kinds

No other state in world history has devoted as large a proportion of its energies and resources in imposing racial segregation as South Africa has done since 1948. While apartheid has been the object of an abundant literature,[1] one of its important aspects has not received much attention, namely the degree of physical distance achieved by measures of segregation. We can distinguish three main degrees of segregation:

1. *Microsegregation*—segregation in public and private facilities (such as waiting rooms, railway carriages, post-office counters, washrooms) located in areas inhabited by members of several "racial" groups;

2. *Mesosegregation*—the physical separation resulting from the existence of racially homogeneous residential ghettos in multiracial urban areas;

3. *Macrosegregation*—the segregation of racial groups in discrete territorial units, such as the "Native Reserves" of South Africa, now being restyled as "Bantustans."

Reprinted from *Cahiers d'Etudes Africaines,* 23, Vol. 6 (1966): 408–418.

The distinction above, however, is one not only of degree but also of kind. Each form of segregation fulfills different purposes from the viewpoint of the ruling albinocracy and entails different consequences for South African society as a whole. Let us first examine the "gains" of the white group from the various forms of segregation, then analyze the internal contradictions inherent in macrosegregation, and finally turn to the differential economic effects of the three types of racial separation.

It is often said that the apartheid policies of the present Afrikaner Nationalist government constitute simply a more systematic and intensified version of traditional practices of racial discrimination and segregation. This statement is true in the sense that large-scale implementation of all three kinds of segregation extends at least as far back as the nineteenth century. However, in recent years the Nationalist government has increasingly stressed macrosegregation. There are two apparent reasons why this should be the case. First, if one accepts the government's premises that interracial contact promotes conflict and that apartheid is the only salvation for the albinocracy, it follows that maximization of physical distance between racial groups is desirable. Second, macrosegregation in the form of the Bantustan policy can be presented, for purposes of international apologetics, as an attempt at equitable partition between separate but equal nations within a happy commonwealth. Indeed, a favorite argument of the apostles of apartheid is that their policy substitutes vertical, non-hierarchical barriers between ethnic groups for a horizontal, discriminatory color bar.

Beyond these obvious considerations, this shift of emphasis in the implementation of apartheid from micro- to macrosegregation is motivated by more basic factors. To be sure, microsegregation is still as rigidly enforced as ever before, but not with the same order of priority. Microsegregation with grossly unequal facilities is a constant symbol of the racial status hierarchy and is a source of emotional gratification, economic advantages, and other practical conveniences for the white group. Substantial as the gains accruing from microsegregation for the whites are, however, this aspect of apartheid is a "luxury," in the sense that it contributes

little to the maintenance of white supremacy and that it further
exacerbates the nonwhite masses. (The Portuguese, for example,
still maintain their rule in Angola and Mozambique without any
resort to legal microsegregation, thus claiming to be free of racial
prejudice; similarly, the white-settler regime of Rhodesia has
gone some way toward the elimination of microsegregation without in any way jeopardizing its power monopoly.) The preservation of microsegregation in South Africa serves mostly to
indulge the albinocracy's phobia of racial pollution, but microsegregation is definitely not a cornerstone of the sociopolitical
order.

Mesosegregation, or the maintenance of racial ghettos, arose in
the nineteenth century as a way of making the nonwhite helotry
as invisible as possible to the *Herrenvolk* and of preserving the
latter from the moral and physical contamination of congested,
unhygienic slums. The presence of many domestic servants living
on their employers' premises, however, made most white sections
of town *de facto* interracial. In addition, there were a number of
racially mixed residential areas in Cape Town, Durban, Johannesburg, and many smaller cities.

When the Nationalists came to power in 1948, they proceeded
to make mesosegregation as impermeable as possible through the
policy of "Group Areas." Tens of thousands of people were expropriated, expelled from their domiciles, and "relocated" according to their pigmentation. Even the number of nonwhite domestic
servants allowed to live with their white employers was sharply
reduced, a distinct departure from earlier practices. The enforcement of mesosegregation involves many hardships for nonwhites,
threatens much of the Indian and Coloured middle class with
economic ruin, and entails considerable profits for many thousands of whites. But, beyond these side effects, the complete
ghettoization of South African cities is ostensibly being promoted
as a cornerstone in the maintenance of the status quo.

The presence of millions of nonwhites in cities is deplored by
the government, but reluctantly accepted as an economic necessity. Given the latter, the government endeavors to enforce a
new style of rigid mesosegregation, in great part for reasons of

internal security. With mounting unrest among Africans, military and police control become increasingly crucial. The older non-white shanty towns with their maze of narrow, tortuous alleys were often located close to white residential or business districts; they are now systematically being razed as a major military hazard. They are being replaced with "model townships" with un-obstructed, rectilinear fields of fire, and wide streets for the passage of police vans and armored cars. The new ghettos are typically situated several miles from the white towns, with a buffer zone between; they are sprinkled with strategically located police stations and often enclosed by barbed wire.

Macrosegregation, because of its many practical and ideological implications, is perhaps the most interesting aspect of Nationalist racial policy and hence deserves closer attention.[2] Total territorial separation is the avowed ideal which apartheid seeks to achieve for all racial groups. Ideally, the government would like to cram the eleven million Africans into the impoverished, eroded, and entirely rural Native Reserves which constitute 13 per cent of the nation's territory. The rest of the country would then acquire a pristine white purity. While the government realizes that this aim is Utopian, it is nevertheless implementing an elaborate scheme, the so-called Bantustan policy, to keep as large a percentage of Africans as possible in these rural slums. Africans deemed to be redundant in the white areas are constantly being "endorsed out" of them and sent to their "Bantu homelands." The Bantustans have several obvious security advantages: they are relatively isolated, dispersed, ethnically homogeneous, distant from the white cities, and devoid of any urban concentrations of more than a few thousand people; and communication within and be-tween them is difficult.

In its basic conception, the Bantustan policy of the South African government is not new. Interpretations of its real inten-tion vary, but the limits of actual variability in implementation which the government is prepared to tolerate can be determined with a fair degree of precision. In "minimum" form, the Bantus-tans are a revamping of the Native Reserves along the following main lines:

1. Geographical segregation of as many Africans as possible from non-Africans and of specific African ethnic groups from each other.

2. Pretoria-sponsored cultural revivalism and the elaboration of pseudo-traditional authority structures.

3. An extension of the sphere of local autonomy under the authority of government-appointed chiefs, which, in effect, amounts to a shift from "direct" to "indirect" rule.

Leo Kuper gives a vivid description of the "minimum" Bantustan scheme as it is presently being implemented:

> Here the power of the White man is displayed in a comic opera of equality with the Black man, indeed of homage to his tribal essence. Here backward tribal reserves are in a state of Messianic transformation to satellite bucolic Ruritanias. . . . The policy is to retribalize Africans and to fragment them into separate tribal entities, self-policed, introspectively detached from each other and from the White man's world, and self-perpetuated by the insemination of tribal ardor.[3]

In this sense, the Bantustan concept amounts to the transformation of the South African colonial empire from an internal one, as analyzed by Leo Marquard,[4] to an external one: the Native Reserves are being restyled into semiautonomous puppet states or protectorates under a quasi-traditional aristocracy.

At the other end of the "tolerable" spectrum from the government's viewpoint is the "maximum" notion of Bantustans as "separate Black States." While this alternative is clearly distasteful to the government, it was being envisaged, as early as 1961, as a possible line of retreat in response to external and internal pressures. Thus, Prime Minister Verwoerd said in reaction to this possibility: "This is not what we would have preferred to see. This is a form of fragmentation which we would rather not have had if it was within our control to avoid it."[5] Even under nominal political "sovereignty" the Nationalist government counts on the ethnic division, small size, and utter economic dependence of the Bantustans to maintain them in a colonial relationship.

Developments in the High Commission Territories in the near future may provide reasonably good predictors of the possible political behavior of the independent Bantustans and thus indirectly influence Nationalist policies.

The basic question concerning the future of the Bantustans, and indeed of the Republic as a whole, then becomes: Will the government be able to contain the Bantustan scheme within these fairly narrow limits? My argument is that it will not, in part because of international pressures, in part because of mounting conflicts in the white areas of the Republic, and lastly because of the dialectic unleashed by contradictions within the Bantustan scheme itself. We shall focus here on this last point.

There are four major aspects to the contradictions evident in the Bantustan policy; all of these are, to a large degree, unanticipated consequences of that policy, threatening to make its implementation in the Transkei the opening of Pandora's box from the government's point of view.

The first aspect concerns the use of the magic word "independence." In 1951, Verwoerd was careful to emphasize: "Now a Senator wants to know whether the series of self-governing Native areas would be sovereign. The answer is obvious. . . . It stands to reason that White South Africa must remain their guardian. . . . We cannot mean that we intend by that to cut large slices out of South Africa and turn them into independent States."[6] Later, he ostensibly reversed his stand by stating eventual "independence" as a possibility. The lack of a timetable, or indeed of an even approximate definition of the term, made the statement vacuous, particularly in conjunction with Verwoerd's 1963 statement: "We want to make South Africa White. . . . Keeping it White can only mean one thing, namely White domination, not leadership, not guidance, but control, supremacy."[7] However, the magic word has been spoken, partly, no doubt, as a carrot to the collaborationist African chiefs, and perhaps also on the assumption that the statement would be taken at face value by some leaders of Western powers on whose nonintervention the future of apartheid hinges to a considerable degree.

It seems likely that the independence pronouncement, however vague, will exacerbate, or even create, rather than mollify opposition. There are already signs that this is happening in two opposite ways. The strategy of many African chiefs who have decided to further their power and pursue their interests within the Bantustan framework is to exert whatever pressure they can against the government in terms of the avowed goal of "independence." This most cautious form of "subversion from within" involves little danger to its advocates since it is couched in government rhetoric and ostensibly follows government logic. The sheer use of the term "independence" represents a retreat, if only a verbal one, on the part of the government, and it is in the nature of tightly oppressive regimes that concessions easily lead to an escalation of demands, as already shown by several tremors of protest among Transkeian chiefs.

The rhetoric of independence has also opened up a new avenue of opposition to government policy. Unlikely as this may have seemed until 1961, Verwoerd is now under attack *from the right,* both from the rural, *platteland* element in his own party and from the United party. The latter in particular claims to accept the independence pronouncements at face value and takes the government to task for partitioning the Republic and creating hostile black states in its midst. Thus, de Villiers Graaff recently proclaimed:

> We would scrap the Bantustan plan. We shall retain South Africa as one integral unit with fifteen million people. We shall not fragment it into a group of States, some of which may become, and indeed are likely to become, hostile to White South Africa. We reject the idea of one man one vote, and we shall retain White leadership all over South Africa and not only in parts, as Dr. Verwoerd would have us do.[8]

Consequently, the government faces an interesting dilemma. On the one hand, if it refuses to transfer sovereignty to the Bantustans, the latter will be exposed more and more clearly as elaborate shams, and this may even precipitate a revolt of the puppet chiefs. On the other hand, should Verwoerd take definite steps toward granting political independence to the Transkei and other future Bantustans, he must face the danger of losing the support of his reactionary Afrikaner electorate.

The second contradiction in the Bantustan scheme is somewhat related to the first. It concerns the extension of universal adult franchise to Africans of the Xhosa and Sotho groups, who live in the Transkei or whose theoretical "homeland" is supposed to be located therein. The government may have assumed that the cathartic effect of casting a ballot would reduce the hostility of Africans and that this franchise would meet demands for "one-man-one-vote." It is clear, however, that few Africans are satisfied with virtually meaningless voting rights which entitle some ethnic groups to elect a minority of members in a Legislative Assembly, which is itself subject to Pretoria's veto and the jurisdiction of which is restricted to only *some* of the people living in 3.2 per cent of the Republic's territory. If anything, it seems probable that the exercise of an ineffective franchise heightens the level of discontent. What can be more frustrating than to be allowed to express one's hostility to apartheid, only to witness the forcible establishment, during a state of emergency, of a "self-government" led by appointed chiefs whose position was overwhelmingly defeated at the polls?

In this respect, the Transkei scheme is fundamentally different from a Fascist-type regime where ritualistic plebiscites, propaganda, mass rallies, and the like are used to create the illusion of consensus. In the Transkei, Africans have been allowed to express their strong opposition to apartheid at the polls, only to see their views disregarded and overridden. This use of the franchise seems to maximize discontent, in that it reflects the government's contempt of African opinion. Implicitly, the latter is regarded as so inconsequential as not even to be worthy of a concerted propaganda effort to "sell" apartheid.[9]

The third, and perhaps most interesting, contradiction in the Bantustan scheme concerns the stand on the racial issue taken respectively by the collaborators and by those in opposition. Ironically, the opponents of apartheid, as represented by Victor Poto, take what is ostensibly a "pro-white" position. They protest against the plan to make the Transkei an exclusively black state and favor "multiracialism" with equal opportunities and rights to all, including whites. Conversely, the collaborating chiefs, under the leadership of Kaiser Matanzima, express their uneasy agreement with apartheid by raising the thinly veiled specter of antiwhitism.

Since apartheid is the product of white racism, it is not surprising that it calls forth black counterracism. The latter is, of course, repressed by the South African government when it takes a militant nationalist form as in the Pan-African Congress. However, black racism can also be couched in apartheid phraseology and take the form of extolling narrow ethnic nationalism and giving vent to xenophobia. Indeed, there is no safer way for an African to express his hostility to whites than to make use of the official hate ideology. The government keeps warning Africans of outside "hyenas" and "jackals" who come to exploit or deceive them; it tells them what noble savages they are so long as they do not let themselves be spoiled by Western culture, and so on.

Thus, apartheid and the Bantustan concept can easily become latent platforms for a surreptitious and insidious variety of ethnic particularism and antiwhitism. Such is Mbeki's interpretation of the Transkeian Chief Minister's motives: "A cold, haughty man who nurses an enmity towards whites and wishes to escape their oppressive presence, Matanzima has chosen to try to do this by using apartheid. . . ."[10]

The fourth contradiction inherent in the Bantustans is the most basic of all and indeed underlies the other three. Both the practicability of the Bantustans and their acceptability to sufficient numbers of Africans hinge on a massive redistribution of wealth and power at the expense of the albinocracy.[11] More specifically, the economic viability of partition in South Africa depends on the manifold enlargement of the African (and indeed other nonwhite) areas, on the large-scale subsidization of subsistence agriculture by the money sector of the economy, and, consequently, on drastic land and income redistribution. Politically, if the partitioned areas are to retain any federal association, the basis of such association must clearly be an effective sharing of power between the constituent racial groups in the joint government rather than the Bantustan blueprint of a white colonial state dominating a half-dozen or more labor reservoirs administered by puppet chiefs.

However, it is obvious that these necessary conditions to any viable partition scheme are precisely those which the Nationalist government desperately seeks to avert through its Bantustan scheme. The latter is apparently based on the assumption or the hope that Africans and the outside world are mistaking the comic opera of equality and the shadow of economic development for the real things. The Bantustan scheme is thus in part an ineffective attempt to mollify internal and external opposition at minimal cost to the ruling caste, and in part a blueprint for the improvement of the state's repressive apparatus.

All four paradoxes or contradictions in Bantustan policy which we have briefly examined raise doubt as to the goverment's ability to control apartheid's latest litter of feral children.

In summary, apartheid aims to introduce between racial groups the greatest degree of physical separation consistent with economic imperatives in a highly industrialized society. Macrosegregation is deemed by the government to offer the greatest chance of continued white supremacy, but, where white industry, mining, and agriculture require nonwhite labor, lesser degrees of segregation are acceptable.

The last aspect of our analysis concerns the differential economic consequences of micro-, meso-, and macrosegregation. Many analysts of the South African scene have observed that apartheid involves a great economic cost and interferes with economic development. Apartheid certainly conflicts with principles of economic "rationality," and government policies often assign priority to political as opposed to economic aims. Directly and indirectly, the economic cost of apartheid is no lesser for being difficult to assess with any degree of precision. However, the three degrees of segregation have different effects and entail different economic costs.

Microsegregation is certainly the least costly of the three. Segregated nonwhite facilities are either vastly inferior to the white ones or altogether nonexistent. To avoid any suggestion of a "separate but equal" doctrine, a law was passed (the Reservation of Separate Amenities Act) providing for segregated *and* unequal facilities. True duplication of public conveniences is highly exceptional, and segregation often means nothing more than the exclusion of nonwhites from many places. Thus microsegregation frequently involves a saving over what it would cost to provide adequate facilities for the entire population, and there is little or no economic incentive for the white group to abolish it.

With the introduction of the new style of mesosegregation, the government is deliberately paying an economic price for the maintenance of white supremacy. Much of that price, however, is paid, not by the government, but by the Africans who have to finance many of the amenities in their streamlined ghettos and bear the cost of transport to and from the white areas where they work. In addition, white employers of nonwhite labor suffer indirectly from the lower labor efficiency resulting from employee fatigue and time wasted in transit. Consequently, while the total economic cost of ghettoization is quite high, the direct price paid by the government and the bulk of the white electorate which votes for the Nationalists is relatively low.

Macrosegregation is potentially the most expensive for the government. The sums required to subsidize economic development in the Bantustans in order to raise the standard of living above starvation would run into hundreds of millions of dollars. But, here again, the government spends only a small fraction of the necessary sum on the development of the "Bantu homelands."[12] What the Bantustan policy does, in effect, achieve economically is to perpetuate the sharp distinction in the South African economy between a high production money sector and a *sub*subsistence one. The productive potential of the one-third of the African population which is kept in or even forced back into the Reserves is thus vastly underutilized. In the same way as South Africa combines politically the properties of a quasi-democracy for the *Herrenvolk* and a colonial tyranny for the Africans, economically the country is, at once, a booming industrial nation and one of the most destitute of the "underdeveloped" countries.

From the analysis above, it seems that all three levels of segregation on which the policy of apartheid rests are doomed to economic and political failure for a combination of reasons. Microsegregation serves little purpose in the preservation of the status quo, but also involves a minimum of cost to the government. Its major function is to provide a bigoted albinocracy with some psychological and material "fringe benefits" of oppression.

Mesosegregation is considerably costlier, but on it rests the political control of the highly explosive urban areas. From the viewpoint of the maintenance of white supremacy, mesosegregation is thus essential. Only through the compartmentalization of racial groups into streamlined ghettos can the dominant white minority hope to combat open insurgency. On the other hand, the implementation of mesosegregation with the entire repressive machinery of "reference books," "influx control," "job reservation," "population registration," and "group areas" is directly responsible for the overwhelming majority of acts of protest and revolt against apartheid. Thus, the ghettoization of urban life brings with it the growing hypertrophy of the police and military apparatus. Not only is the militarization of an ever growing proportion of the white population expensive but its effectiveness is limited by at least two factors. First, the open and unrestrained use of military violence, given the climate of world opinion, threatens the government with outside intervention. Second, as the whites monopolize all key positions in government, industry, transport, communications, and the like, and as many whites hold such key positions, the simultaneous mobilization of the albinocracy on any sizable scale would bring about considerable disruption of civilian activities, not to mention the problem of the protection of dependents.

In the foregoing analysis, I have tried to show that the continued enforcement of meso- and macrosegregation is essential to the preservation of white supremacy. However, apartheid also generates conflicts and contradictions, the control of which involves an ever rising cost in economic, human, and military resources. Micro- and mesosegregation in urban areas create an undercurrent of revolt precariously held in check by a growing police and army apparatus, and the Bantustan scheme unwittingly threatens to destroy the entire edifice of white supremacy.

NOTES

1. Among the many books on contemporary South Africa, the following provide particularly valuable background information: Gwendolen M. Carter, *The Politics of Inequality, South Africa since 1948* (New York: Praeger, 1958); J. S. Marais, *The Cape Coloured People, 1652–1937* (London: Longmans, Green, 1939); C. W. de Kiewiet, *A History of South Africa, Social and Economic* (Oxford: Clarendon Press, 1941); I. D. MacCrone, *Race Attitudes in South Africa* (London: Oxford University Press, 1937); Ellen Hellmann, ed., *Handbook of Race Relations in South Africa* (Cape Town: Oxford University Press, 1949); Leo Marquard, *The Peoples and Policies of South Africa* (London: Oxford University Press, 1962); Sheila Patterson, *Colour and Culture in South Africa* (London: Routledge and Kegan Paul, 1953); Sheila Patterson, *The Last Trek* (London: Routledge and Kegan Paul, 1957). For information concerning the ideology and implementation of apartheid, the publications of the South African Institute of Race Relations and the South African Bureau of Racial Affairs are useful. See in particular Muriel Horrell's yearly *Survey of Race Relations in South Africa* (Johannesburg: South African Institute of Race Relations). Other publications include S. Pienaar and Anthony Sampson, *South Africa, Two Views of Separate Development* (London: Oxford University Press, 1960); C. W. de Kiewiet, *The Anatomy of South African Misery* (London: Oxford University Press, 1956); N. J. J. Olivier, "Apartheid or Integration?" in P. Smith, ed., *Africa in Transition* (London: Reinhardt, 1958); Leo Kuper, *Passive Resistance in South Africa* (New Haven: Yale University Press, 1957); Patrick van Rensburg, *Guilty Land, The History of Apartheid* (New York: Praeger, 1962); and Pierre L. van den Berghe, *South Africa, A Study in Conflict* (Berkeley: University of California Press, 1967).

2. For an analysis of the role of African chiefs in the Transkei, see

David Hammond-Tooke, "Chieftainship in Transkeian Political Development," *Journal of Modern African Studies* 2 (December 1964): 513–529.

3. Leo Kuper, *An African Bourgeoisie* (New Haven: Yale University Press, 1965), pp. 22–23.

4. Leo Marquard, *South Africa's Colonial Policy* (Johannesburg: South African Institute of Race Relations, 1957).

5. Quoted in Brian Bunting, *The Rise of the South African Reich* (Baltimore: Penguin, 1964), p. 310.

6. Quoted in van den Berghe, *op cit.,* p. 118.

7. *Ibid.*

8. *Africa Digest* 12, no. 3 (December 1964): 81.

9. This is but one of several ways in which South Africa differs from a Fascist-type regime. See van den Berghe, *op. cit.,* for a more extensive treatment of this point. Bunting, on the other hand, stresses, and indeed overstresses, the similarities of South Africa with Nazi Germany. See Bunting, *op. cit.* The southern United States constitute a closer parallel to South Africa than does Nazi Germany, Fascist Italy, or Franco's Spain.

10. Govan Mbeki, *South Africa, The Peasants' Revolt* (Baltimore: Penguin, 1964), p. 137.

11. Although the vast majority of African leaders have rejected the partition of South Africa on any terms, there have been a few dissenting voices. For example, Jordan Ngubane has advocated an ethnic confederation accompanied by drastic land reform. Cf. his book, *An African Explains Apartheid* (New York: Praeger, 1963), pp. 220–232.

12. Only a small fraction of the conservative 1956 estimate of £104 million recommended by the Tomlinson commission for a ten-year period has so far been expended. On the other hand, defense expenditures aimed primarily at the repression of internal unrest have climbed from £40 million a year in 1960–1961 to £104 million in 1963–1964.

13

Miscegenation in South Africa

A number of related factors make the Union of South Africa an ideal object of investigation in the field of miscegenation. The exceptionally virulent brand of racism that has developed in South Africa since the beginning of the twentieth century was accompanied by an increasingly morbid fear of miscegenation unparalleled in intensity anywhere else in the world.[1] As a consequence of this miscegenophobia, South Africa went further than any other country in recent times in prohibiting by law all sexual relations, whether marital or nonmarital, between whites and nonwhites. Finally, the South African government, in its concern over "bastardization," provides the social scientist with the best data on interracial marriage and concubinage of any country known to the author.

The history of miscegenation in South Africa is as old as the first permanent Dutch settlement at the Cape in 1652. In the first few decades, some instances of marriage between Dutchmen and Christianized Hottentot women took place, as well as extensive nonmarital relations between masters and female slaves.[2] In the 1670's, an estimated three-fourths of all children of female slaves had white fathers.[3] With the rise of color prejudice in the

Reprinted from *Cahiers d'Etudes Africaines*, 4 (1960): 68–84.

latter decades of the seventeenth century, legal unions of whites and nonwhites became rare. A 1685 law prohibited marriage between white men and slave women; some legal unions of white men with free women of color continued to take place, but with decreasing frequency. Miscegenation, however, continued to flourish in the form common to most slave societies, namely institutionalized concubinage between white men and nonwhite women.[4]

The salient fact in the early history of miscegenation in South Africa is that, while intermarriage became rapidly condemned, extramarital relations between white men and women of color were not only tolerated but even looked upon with amusement. The slave lodge of the Dutch East India Company at the Cape was a wide-open brothel of which Mentzel gives an interesting account:

> Female slaves are always ready to offer their bodies for a trifle; and towards evening, one can see a string of soldiers and sailors entering the lodge where they misspend their time until the clock strikes 9. . . . The Company does nothing to prevent this promiscuous intercourse, since, for one thing it tends to multiply the slave population, and does away with the necessity of importing fresh slaves. Three or four generations of this admixture (for the daughters follow their mothers' footsteps) have produced a half-caste population—a mestizo class—but a slight shade darker than some Europeans.[5]

Among the European bourgeoisie, interracial concubinage was also common:

> Boys who, through force of cirmumstances, have to remain at home during these impressionable years between 16 and 21 more often than not commit some folly, and get entangled with a handsome slave-girl belonging to the household. These affairs are not regarded as very serious . . . the offence is venial in the public estimation. It does not hurt the boy's prospects; his escapade is a source of amusement, and he is dubbed a young fellow who has shown the stuff he is made of.[6]

A British visitor to the Cape in the beginning of the nineteenth century tells that slave girls were routinely assigned to the bedroom of white guests to enliven the latters' nights.[7] Slave girls were "loaned out" to Europeans by their masters:

> Female slaves sometimes live with Europeans as husband and wife with the permission of their masters who benefit in two ways: the cost of upkeep of the slave is reduced through the presents she receives from the man, and her children are the property of her master since children of female slaves are themselves slaves. . . . In this manner, the slave population is always increasing. . . .[8]

Similarly, the whites interbred extensively with the nominally free Hottentots. Vaillant estimates the number of *Bastards* (for such was the contemporary designation of white-Hottentot half-breeds) in the 1780's at one-sixth of the inhabitants of the whole Cape Colony.[9] In the first half of the nineteenth century, entire communities of Bastards settled along the Orange River, where they established autonomous "states." The offspring of these white-slave and white-Hottentot unions, as well as interbreeding between slaves and Hottentots, gave rise to the people known today as the "Cape Coloureds."[10]

In this early period, then, miscegenation was not only common but sanctioned, so long as it took the form of concubinage between higher-status men and lower-status women. There was no trace of a feeling of horror against miscegenation per se. The main concern of the dominant white group was the preservation of its superior status, and the latter was left unthreatened by master-slave concubinage. Intermarriage, on the other hand, entailed a measure of social equality and was consequently opposed.

During the nineteenth century, miscegenation continued, as witnessed by people like De Buys and Dunn, whose descendants now constitute entire communities of Coloureds. The majority of the *Voortrekkers,* however, who settled the Orange Free State and the Transvaal in the first half of the nineteenth century do not seem to have shared the amused tolerance of miscegenation found at the Cape in the eighteenth century. Their rigid Calvinist

TABLE 13-2   Number of Whites Marrying and Percentage
Marrying Outside Their Race, 1925-1946

Year	Number Marrying	Number Marrying Outside Their Race	% Exogamous
1925	28,137	133	0.47
1930	33,307	97	0.29
1935	41,289	91	0.22
1940	56,774	105	0.18
1945	48,234	92	0.19
1946	56,693	77	0.14

Adapted from Sonnabend and Sofer, *op. cit.*, p. 26.

over the years. It is interesting to note that the greatest drop occurred between 1925 and 1930, coinciding with the passage of the Immorality Act of 1927. A direct causation between the two events is unlikely since the Act only affected nonmarital relations between Africans and Europeans. Both events can be interpreted more plausibly as independent indices of the rising prejudice against miscegenation.

The breakdown by sex given in Table 13–3 shows that European men are much more likely to marry outside their race than are European women. Between three-fourths and four-fifths of all interracial marriages involving whites are of the hypergamous variety. Disapproved as all interracial marriages are in South Africa, the prejudice against a white woman's entering such a union is even greater than that encountered by a white man.

TABLE 13-3   Mixed Marriages of Whites by Sex, 1925-1946

Year	White Male to Nonwhite Female	White Female to Nonwhite Male	Total	% Hypergamous
1925	98	35	133	73.7
1930	76	21	97	78.4
1935	75	16	91	82.4
1940	87	18	105	82.9
1945	71	21	92	77.2
1946	60	17	77	77.9

Adapted from Sonnabend and Sofer, *op. cit.*, p. 26.

Table 13–4 gives the relative frequency of the six racial combinations of intermarriage for the sum of all cases occurring between 1925 and 1946, while Table 13–5 shows the trend over time for each racial combination. The discrepancies between expected and actual percentages in Table 13–4 show that three combinations are overrepresented. One of these is between members of racial groups of roughly equivalent status (Coloured-Indians), and the other two are between members of racial groups adjacent in the South African status scale (African-Coloured and white-Coloured).

TABLE 13-4 Number and Percentage of Interracial Marriages by Race, 1925-1946

Racial Combination	Number of Marriages 1925-1946	% of Total	Expected %[a]
White-Coloured	1,766	13.33	7.60
White-Indian	116	0.88	2.53
White-African	277	2.09	56.51
African-Coloured	9,255	69.87	24.22
African-Indian	170	1.28	8.07
Indian-Coloured	1,662	12.55	1.08
TOTAL	13,246	100.00	100.01

[a]The expected proportion for any given combination is:

$$P = \frac{p_i \cdot p_j}{\Sigma p_i \cdot p_j}$$

where p_i and p_j are the proportions of the groups in the total population. The same assumptions are made as in computing the expected proportion of intermarriage.

Adapted from Hellmann, *op. cit.*, p. 11; Sonnabend and Sofer, *op. cit.*, p. 24.

Intermarriages between whites and Africans (the two extreme groups on the color scale) occur 28 times less frequently than one would expect if *intermarriage* occurred randomly. The remaining two combinations are between adjacent groups (Indians-whites and Indians-Africans) and are also underrepresented, but not nearly as much as African-white unions. In short, then, the overwhelming majority (98 per cent) of all intermarriages occur between persons belonging to racial groups of

either equivalent or adjacent status. Conversely, marriage between the two extreme groups on the racial status scale is very
rare. Indians, when they intermarry, tend to restrict their choice
to the Coloureds, a group of approximately equal status. Indians
tend to marry either "up" or "down" to a lesser extent than
the Coloureds.

The total incidence of interracial marriage increased somewhat
faster than the general population. Between 1925 and 1946, the
total number of intermarriages grew by 84.53 per cent, whereas
the total population of the Union showed an increase of only
64.79 per cent between 1921 and 1946. As Europeans became
increasingly endogamous over the years, and as the Coloured
endogamy rate remained almost constant, the slight increase in
the incidence of intermarriage is attributable to the Africans.
Turning to Table 13–5 we see that African-Coloured unions
constituted an ever greater percentage of all intermarriages. By
1946, such unions accounted for over three-fourths of the total.

TABLE 13-5   Percentage of Each Racial Combination of Intermarriage in
Total Number of Intermarriages, 1925-1946

Year	White- Col.	White- Indian	White- African	African- Col.	African- Indian	Indian- Col.	Total %	Total No. of Mixed Marriages
1925	25.34	0.22	4.26	58.74	0.90	10.54	100.00	446
1930	16.78	1.12	3.80	63.53	0.67	14.10	100.00	447
1935	15.70	0.58	1.36	70.35	0.78	11.24	100.01	516
1940	13.24	0.27	0.53	71.93	1.74	12.30	100.01	748
1945	9.54	0.82	0.47	72.79	0.71	15.67	100.00	849
1946	8.02	0.73	0.61	76.55	1.70	12.39	100.00	823

Adapted from Hellmann, *op. cit.*, p. 11; Sonnabend and Sofer, *op. cit.*, p. 24.

White-Coloured and white-African marriages declined both
relatively and absolutely long before the passage of the 1949
Act. Not only are white-African marriages rare but they have
become increasingly so over time. By 1946, only 0.61 per cent
of the mixed unions were between these two extreme groups,
compared to 4.26 per cent in 1925. Indian-Coloured unions show

no trend toward either an increase or a decrease, while white-Indian and African-Indian percentages are based on too few cases to draw any conclusions.

There exist, of course, no statistics on the extent of non-marital miscegenation, but prosecutions under the Immorality Acts constitute a source of data unique to South Africa. Such prosecutions have averaged some 300 cases each year since 1951.[21] Naturally, not all cases of miscegenation reach the courts. For one thing, sexual relations between members of the three nonwhite groups are not included; these unions are not prohibited by the law, which is concerned with the "purity" of the white ruling group only. Even of the illicit miscegenation between whites and nonwhites, it may safely be assumed that the great majority of such cases are never prosecuted, either because they escape detection or because they are suppressed, through bribery or otherwise, before they reach courts. The proportion of actual cases being tried and the selective factors operating are entirely a matter for speculation.

For purposes of this study all "immorality" cases reported in a non-European weekly newspaper between January 1958 and April 1960 were analyzed. This procedure yielded a sample of 175 cases.[22] While the newspaper does not report all immorality cases tried in court, it probably has a more extensive coverage than any other paper in the country. According to the editors, most cases tried in the large cities, particularly in Johannesburg, Durban, and Cape Town, are covered, while most rural cases are not published. This urban bias does affect some of the findings and must therefore be kept in mind. Due to the elusive nature of the universe in this instance, one has to be content with a sample, however open to question that sample may be.

Of 175 cases, 13 involved European women, and 162, European men. As in the case of interracial marriage, hypergamous (or better, "hypergenous") unions are overwhelmingly more frequent than "hypogenous" relationships. The complete breakdown by race given in Table 13–6 reveals that the Coloureds are heavily overrepresented (64 cases out of 175, or 36.6 per cent of all unions for a group which represents only 9 per cent of the total population). The small number of cases involving

Indians does not permit any reliable conclusions. Africans are correspondingly underrepresented. These findings corroborate the intermarriage data which likewise show that relations tend to take place between racial groups of adjacent status in the color scale. However, the tendency is not nearly so clear-cut as for the intermarriage data. Whereas, in 1945, only 0.5 per cent of the *mixed* marriages occurred between whites and Africans, in 1958–1960, 51.4 per cent of the nonmarital unions in our sample took place between these two extreme groups on the South Africa color scale.

TABLE 13-6 Racial Distribution of a Sample of Persons Involved in "Immorality" Cases, 1958-1960

		Race of Male Partner				
		White	Indian	Coloured	African	Total
Race of Female Partner	White	0[a]	3	4	6	13
	Indian	11	0	0	0	11
	Coloured	60	0	0	0	60
	African	84	0	0	0	84
	"Nonwhite"	7	0	0	0	7
	TOTAL	162	3	4	6	175

[a]All cells with a frequency of zero do not fall under the legal definition of "immorality," and hence are not prosecuted.

Many South Africans believe that of the two main white language groups, Afrikaners are overwhelmingly overrepresented in "immorality" cases. Table 13–7 shows that this is not the case in the present sample. Of the 79 white South African na-

TABLE 13-7 Language and Nationality of White Partners in "Immorality" Cases, 1958-1960

	Male	Female	Total
Afrikaans-speaking South Africans	45	5	50
English-speaking South Africans	28	1	29
Aliens	43	0	43
Policemen on "trap" duty	27	0	27
Not ascertainable	19	7	26
TOTAL	162	13	175

tionals whose language group could be determined, there are 50 Afrikaners (63.3 per cent) and 29 English-speaking whites (36.7 per cent), that is, a close approximation to the proportion of these two groups in the white population.[23] Many more aliens were convicted under the Act than one would expect on the basis of their proportion in the white population. Of the 43 cases, however, 32 involved transient foreign sailors in the harbors of Cape Town and Durban, some of whom were ignorant of the law.[24]

Insofar as possible, the nature of the sexual relationship was determined as shown in Table 13–8. In 27 cases, white policemen acted as "decoy" to trap nonwhite prostitutes. Fifteen cases involved sexual assault or "improper advances" without the consent of the women. In the 42 cases above, only one of the parties was tried. There was insufficient evidence to determine the nature of the relationship in another 46 cases. Of the remaining 87 instances, 70 cases involved short-term, casual relations, either of a mercenary nature with prostitutes or of an exploitative nature between masters and servants. Evidence of a deeper, long-standing relationship existed in only 17 cases. In only 5 out of these 17 cases did one or more children result from the relationship, thereby indicating the largely sterile character of nonmarital miscegenation under recent South African conditions.[25] Although the small number of white women involved does not permit any definite statistical conclusions, it seems that such relations tend to be of longer duration than cases involving white men. This

TABLE 13-8   Type of Relationship between Partners in "Immorality" Cases, 1958-1960

Type of Relationship	White Female-Nonwhite Male	White Male-Nonwhite Female	Total
Long-term	4	13	17
Short-term	1	69	70
One-sided, assault	3	12	15
One-sided, police trap	0	27	27
Not ascertainable	5	41	46
TOTAL	13	162	175

finding is to be expected since the racial structure of South Africa makes for few European prostitutes, and the few who exist restrict their practice principally to the more profitable white clientele.

Sentences imposed under the Immorality Act, though stringent by normal Western standards of equity, are well below the maximum of seven years that the law establishes. The bulk of the sentences lies between 3 and 6 months in prison. The most salient conclusion from Table 13-9 is that non-Europeans tend to be sentenced more heavily than Europeans. A greater proportion of nonwhites are given prison terms, and these prison terms are longer than for the whites on the average. Out of 67 cases where both parties were convicted, the non-European partners received a heavier sentence in 24 cases, both partners received equal sentences in 34 cases, and the Europeans were more heavily sentenced only 9 times. These findings will, of course, not surprise anyone familiar with the South African system of government.

TABLE 13-9 Types of Sentences Imposed on Persons Accused of "Immorality," 1958-1960

Type of Sentence	Whites	Nonwhites	Total
Physical punishment only	12	0	12
Fine	1	1	2
Suspended prison term	17	5	22
1 to 3 months in prison	15	14	29
4 to 6 months in prison	40	57	97
Over 6 months in prison	4	6	10
Deportation	0	8	8
Case dismissed	17	18	35
Not charged (one-sided case)	30	12	42
No information	39	54	93
TOTAL	175	175	350

The occupational distribution of the European males and non-European females is given in Table 13–10.[26] On the female side, prostitutes are by far the largest group, thereby confirming our

TABLE 13-10   Occupational Distribution of White Males and
Nonwhite Females in "Immorality" Cases, 1958-1960

Occupation	White Males	Nonwhite Females	Total
Business and professional	4	0	4
Semiprofessional	4	3	7
Farming	3	0	3
Police and civil service	24	0	24
Other clerical and white collar	7	1	8
Sailors	32	0	32
Domestic servants	0	12	12
Prostitutes	0	83	83
Other manual	11	0	11
Retired or unemployed	8	0	8
Police trap	27	0	27
No information	42	63	105
TOTAL	162	162	324

previous finding on the transitory and mercenary character of much nonmarital miscegenation in our sample.[27] The second most frequent female occupation is that of servant. Among white males, farmers are probably underrepresented because of the urban bias of the sample. The male distribution is slanted toward the lower-prestige occupations, but not as exclusively as is generally believed. A few prominent business and professional men were involved, including a physician, a minister of the Dutch Reformed Church, and the brother of the Prime Minister's son-in-law. It may, of course, be cogently argued that cases involving prominent persons are given more publicity and hence that they are overrepresented in our sample. The prominence of the police and civil service (including the state railways) among the occupations is noteworthy.[28] This fact lends indirect support to Lewin's contention that nonmarital miscegenation is found more frequently among highly prejudiced Europeans, who treat nonwhites as tools for the white man's convenience, than among liberals preaching racial equality.[29] Since the Nationalist Party came into power in 1948, the civil service has been increasingly recruited among government supporters who are most likely to be strongly prejudiced against non-Europeans. Policemen and railway workers come predominantly from the Afrikaner lower class among whom racial prejudice is deeply rooted.

Table 13–11 summarizes the data on age. As might be expected, the men are 9 years older than the women on the average. Only 16.6 per cent of the women are 30 years of age or more, compared to 56.3 per cent of the men. A different picture emerges, however, if one separates the cases involving white men from those involving white women. Now it appears that the white partners, whether male or female, are older than the nonwhite partners. One-third of the white women (4 out of 12) are 40 or above, compared to 5 per cent of the nonwhite women (5 out of 102). Those white women in their forties all had nonwhite lovers in their twenties and thirties. Conversely, only 2 of the 27 white men of age 40 or above had affairs with nonwhite women older than themselves. Conclusions drawn on such a small and selective sample must, by necessity, be highly tentative. However, this age differential suggests the hypothesis that the white partner, whether male or female, is dominant in the relationship and is the "sexual exploiter" of the nonwhite partner.

TABLE 13-11   Mean Age in Years by Sex for Partners in "Immorality" Cases, 1958-1960

| | Mean Age of: | | |
Cases Involving:	Males	Females	Total
White female and nonwhite male	28.4	30.2	29.3
White male and nonwhite female	34.4	24.2	29.0
Mean for total	33.8	24.8	29.1

Summary

The feeling of aversion that most white South Africans manifest at the mere mention of miscegenation did not exist before the nineteenth century. Previous to that time, interracial concubinage between white men and women of color was not only common but also viewed with tolerance and amusement.

Beginning in the nineteenth century, and becoming even more

sharply defined in the twentieth century, a new and much more virulent phase of race relations was entered in South Africa. One aspect of that new phase was the spreading of antimiscegenation attitudes. More and more stringent legislation against interracial sexual relations, whether marital or nonmarital, is one of the indices of this change in attitudes.

The data on interracial marriage show that:

1. All four "racial" groups are almost entirely endogamous. Less than 1 per cent of all marriages take place across color lines.

2. The Europeans are the most endogamous of the four groups, and the Coloureds the least so. This finding is not consistent with the numerical size of these groups in the total population.

3. Interracial marriages increased somewhat faster than the total population between 1925 and 1946, but the increase was due almost entirely to African-Coloured marriages.

4. Marriages between whites and nonwhites showed a consistent downward trend long before they became illegal.

5. White-nonwhite unions tend to be predominantly hypergamous (between white men and nonwhite women).

6. Intermarriage is almost entirely (98 per cent) confined to persons belonging to groups of adjacent or equivalent racial status, according to the South African "pigmentocracy." African-Coloured marriages alone account for over three-fourths of mixed unions in 1946.

The data on nonmarital miscegenation showed as marked a hypergamous (or better hypergenous) trend as the intermarriage statistics. Nonmarital relations also show a tendency to occur more frequently between members of adjacent color groups, but not nearly to the extent that intermarriage does. The vast majority of nonmarital relations across color lines is of a short-term and mercenary nature. Such relations also tend to be sterile; children resulted in only 5 out of 175 cases. The European men involved are of low occupational status on the average, but not exclusively so. The police and civil service are heavily represented among male occupations. Non-European females are over-whelmingly prostitutes and domestic servants. Afrikaners are not significantly overrepresented in relation to English speaking whites. European men are 10 years older than nonwhite females on the average, whereas European women are 2 years older than their male nonwhite partners.

NOTES

1. Alan Paton's novel, *Too Late the Phalarope* (New York: Scribner, 1953), besides being a masterful work of literature, gives a perceptive analysis of this "miscegenophobia." We are indebted to our colleagues S. E. Cruise, H. Dickie-Clark, K. Hill, J. Horton, E. Krige, H. Kuper, L. Kuper, and J. Mann for help and advice, but the responsibility for the views contained in this chapter is entirely our own.

2. Cf. I. D. MacCrone, *Race Attitudes in South Africa* (London: Oxford University Press, 1937), p. 42; M. W. Spilhaus, *The First South Africans* (Cape Town: Juta, 1949), p. 127; M. Jeffreys, "Where Do Coloureds Come From?" *Drum* (August and September 1959). Simon van der Steel, the Dutch governor of the Cape, had a Javanese grandmother. At that time, culture and religion were the criteria of status at the Cape rather than race, so that Christianized half-castes enjoyed equal status with the white burghers.

3. MacCrone, *op. cit.,* p. 68; Spilhaus, *op. cit.,* p. 130.

4. For a theoretical discussion of hypergamy, see Chapter 3.

5. O. F. Mentzel, *A Description of the African Cape of Good Hope, 1787* (Cape Town: The van Riebeeck Society, 1944), II, 125.

6. *Ibid.,* II, 109.

7. Robert Percival, *An Account of the Cape of Good Hope* (London: C. and R. Baldwin, 1804), p. 291.

8. Mentzel, *op. cit.,* II, 130.

9. Jacques Boulenger, *Voyages de F. Vaillant dans l'Intérieur de l'Afrique, 1781–1785* (Paris; Plon, 1932), pp. 160–162. The term *Bastard* was not derogatory at the time.

10. J. S. Marais, *The Cape Coloured People, 1652–1937* (London: Longmans, Green, 1939).

11. This change in attitudes is part of what we have described elsewhere as a transition from a "paternalistic" to a "competitive" type of race relations. Cf. Pierre L. van den Berghe, "The Dynamics of Racial Prejudice," *Social Forces* 37 (1958); and in Chapter 1 in this volume.

12. Cf. Paton, *op. cit.*, pp. 249–254, 267–269.

13. The four major racial groups in South Africa in the 1951 census were as follows: Europeans or whites (2.6 million, 21 per cent of total), Asiatics or Indians (370,000, 3 per cent of total), Natives or Africans (8.5 million, 67 per cent of total), and Coloureds, that is, the people of mixed ancestry (1.1 million, 9 per cent of total). The Europeans have imposed a hierarchy of political power and rights, of economic position, and of "racial" status with themselves clearly at the top, the Coloureds and the Indians in an intermediate but rapidly deteriorating position, and the Africans at the bottom. It is interesting to note that sexual intercourse with Africans was prohibited over twenty years before intercourse with Coloureds and Indians was forbidden.

14. However, intermarriage between Coloureds, Indians, and Africans is still allowed. The same is true for nonmarital miscegenation. Cf. J. Lewin, "Sex, Colour, and the Law," *Africa South* 4: 63–66.

15. H. Gibbs, *Twilight in South Africa* (London: Jarrolds, 1949), p. 27.

16. J. Hoge, *Bydraes tot die genealogie van ou Afrikaanse families* (Balkema: 1958); Jeffreys, *op. cit.*

17. Racialist policies in South Africa have at least the useful by-product of providing the social scientist with an impressive set of racial statistics.

18. The expected proportion of intermarriages is based on the formula:

$$P = 1 - \Sigma\, p_i{}^2$$

where p_i is the proportion of group i in the total population. The formula assumes an equal sex ratio, an equal marriage rate between the various groups, and a constancy of proportion of the four racial groups in the total population between 1925 and 1946.

19. Registered marriages in the Union are monogamous.

20. Cf. Hilda Kuper, *Indian People in Natal* (Durban: Natal University Press, 1960).

21. Lewin, *op. cit.*, p. 67. As will be seen from our sample, a num-

ber of those cases involve foreign sailors in Durban and Cape-town.

22. A "case" is defined here as an actual or an attempted sexual re-lationship between a white and a nonwhite, insofar as at least one of the two parties involved was tried in a court of law. When-ever one party had relations with more than one person, each dyadic relationship was treated as a case. We are indebted to the staff of the *Golden City Post* for giving us full access to their newspaper's files.

23. A person was classified as belonging to one of the two language groups if *all* of his names were of that language. When given names and surnames were not of the same language, the case was classified as doubtful. This classification does not exclude any possibility of error since a number of persons with Afri-kaner names are fully anglicized, and the reverse also happens, though more rarely. The urban bias of the sample may account in part for the results, as over 80 per cent of the white *rural* population are Afrikaans-speaking. Since some 80 per cent of the *total* white population are urban, however, it is unlikely that the relative numerical position of the two groups would be greatly altered in an unbiased sample. Another indication that miscege-nation is not confined to Afrikaners is that many, though not most, Coloureds have English surnames, particularly in Natal.

24. One sailor pleaded that, although he had been warned about the Immorality Act, he thought that his shipmates had played him a joke.

25. Some of the women may have been pregnant at the time they were tried, but it is doubtful that this factor affects the conclu-sion about the sterility of most unions.

26. Occupation was given in only one case involving a European woman (prostitute) and in only 3 cases of non-European men (one policeman, two servants).

27. The urban bias of the sample may account in part for this finding.

28. These cases do not include the policemen on trap duty, who are listed separately.

29. Lewin, *op. cit.,* p. 70.

14

Language and Nationalism
in South Africa

To state that language and nationalism are closely related is a tautology, but one that needs restating in view of the loose usage of the term "nationalism" in the Third World and particularly in the African literature. In the nineteenth-century European sense of the word, "nationalism" referred to a political movement or a process of growing self-consciousness based on a feeling of common ethnicity. Of the several criteria of ethnicity, a common language has often been the paramount one, with religion coming in second place. Thus, when one speaks of German or Italian nationalism, one means primarily the growth of political consciousness by people sharing the same language.

Nationalism in Africa

In dealing with contemporary Africa, social scientists have greatly confused political analysis by using "nationalism" to mean broadly "anti-colonialism."[1] If the confusion had stopped there, not too much damage would have been made, but, faced with the problem of having to use a descriptive term to refer to true nationalism in Africa, the word "tribalism" was resorted to.

Reprinted from *Race* 9, no. 1 (July 1967): 37–46.

Apart from the invidious connotations of "tribalism," the word "tribe" and its derivatives have been used in at least half a dozen unrelated senses. A tribe has meant a group speaking the same language, a group inhabiting a certain area, or a traditional state, even though the three criteria often did not coincide. "Tribalism" has meant federalism as opposed to centralism, nationalism as opposed to internationalism, traditionalism as distinguished from modernism, or a rural orientation as opposed to an urban one.

In conclusion, I would suggest that "tribe" and its derivatives be scrapped altogether. To refer to a political movement based on ethnicity, I shall use the term "nationalism" (for example, Yoruba nationalism, Ewe nationalism, Kikuyu nationalism). To refer to political movements that use the multinational state as their defining unit, I shall speak of "territorialism" (for example, Nigerian territorialism, Congolese territorialism). Only in the few cases of true African nation-states, in the few instances of culturally homogeneous or nearly homogeneous states, can the term "nationalism" properly be applied at the level of the sovereign polity (for example, Somali nationalism, Egyptian nationalism, or Rwanda nationalism). Finally, where the defining unit is larger than both the sovereign state and the ethnic group, I shall speak of "internationalism" (thus European internationalism, African internationalism, Pan-Islamic internationalism). However, movements aimed at uniting in a single state an ethnic group divided between several polities are properly "nationalist" (for example, Bakongo nationalism, or German nationalism prior to Bismarck).

The Political Role of Language in South Africa

Having hopefully given back to the term "nationalism" the reasonably clear meaning it had until my Africanist colleagues confused the issue, I shall turn to an analysis of the political role of language in the Republic of South Africa.[2] According to the definitions above, there is no political movement in contemporary South Africa which can properly be called nationalist, although I confess to having loosely used the term in my previous writings about South Africa.

Whatever nationalism existed among the African nation-states of the nineteenth century (the Zulu, the Xhosa, the Sotho, the Swazi, the Ndebele) has all but disappeared by now. Although the indigenous languages are spoken by more people than ever before, and although feelings of ethnic particularism and prejudice persist between African ethnic groups, these feelings have little if any political meaning in the modern context. (They are analogous to ethnic feelings of people of Italian, Irish, or Jewish descent in the United States, for example.) What is often called African nationalism or black nationalism in South Africa is the movement aiming at the overthrow of white supremacy, represented by such organizations as the Pan-Africanist Congress and the African National Congress. In our terminology, this is an instance of territorialism. Similarly, "white nationalism" is simply a racist ideology for the maintenance of the status quo.

Of course, some scholars would argue that Afrikaner nationalism, that is, the political movement of people of Dutch or Boer descent, is an authentic case of nationalism as I have defined it.[3] Afrikaner nationalism does indeed have many characteristics of classical nationalism and, of all political movements in South Africa, comes closest to being truly nationalist. Yet, the added element of racism complicates the picture. Speaking Afrikaans as one's mother tongue is a *necessary* condition for membership in the *Volk*. But it is not a *sufficient* condition; one must also meet the test of racial "purity." For every six "white" people who are ethnically Afrikaners, there are five "Coloured" Afrikaners who are denied membership in the *Volk*. That race is an even more important criterion than ethnicity is shown by the fact that, *de jure,* a non-Afrikaans-speaking white may belong to the governing Nationalist Party (and *de facto* quite a number of German and a few English-speaking whites do belong to the Party), whereas an Afrikaans-speaking Coloured may not. While there is a strong ethnic component to "Afrikaner nationalism" (probably over 95 per cent of the Nationalist Party members are Afrikaans-speaking), that movement is first and foremost racial and only secondarily nationalist. Yet, the Afrikaners, of any ethnic group in South Africa, have come closest to developing a nationalist movement.

Although no South African political movement is, strictly speaking, nationalist, ethnicity has been, next to race, the most important line of cleavage in South African society. More specifically, the English-Afrikaner conflict which goes back to the first years of the nineteenth century has an important linguistic dimension, and the official status and use of the two main European languages has long been a football of white politics.

Here I should like to deal briefly with four main aspects of the political significance of language in contemporary South Africa: (1) traditional Afrikaner "nationalism"; (2) the reaction of other ethnic and racial groups to Afrikaner nationalism; (3) the use of ethnic revivalism and the attempt to revive African linguistic nationalism in the apartheid program of the government; (4) problems presented by multilingualism in the future development of South Africa as a unitary state under majority control.

Traditional Afrikaner Nationalism

The division of the dominant white group into English and Afrikaners is based mainly on ethnicity as symbolized mostly by language.[4] The long-standing conflict between these two ethnic groups goes back to the early nineteenth century and has a long and complex history, involving many interrelated aspects. With the advent of British hegemony at the Cape in the first years of the nineteenth century, the Afrikaners found themselves in a politically, economically, socially, and culturally subordinate position vis-à-vis the English, although they remained dominant in relation to the nonwhite population. In this respect, their position became analogous to that of the French Canadians after the British conquest, and language became much the same kind of rallying point for the development of a politicocultural nationalism. Due to the presence of a large nonwhite majority, however, policy toward Africans, Coloureds, and Indians became a major dimension of English-Afrikaner conflicts in a somewhat analogous way to the North-South conflict over the extension of slavery in the nineteenth-century United States. Thus, Afrikaner nationalism acquired a strong racial as well as ethnic component.

The feeling of ethnic and racial identity of the Afrikaners led to a growing "nationalism" which had the characteristics outlined in the following paragraphs.

First, an origin myth with an idealized, quasi-sacred, heroic, and epic version of Afrikaner history. The Boer fights against British imperialism and the African nations, the frontier, the Great Trek, the two Anglo-Boer Wars, and other events are glorified and legitimized in biblical terms. The themes of the Chosen People, the flight from Egypt, the Promised Land, and divine guidance appear frequently in Afrikaner-Calvinist historiography. This heroic conception of the *Volk's* history has its great temple (the Voortrekkers Monument near Pretoria), its demigod (Paul Kruger), its atrocity stories (the British concentration camps), its martyrs (Piet Retief), its traitors (Jan Smuts), and its holidays (Day of the Covenant).

Next, an ideology which is a complex blend of rugged individualism, egalitarianism among the Chosen People, anticapitalist agrarianism, fundamentalistic Calvinism, anticosmopolitan isolationism, white supremacy and racism, xenophobia, fear of miscegenation and cultural assimilation, anti-Communism, ascriptive exclusion, and narrow provincialism and ethnocentrism.

Third, a distinctive culture symbolized by Voortrekker costumes, diet, the Dutch Reformed churches, and, above all, by the Afrikaans language.[5] Concern for the maintenance of this distinctive culture and for resisting anglicization has centered around the recognition of Afrikaans as a national language of equal status to English, the actual use of Afrikaans in government, and the use of that language as a medium of instruction in the racially and ethnically segregated schools. Feelings toward Afrikaner culture have often consisted of an ambivalent mixture of pride and shame vis-à-vis the more cosmopolitan and dynamic English culture.

Last, a number of political or quasi-political organizations, the major ones being the old and the "purified" Nationalist Party and the latter's elite secret society, the *Broederbond*. In addition, quasi-Fascist organizations like the New Order and the Ossewa Brandwag and splinter parties like the Afrikaner Party rose and fell in the 1930's and 1940's. Today, the Nationalist Party has effectively rallied the great majority of the Afrikaners and has ruled the country since 1948. All these political organizations have shared the aims of emancipation from Britain as a foreign power, of ethnic paramountcy over English South Africans, and of racial supremacy over all nonwhites, including those who are ethnically Afrikaners.

Except for the added element of racism, which is, of course, quite salient and gives Afrikaner nationalism a special character, that movement has all the main hallmarks of "classical" nationalism as defined earlier. Insofar as this is true, Afrikaner nationalism is distinctly unlike most political movements of independence and anticolonialism in black Africa and is especially different from the so-called African nationalism in South Africa itself.

The Reaction of Other Ethnic and Racial Groups

It might be expected that militant Afrikaner nationalism would have excited similar movements among the other main ethnic and racial groups in South Africa. In fact, for diverse reasons, this has not been the case to any significant extent.

Of the three main nonwhite racial groups, the Coloureds have been most completely westernized and have most aspired to social assimiliation into the dominant white group. Although long frustrated in their assimilationist aspirations, most Coloureds, far from wanting to maintain a separate identity, continue to seek acceptance into the two main white ethnic groups whose culture they share.

Indians have been divided into two main religious groups, five language groups, and many more caste groups, any of which would be far too small to constitute a basis for a politically successful nationalist movement. Furthermore, South African Indians have been rapidly anglicized, and although they do not, by and large, seek assimilation to the whites, they do seek equal, nondiscriminatory acceptance into a multiracial and multiethnic South Africa. Since the days of Mahatma Gandhi, South African Indian politics have been secular, universalistic, and opposed to any ethnic or racial divisions.

English-speaking whites did develop a slight degree of nationalist feelings in response to Afrikaner nationalism. Some cultural and political organizations (including small splinter parties) did form along English ethnic lines, and, in the Province of Natal, there is a modicum of English nationalist sentiment. However, English nationalism remained a very subdued phenomenon compared to Afrikaner nationalism. There are two major reasons for this state of affairs. First, being a minority within a minority, English South Africans could achieve power only by allying themselves with nonnationalist Afrikaners, by taking a racist but antinationalist stand in politics. The major parties in which the English have gained a share of political power (such as the South African Party and the United Party) have consistently based their appeal on all whites irrespective of ethnicity.

Second, English South Africans have not developed a distinctive culture to the same extent as the Afrikaners, and, consequently, any attempt to stress English ethnicity has been stigmatized by Afrikaners as a disloyal attachment to a foreign colonial power. Local South African English has, of course, some dialectical idiosyncrasies, but remains closer to standard British English than American English and hence cannot qualify for separate language status as Afrikaans does in relation to Dutch. In addition, no single religion (comparable to the Dutch Reformed churches for Afrikaners) unites English South Africans, who are split between Anglicans, Methodists, Catholics, and Jews, not to mention many smaller Protestant denominations.

Among the various African language groups, there still exists some degree of ethnic particularism, and the vast majority of black South Africans speak one of the Bantu tongues as their home language. Furthermore, three of these language groups are quite large, both absolutely (two to three millions each) and relatively (between 14 and 20 per cent of the total population). Yet, what has been called "African nationalism" has, from its inception in the first years of the twentieth century, shown few nationalist characteristics and many hallmarks of "territorialism." The African National Congress, the All-African Convention, the Pan-African Congress, and African trade-unionism have all been militantly opposed to white supremacy, to racial segregation and discrimination, to ethnic particularism (which they have stigmatized as "tribalism"), and to any program of cultural distinctiveness or revivalism.

Generally, the ideology of the African political movements has stressed equality regardless of race or ethnicity, and, although tolerant of cultural pluralism, it has never based its appeal on ethnic distinctions. Faced with an acutely racist dominant group, African political movements have sometimes made a racially based appeal to Africans or to all nonwhites, but scarcely ever to specific cultural groups. European culture has rarely been disparaged (a fact which is hardly surprising since the vast majority of leaders are Western-educated, mostly in Christian mission schools), and any divisive feelings of ethnic separation between Africans have been regarded as a political liability. If anything, the black South African intelligentsia has shown a considerable drive toward westernization and attitudes of "cultural shame" toward indigenous cultures. Unlike in other parts of Africa where "nationalist" movements have adopted some traditional symbols and have sought to Africanize their ideology, the South African freedom movements have been unashamedly eclectic in ideology and organization (borrowing freely from America, Europe, and Asia) and Western, "modern," and anti-traditional in both their tactics and their aims. They have challenged racism and white supremacy largely in terms of Christian ethics and a Western-inspired liberal or socialist philosophy of democracy, equality, and freedom.

Thus, the only people of South Africa (and one of the few in the sub-Saharan part of the continent) to have developed a nationalism based, at least partly, on ethnicity and language are the Afrikaners. We shall now turn to the implications of that fact for apartheid policy toward the other ethnic groups of South Africa.

The Use of Ethnic Revivalism and the Attempt to Revive African Linguistic Nationalism

The attempt by the ruling Afrikaner nationalists to impose upon the other groups a policy of rigid racial and ethnic separation is the result of complex motivations. It is partly a systematic method of dividing Africans, some two-thirds of whom have now become "detribalized," into mutually antagonistic ethnic groups. To the extent that Africans of various language groups have intermixed, intermarried, learned each other's tongues, and lived and worked side by side in the cities under identical conditions of oppression and destitution, they have developed a common consciousness which transcends ethnicity. The government policy of "retribalization" is in part a conscious effort to counteract these universalistic trends and to isolate each ethnic group in a cultural and political desert.

Beyond this rather obvious motive, Pretoria-sponsored cultural revivalism for Africans arises from a confusion between race and culture on the part of the ruling Afrikaners. In spite of considerable contrary evidence in their own country, most South African whites believe that culture is in part racially determined and, hence, that a given culture reflects the innate abilities and propensities of its members. Consequently, the allegedly "primitive" Bantu cultures are held to be peculiarly suited to the supposedly "primitive" mentality of Africans.

A third source of cultural revivalism arises from the projection of the Afrikaner's sense of ethnic particularism and linguistic chauvinism onto other people. Since the preservation of ethnic and racial identity has been a paramount value in Afrikaner nationalism, many Afrikaners have assumed that other ethnic groups would feel likewise.

Pretoria-sponsored revivalism vis-à-vis Africans is reflected in a number of apartheid programs. In urban areas, an attempt is made to segregate Africans of different language groups from each other, as well as Africans from non-Africans. In the rural areas, the Bantustan policy consists of consolidating and reconstructing monoethnic areas with a semiautonomous political structure modeled in part on traditional chieftainship. Such insignificant voting rights as Africans enjoy are based on ethnicity. In the Transkei, Xhosa-speaking people vote for Xhosa candidates to the Xhosa Assembly.

Similarly, the entire educational system for Africans has been "tribalized" by the Bantu Education Department. Mother-tongue instruction is stressed at all levels of schooling despite overwhelming opposition of Africans who would prefer to be taught in English, at least beyond the lower primary grades. Ethnically segregated pseudo universities have been created for the Zulu, Xhosa, and Sotho, and these "bush colleges" are practically the only places where Africans of a given language group can receive any form of postsecondary education. In these institutions, attempts are made to use Bantu languages as media of instruction, to modify the curriculum in line with Pretoria's conception of what is good for Africans, to create an artificial technical vocabulary in the Bantu languages, to incorporate Bantu elements into the architecture, and to instill ethnic chauvinism into the students.[6]

Multilingualism in the Future Development of South Africa

The significance of language in South African politics is, of course, not limited to the past and present. Assuming that the status quo is unlikely to continue for much longer and that South Africa will continue to exist as a unitary state, but under a government representing the majority of the people, the use of official languages will have immediate educational and political implications. Obviously, the present situation where only the two main European languages are granted official status is unlikely to be acceptable to most South Africans under a majority government. Many Africans have developed negative feelings toward Afrikaans as the language of the oppressors. But, as the home language of nearly four million people, nearly half of whom are nonwhites, Afrikaans cannot easily be eliminated.

Most educated Africans, who are likely to play prominent roles in the future, would probably be reluctant to substitute a Bantu language as the official tongue. To do so would revive ethnic rivalries and raise a host of other problems. No single language is spoken as a mother tongue by more than 20 per cent of the total population, and three Bantu languages are spoken by nearly equal numbers of people (between two and three millions). Some African languages (notably Zulu, Swazi, and Xhosa) are closely enough related so that they could conceivably be fused into a single official written tongue; but, even so, the latter would encompass only some 40 per cent of the total population.

Alternatively, to make English the only national language would also be unacceptable. Most African leaders recognize the importance and practical superiority of English as a medium of interethnic communication, of trade, of intellectual life, and of contact with the rest of Africa and of the world. Yet, English comes only in fifth place (after Afrikaans, Xhosa, Zulu, and Sotho) in terms of numbers of native speakers. Furthermore, English is also associated with a segment of the dominant racial minority.

Another possibility would be to grant equal status to all five major languages; but this would present great practical problems which, while not insuperable, would lead to high cost and inefficiency of administration. Alone the cost of translating and printing official documents in five tongues and of simultaneously translating legislative debates would be prohibitive for a none-too-affluent country. In terms of education, a five-language policy would mean one of two things. Either children of the five main groups would be taught in their mother tongue, or all five languages would have to be taught in all schools. The second possibility is clearly unworkable, and the first one would meet with strong African opposition because it would perpetuate *de facto* racial segregation and unequal educational opportunities.

One workable solution seems to meet pragmatic exigencies as well as to resolve at least some of the major political problems raised by language in a reconstructed South Africa of the future. English should be recognized as the national language, to be taught in all schools and used in the central legislature and in official documents. At the same time, the other four main languages should also have official recognition as regional second languages. Thus, in the Western Cape, Afrikaans would be the second language; in the Eastern Cape, Xhosa; in the Orange Free State and the Transvaal, Sotho; and in Natal, Zulu. In any given area, two languages (one of them English) would be used in schools and in government offices. Signs, ordinances, forms, and other written documents would be published in English and in the local second language.

Here is not the place to elaborate on this brief linguistic blueprint for a reconstructed South Africa. Two things, however, are certain, if one assumes that South Africa will continue to exist as a unitary multinational state, but under majority government. First, the official use of one or more languages is going to create difficult and unavoidable problems with both ethnic and racial ramifications. Second, any satisfactory solution of linguistic problems will have to take both "nonrational" and "rational" factors into account. The former include such things as the demographic, educational, and other forces affecting the ethnic distribution of power and the subjective attitudes and values of people concerning the various languages. The latter, which are likely to clash with political contingencies, involve considerations of administrative cost and efficiency, of relative usefulness of tongues in various forms and fields of communication, and of the feasibility of guided linguistic change ranging from minor standardization of orthography to major fusion between existing tongues.

Clearly, South Africa offers fascinating prospects for both theoretical and applied social linguistics; and, equally clearly, sociolinguistics will have to assign to each set of factors its proper weight in the total equation. For such an embryonic discipline, the difficulty will be as great as the opportunity.

NOTES

1. There is an abundant literature on African "nationalism." For political analysis using various definitions of nationalism, see Section VII of Pierre L. van den Berghe, ed., *Africa, Social Problems of*

Change and Conflict (San Francisco: Chandler, 1965). This work also contains a bibliography. See also Immanuel Wallerstein, ed., *Social Change, The Colonial Situation* (New York: Wiley, 1966).

2. The social science literature on South Africa is abundant. An extensive and recent bibliography can be found in my book *South Africa, A Study in Conflict* (Berkeley: University of California Press, 1967). Among other germane books on the subject are Gwendolen M. Carter, *The Politics of Inequality* (New York: Praeger, 1958); C. W. de Kiewiet, *A History of South Africa, Social and Economic* (Oxford: Clarendon Press, 1941); Muriel Horrell, *A Survey of Race Relations in South Africa* (Johannesburg: South African Institute of Race Relations, 1951–1952, continuing annually); Leo Kuper, *An African Bourgeoisie* (New Haven: Yale University Press, 1965); Leo Marquard, *The Peoples and Policies of South Africa* (London: Oxford University Press, 1962); Sheila Patterson, *Colour and Culture in South Africa* (London: Routledge and Kegan Paul, 1953); Sheila Patterson, *The Last Trek* (London: Routledge and Kegan Paul, 1957); Michael Roberts and A. E. G. Trollip, *The South African Opposition, 1939–1945* (London: Longmans, 1947); and William Henry Vatcher, *White Laager, The Rise of Afrikaner Nationalism* (New York: Praeger, 1965).

3. In this connection Vatcher makes a twofold error when he states, "Afrikaner nationalism is the classic form of all the nationalisms that now flourish on the continent of Africa" (Vatcher, *op. cit.,* p. ix). Afrikaner "nationalism" is unlike most other African "nationalisms" in that it does have both an ethnic and a racial basis.

4. The racial breakdown of the population is as follows: Whites or "Europeans," 19.4 per cent; Africans, 68.2 per cent; Indians, 3.0 per cent; and Coloureds, 9.4 per cent. Of the whites, some 57 per cent speak Afrikaans as their mother tongue, 39 per cent English, and 4 per cent other tongues, mostly German and Dutch. The 1951 census classified 73 per cent of the whites as bilingual, but only 2 per cent habitually speak both languages at home. Of the Coloureds, 89 per cent speak Afrikaans as their home language, and the remainder English; 46.5 per cent of the Coloureds are bilingual. The two largest language groups among Indians are Tamil and Hindi, spoken by some 40 per cent each; the remaining 20 per cent speak Telugu, Urdu, and Gujarati. In addition to those Indian languages, some 77 per cent of the Indians know English

and 16 per cent, Afrikaans. Among Africans, 29 per cent speak Xhosa, 26 per cent Zulu, 22 per cent Sotho, 8 per cent Tswana, 5 per cent Tsonga, 3 per cent Swazi, 3 per cent Ndebele, 2 per cent Venda, and 2 per cent a sprinkling of other Bantu languages. In addition, 15 per cent speak English and 21 per cent Afrikaans.

5. Afrikaans, originally a dialect of Dutch with indigenous and Malay admixtures, gained the status of a distinct written language in the nineteenth century.

6. Leo Kuper has written a true-to-life satire of these bush colleges: *The College Brew* (Durban: privately printed, 1960).

Part IV

THE INDIAN DIASPORA

15

Indians in Natal and Fiji: A "Controlled Experiment" in Culture Contact

The South African population of Indian origin, which is largely concentrated in the coastal area of Natal, is already well known through a number of studies.[1] The recent study of an Indian group on the Fiji Islands now offers an opportunity for detailed comparison.[2] Indeed, the near identity of environment, history, and composition of two immigrant communities separated by some nine thousand miles of ocean and without direct contact with each other makes for a situation as close to a large-scale controlled experiment as can be hoped for in the social sciences. At the same time, a few salient differences allow one to isolate relationships that may otherwise have been obscured.

In trying to make the best of this unusual opportunity, we shall apply ex post facto the experimental model to the two situations.[3] The central problem of interest here is the adaptive response of the two immigrant communities to their new social environment. The two cases will thus be treated as an experiment in culture contact, in which structural changes in the Indian groups will be considered as dependent variables. But the experi-

Reprinted from *Civilisations* 12, no. 1 (1962): 75–84.

ment takes place on two levels. First, treating India as the control group, one can trace adaptive changes common to both immigrant groups. These changes then become dependent variables while the new conditions common to Fiji and Natal can be treated as independent variables. Second, one can contrast the two immigrant groups. In this case, the elements common to both new situations become control variables, the factors specific to each of the two situations can be viewed as independent variables, and the resulting adaptive differences between the two groups constitute the dependent variables.

The origins of the Fiji and Natal Indian communities are virtually identical. The humid and warm climate of the two territories proved suitable to the growth of sugar cane. Within less than twenty years of one another (Natal: 1860, Fiji: 1879), these two British colonies began introducing indentured laborers to work on sugar-cane plantations.[4] Indentured Indian immigration was stopped in Natal in 1911 and in Fiji in 1916. The nonliterate natives (Fijians and Zulu) were in both cases reluctant to engage in heavy and routinized agricultural labor. Conditions of indenture were practically the same in Fiji and Natal and amounted to virtual chattel slavery. The "coolies" had to serve a five-year term at very low wages, after which they had the option of returning to India, reindenturing themselves for a further five years, or settling in the respective colonies as free men. In both cases the majority of the Indians chose the latter alternative. A minimum of forty females to one hundred male migrants was required by law. Only slowly did the sex ratio approach unity in the twentieth century. Recruiting was often made under false or misleading pretenses. After a long sea voyage under crowded and promiscuous conditions, the workers were housed in extremely primitive dwellings, typically in rows of mud or corrugated-iron barracks. Entire families were housed in single rooms as small as 7 by 10 feet and at best 10 by 12. Flogging by white overseers was a daily occurrence. Gangs of workers were directly supervised by Indian sirdars.

The Indian migrants to Fiji and Natal came from very similar social origins. They were mostly illiterate and rural people, driven to emigration largely by destitution. In both cases, over 80 per cent of the Indians were Hindus, some 15 per cent Muslims, and the rest mostly Christians. Of the Hindus, at least 60 per cent were of low-caste origin (Sudra and Scheduled castes), but there were also some Kshatriyas and Brahmins among the immigrants. In both territories, a minority of free Indians, who were mainly Gujarati Hindus or Muslims, followed the indentured laborers and settled mostly as merchants. Hindi-speaking Northerners and Tamil- and Telugu-speaking Southerners are found in both Fiji and Natal (though in different proportions), so that the linguistic and cultural composition of the two Indian groups is as similar as their religious and social background.

In addition to similar social and cultural origins and conditions of immigration and employment, the two Indian communities also shared and continue to share similar positions in the sociopolitical structure of their countries of adoption. Both groups came to occupy an intermediate position in status and economic standard between, on the one hand, a dominant white minority holding a monopoly or near monopoly of economic and political power, and, on the other hand, a subjugated, nonliterate, native majority.[5] While British colonialism and white domination were nothing new to the immigrants, the presence of an indigenous majority was a new factor. In Fiji as in Natal, Indians met with mistrust and hostility on the part of the whites and the natives and with official discrimination at the hand of the government. In both territories, the Indian's right to acquire land in freehold was stringently limited, and his political rights were practically nonexistent.

Having mentioned briefly the major new conditions common to Fiji and Natal with which the Indian migrants were faced, we must examine the adaptive responses of the two communities to their new environment. As one might expect, these responses have been strikingly similar. In Natal as in Fiji, the Indian population does not represent a cross section in miniature of the parent population of India. Due to the selectivity of migration mentioned earlier, the migrant groups constitute rather the basis of a miniature truncated pyramid, the apex of which remained in

India. The expatriate groups, while coming from a literate and
urban country with a very complex culture, were stripped of their
cultural superstructure of priests, rulers, scholars, and professionals. The result in both cases was that the process of trans-
plantation was accompanied by cultural impoverishment. Quite
apart from new disruptive factors, the folk culture of the migrants, notably in religion, was weaned of much of its intellectual
and philosophical content.

Besides this process of impoverishment, the conditions of migration and resettlement further disrupted the structure of the two
groups and made the preservation even of traditional, folk, rural
culture impossible or very difficult. The initial period of the sea
journey and of resettlement dealt a shattering blow to the social
organization of the indentured laborers. Promiscuity on board
ship and later in the sugar estate barracks made the observance
of the rules of caste purity and of diet impossible. Random as-
signment to the various estates destroyed the occupational basis
of caste and precluded the possibility of regional regroupings.
Most traditional caste occupations became redundant in the new
situation, and the relatively undifferentiated character of field
work on the cane plantations rendered the traditional caste hierarchy functionally groundless. To add to the fluidity of the new
environment, many low-caste persons claimed a higher-caste
status (mostly through name changes), a step which their unknown companions could not easily challenge. Finally, the migrants moved as individuals, not as family units, and the scarcity
of women retarded the reconstitution of the traditional Indian
extended family. Under such conditions, political institutions such
as caste councils or panchayats likewise disappeared.[6] The indentured workers became anonymous numbers in a vast system
of white-controlled, commercial agriculture.

In both Fiji and Natal, the initial period of settlement seems
to have destroyed the main elements of Indian social structure:
caste, family groupings, and political institutions. With the end
of the indenture system, however, social stabilization set in again,
particularly as regards the family. As more Indians were born in
their countries of adoption, the sex ratio approached unity. The

end of indenture also stimulated the growth of family groups. In addition, the free Indians who followed the indentured laborers often came as family units and maintained a greater degree of social cohesion. In both Fiji and Natal, the Gujarati merchants resist westernization and maintain traditional culture to a greater extent than the other groups. While the patrilocal extended family is still the most common type of kin group among Fiji and Natal Indians, there is a tendency toward a Western type of nuclear family. Many families seem to go through a transitory stage akin to what French social scientists have called the *famille souche,* a system where only one married son continues to live with his parents, while the other sons go and live neolocally. This arrangement, which is institutionalized in the peasantry of several European countries, only seems to be emerging as a preferential alternative to the fully patrilocal family among some of the immigrant Indians. In many cases, two or three but not all married sons live in close proximity with their parents.

Caste was so effectively shattered in the early period that it was not revived in the subsequent era of social stabilization. The general attitude toward caste seems to be defensive. Attempts are made to deemphasize the residual remnants of the caste system and to stress the universalistic elements in Hinduism. For practical purposes, caste survives only in rules of endogamy, but, even there, caste is only one of several criteria affecting the choice of spouses. While many people still have a vague idea of caste as a hierarchal factor, other criteria of status are of increasing importance. Few people are aware of the intricacies of the traditional caste system. Only in the Gujarati Hindu minority is caste still an important factor in anything but marriage.[7]

Apart from the breakdown of caste, other elements of Indian culture have shown great resilience in Fiji and Natal, in spite of the fact that over 90 per cent of the Indian population have now been born outside India. Most people retain their allegiance to Hinduism or Islam, and conversions to Christianity have affected less than 5 per cent of the population. While Islam has been largely unaffected by its new environment, Hinduism has however undergone a process of simplification in rituals. The tying of the sacred thread (*janao*) at the initiation of the "twice-born" castes, for example, is now retained only in residual form and combined with marriage ceremonies. Hindu rites involving fire-walking, fasting, piercing of the skin, and other forms of bodily mortification are practiced in both communities, but, whereas in Fiji they are confined to the Southern groups (Tamil and Tel-ugu), in Natal, Hindis also participate.

The barrier between Muslims and Hindus seems equally strong in Fiji and Natal and affects not only intermarriage, which is very rare, but also most forms of intimate social intercourse. Except in intellectual and political circles, this religious barrier shows no signs of weakening. The cultural and linguistic division between Northern (Hindi-speaking) and Southern (Tamil- and Telugu-speaking) Hindus, while not so strong as the Muslim-Hindu division, is still found and reduces intermarriage to a minimum. In some areas, this linguistic factor has given rise to a loose geographical concentration in culturally homogeneous neighborhoods. Free association between Tamils and Telugus, including inter-marriage, is common to both Natal and Fiji. Traditional cooking with the use of curries, Indian music, and the wearing of saris by women have been preserved to the same extent in the two countries.

As may be expected, the two Indian communities have also been strongly influenced by the dominant European culture. For-mal education has been mostly along Western lines, a certain amount of syncretism between Christianity and Hinduism has taken place (as in the identification of Christ and Krishna and the celebration of Christmas by Hindus), men have adopted Western clothing, and English has become a widespread medium of communication. Modern economic conditions encourage the nuclear type of family and militate against the maintenance of large patrilocal kin groups. Customs of preferential marriage (of parallel cousins among Muslims and cross-cousins among the Southern Hindus) are falling into disuse. Western tastes in music and in material objects compete more and more strongly with traditional tastes. A gradual secularization of life is setting in, particularly among young, educated people. Indigenous Zulu and

Fiji cultures on the other hand, seem to have had no perceptible influence on the culture of the immigrants who, in most cases, look down on the native population as "inferior," "primitive," and "savage."

Although most indentured migrants were rural and lowly educated, the literate, urban, and sedentary traditions of the cultures they brought with them (albeit in impoverished form) gave the Indians a notable advantage over the aborigines in adapting to Western culture. This advantage largely accounts for the intermediate position of the Indian group in the raciocultural hierarchy of Natal and Fiji. In both territories, Indians have, as a group, made much more rapid advances in education, retail commerce, and professional and skilled occupations than the native Fijians and Africans. In spite of political, economic, and social discrimination on the part of Europeans, Indians, as a group, occupy a distinctly higher status than the indigenous population. In both cases, however, Indian attitudes toward the dominant Western culture have been ambivalent. While conceding the technological superiority of the West and the need for English education, most Indians possess a strong consciousness of belonging to an ancient civilization. This feeling of cultural pride has received a recent impetus with the independence of India and Pakistan and has contributed to the resilience of some aspects of Eastern culture.

Besides the many similarities between Natal and Fiji, a number of differences in the two situations have made for idiosyncratic responses in the respective Indian communities. One important difference is in the proportion of Northern as opposed to Southern Hindu groups. In Fiji, the Northern Hindi group constitutes over three-fourths of the Indian population, compared to about four-tenths in Natal. The numerical preponderance of Hindi-speaking immigrants in Fiji helped to establish Hindi as a lingua franca among Fiji Indians. Hindi is still the medium of instruction in the lower standards of Indian schools, and the spread of English has thus been less rapid than in Natal. In the latter case, no single language group outnumbered all others, and English became both the medium of instruction in the segregated Indian schools and the lingua franca among Indians. Except for some older people and women from the more conservative families, all Natal Indians speak fluent English. In the younger generation, English is generally spoken much more fluently than the vernacular Indian tongues. This historical accident of language distribution seems to have been one of the major factors making for a slower rate of westernization in Fiji as compared with Natal.

TABLE 15-1   Racial Composition of the Population in Percentage of Total

Racial Group	Fiji (1956)	Natal (1960)
Europeans	1.8	11.3
Indians	49.0	12.4
Indigenous	42.8	75.0
Other	6.4	1.3
TOTAL	100.0	100.0

Another demographic factor which entailed a number of important consequences is the proportion of the Indian population to the dominant whites, on the one hand, and the indigenous blacks, on the other (Table 15–1). In both Natal and Fiji, the Indian group grew faster than the rest of the population, first through immigration and later through a rapid rate of natural increase.[8] But in Fiji the Indians are now the largest group in the population and constitute nearly an absolute majority. In relation to the native population they are nearly equal, while they outnumber the whites by about 27 to 1. In Natal, on the other hand, the African population greatly outnumbers both the Indian and the white populations, while the latter two groups are near parity. The Indian community constitutes only 12.4 per cent of the Natal population and some 3 per cent of the total population of South Africa.

These population statistics are related to other important factors, notably to the political situation. The greater proportion of whites in Natal compared with Fiji reflects the fact that the former is an area of permanent European settlement while the latter is a colony of exploitation. When the white settlers of Natal were granted self-government they embarked on a policy of ever increasing racial discrimination against Indians, starting with disenfranchisement and the notorious £3 tax in 1896, and ending with Group Areas, Job Reservation, Population Registration, and the many other racialistic measures of the Afrikaner Nationalist government.[9] In Fiji, while Indians have always been and still are subject to political and economic disabilities, their share of representation in the Legislative Council has slowly increased. As the largest racial group in the Islands, Fiji Indians occupy a fairly secure position, and prospects for further improvements are favorable. Natal Indians, on the contrary, as a small minority group, are in a precarious situation, caught in between two powerful and antagonistic groups which use them as scapegoats and look upon them as aliens. They are the object of virulent racialism on the part of the whites, who now possess a monopoly of power, and of suspicion and envy on the part of the African majority, which is gaining conscience of its numerical strength. Their position has steadily deteriorated, and their future under either white or black nationalism is laden with uncertainty and danger, as shown by the great anti-Indian pogrom of 1949. Natal Indians are completely deprived of representation, either direct or indirect, in the government of South Africa and are at the mercy of arbitrary action by strongly hostile local and central authorities.

Another major difference between Fiji and Natal concerns economic organization. Whereas Fiji still has a relatively undifferentiated rural economy, Natal and South Africa as a whole are fairly highly industrialized and urbanized. Suva, the capital city of the Islands and the sole urban center of any size, has a population of only 37,000. Durban, the main metropolis and harbor of Natal, is a thriving industrial city of over 600,000 people, over one-third of whom are Indians. While the majority of Fiji Indians are still rural, 73 per cent of the Natal Indians live in towns and engage in industry, commerce, transport, and service and professional occupations.

What consequences have these demographic, political, and economic differences had on the adaptation of the two Indian communities? Culturally, the more rural conditions of Fiji,

coupled with the numerical preponderance of Hindi-speaking
people, made for a slower rate of westernization and for a greater
retention of Indian traits than in Natal. Much the same transformations in traditional culture took place in the two countries, but
the process seems more advanced in Natal. Thus, for example,
the regular appeal to what Mayer call panchayats (five-member
conciliation councils, not caste councils) in settling disputes seems
much more institutionalized in Fiji than in Natal. In the latter
territory, if prominent people are called upon to arbitrate disputes,
the whole procedure is much less formal, the number of people
involved varies, and the very term "panchayat" is only rarely
used in that connection. We have already mentioned that in Fiji,
Hindi is still spoken extensively, while, in Natal, the vernacular
tongues are quickly becoming supplanted by English. One must,
however, remember that the Indian community of Fiji is nearly
twenty years younger than that of Natal. This time factor probably accounts for some of the difference in acculturation.

The urban and industrial society of Natal has, of course, resulted in greater occupational diversification than in Fiji and,
with it, in a greater degree of class stratification along Western
lines. While Fiji Indians engage mostly in either agriculture or
retail trade, Natal Indians have, in addition, a large unskilled
and semiskilled proletariat, a number of white-collar workers,
and a sizable university-educated professional elite. Both Natal
and Fiji Indians have concentrated in commerce to a greater
extent than the other racial groups, but Natal Indian merchants,
due to the importance of European-owned concerns, hold a
smaller share of the total trade than Fiji Indians. Furthermore,
the foothold of Natal Indians in commerce is now seriously
threatened by the apartheid legislation of the Nationalist government.

The greatest contrast between the two communities is probably
to be found in political reactions. In both countries, Indians have
been largely debarred from participation in government. They
have been administered, mostly unsympathetically, by the white-
controlled authorities. In Fiji, a loose and amorphous pattern of
informal leadership emerged at the local rural level. That pattern

centers around the election of sirdars or supervisors to harvest collectively the cane crop and around the informal choice of prominent people to serve on the quasi-judiciary panchayats. In neither instance can one speak of permanent bodies or of a permanent structure of local government. Neither do these fluid forms of leadership transcend the local level. Modern Western forms of political organization such as trade-unions, parties, and ratepayers' associations are either embryonic or nonexistent.

Due to a number of factors, the situation in Natal is markedly different. Local, rural forms of political organization along traditional lines are much less prominent than in Fiji, and modern, Western types of reaction are well developed. Trade-unions, though hampered by restrictive legislation, have drawn in much of the urban proletariat. For lack of parliamentary participation, there are no Indian political parties as such, but two main political bodies (the Natal Indian Congress and the Natal Indian Organization) compete for the support of the population. Furthermore, a number of prominent Indians belong to the interracial Liberal party. Indian ratepayers are organized into associations in urban areas. Several Indian newspapers feature politics prominently, and many Indians participate in campaigns of passive resistance and attend political meetings in opposition to the government. A number of Indian politicians, belonging mostly to the Natal or South African Indian Congress, have recently been arrested, imprisoned, and tried for "treason." Obvious factors such as urbanization and the presence of an intelligentsia help to account for that type of political reaction. But certain conditions special to Natal and South Africa must also be taken into consideration. Oppressive legislation by successive governments has been an important stimulus. South Africa thus became the training ground for Mahatma Gandhi's methods of passive resistance and nonviolence, and the Mahatma's influence is still strongly felt in nonwhite politics. More recently, the potential challenge of militant African nationalism has aroused the fears of many Indians, who view themselves as caught between two hostile and powerful groups.

We have seen how two Indian communities have, under similar

conditions, and without contact with one another, developed in remarkably parallel fashion. This development suggests a high degree of determinism in situations of culture contact. In both cases, the immigrant community made a crucial contribution to the development of its country of adoption. It successfully adapted itself to the new conditions, unfavorable as these have been, acquired the new skills necessary for survival, and fitted into the structure of the new country which it has come to view as its own. Fiji and Natal Indians even succeeded, after the disorganizing conditions of indenture, in restoring a stable and integrated family system and in maintaining many elements of their ancestral culture while effectively shedding those aspects that were unsuited to the new situation, notably the caste system. They did not, to any significant extent, intermarry nor interbreed with either whites or blacks. In all these respects, the Indians have differed markedly from the descendants of Negro slaves in the Americas. Of course, the period of Negro slavery was much longer than that of Indian indenture, and the cultural heterogeneity of the African slaves was even greater than that of the Indian immigrants. These two factors may be sufficient to account for the almost complete disappearance of African culture in the New World. One cannot, however, discount the possibility of a difference in adaptability to Western conditions and in intrinsic resilience or "fragility" between Indian and African cultures.

Debarred by white prejudice and legal discrimination from access to the dominant group, and enjoying certain cultural advantages over the nonliterate native population, the Indians were forced into the position of an intermediate stratum. Like other groups of middlemen, such as Jews in eastern Europe and the overseas Chinese scattered around the Pacific, Fiji and Natal Indians have served as convenient scapegoats for the hostility of the dominant white minority and of the subjugated mass of the population. Kuper aptly expresses the plight of Natal Indians: "Sufficiently wealthy to serve as bait for greed, too few to be feared, and in the main, ideologically opposed to counter aggression with physical violence, their ethnic difference and cultural diversity serve as excuses for discrimination and oppression."[10]

From the point of view of political status and future security, the Fiji Indians are in an incomparably better position than Natal Indians. The former face a colonial government in full retreat, while the latter suffer under a reactionary, tyrannical, and entrenched white-settler regime. Fiji, through demography alone, is already, like Mauritius, a "little India." The relatively smaller and politically unaware indigenous population is unlikely to present a serious challenge to the permanence of the Indians on the Islands. On the other hand, the survival of Asian communities on African soil is much more problematical. While physical extermination is hopefully unlikely, conditions for Indians under emerging African nationalist governments from Kenya to South Africa may conceivably become even more intolerable than under the present colonial or white-settler regimes. South African Indians can only hope that the African rulers of the future will prove more humane, tolerant, and civilized than their European predecessors.

FOR FURTHER READING

Raymond Burrows, *Indian Life and Labour in Natal*. Johannesburg: South African Institute of Race Relations, 1952.

G. H. Calpin, *Indians in South Africa*. Pietermaritzburg: Shuter and Shooter, 1949.

Ernest Greenwood, *Experimental Sociology*. New York: King's Crown Press, 1945.

P. S. Joshi, *The Tyranny of Colour*. Durban: Commercial Printing Co., 1942.

C. Kondapi, *Indians Overseas, 1838–1949*. New Delhi: Oxford University Press, 1951.

Hilda Kuper, *Indian People in Natal*. Durban: Natal University Press, 1960.

Adrian C. Mayer, *Peasants in the Pacific, A Study of Fiji Indian Rural Society*. London: Routledge and Kegan Paul, 1961.

Birbal Rambiritch and Pierre L. van den Berghe. "Caste in a Natal Hindu Community," *African Studies* 20, no. 4 (1961).

Pierre L. van den Berghe, *Caneville, The Social Structure of a South African Town*. Middletown, Conn.: Wesleyan University Press, 1964.

Pierre L. van den Berghe and Edna Miller, "Some Factors Affecting Social Relations in a Natal North Coast Community," *Race Relations Journal* 28, no. 2 (1961).

C. A. Woods, *The Indian Community of Natal.* Cape Town: Oxford University Press, 1954.

NOTES

1. See appended Bibliography. A more exhaustive and up-to-date bibliography can be found in Hilda Kuper, *Indian People in Natal* (Durban: Natal University Press, 1960).

2. Adrian C. Mayer, *Peasants in the Pacific, A Study of Fiji Indian Rural Society* (London, Routledge and Kegan Paul, 1961). To avoid overburdening the text with footnotes, specific factual references will be minimized.

3. For suggestions on the use of ex post facto experiments, see Ernest Greenwood, *Experimental Sociology* (New York: King's Crown Press, 1945).

4. Indian indenture immigration started in Mauritius in 1839. Cf. C. Kondapi, *Indians Overseas, 1838–1949* (New Delhi: Oxford University Press, 1951), p. 8.

5. In the last twenty-five years, Fiji Indians have begun to outnumber the native Fijians. Cf. Mayer, *op. cit.*, p. 7.

6. What Mayer calls panchayats in Fiji are not caste councils in the traditional sense at all, but rather arbitration bodies of five members called together for the purpose of settling disputes without resorting to the regular courts. Cf. *ibid.*, pp. 116–120.

7. For more detailed discussions of caste in Fiji and Natal, see Kuper, *op. cit.*, pp. 18–43; Mayer, *op. cit.*, pp. 156–164; and B. Rambiritch and Pierre L. van den Berghe, "Caste in a Natal Hindu Community," *African Studies* 20, no. 4 (1961). Of course, caste is also breaking down in India since World War II. But, in India, the breakdown of caste is more a consequence of deliberate government policy since independence than a response to changed conditions as in Fiji and Natal. In these latter territories, the British government made no more effort to discourage caste than it did in India itself.

8. In both countries, the Indian population is in the high-birth-rate low-death-rate phase of their demographic history, while the

whites are in the low-birth-rate low-death-rate phase, and the blacks mostly in the high-birth-rate high-death-rate phase. Hence the relatively high rate of Indian natural increase.

9. A former Prime Minister, Dr. Malan, declared, for example, "that the Indian as a race in this country is an alien element in the population and that no solution of this question will be acceptable to the country unless it results in a very considerable reduction of the Indian population in the country." The attitude of the main opposition United Party is fully as hostile to Indians as that of the ruling Nationalist Party. Only recently have these two parties condescended to "recognize the existence" of South African Indians, but only as a disenfranchised, segregated group of second-class citizens.

10. Kuper, *op. cit.,* p. 271.

16

Asians in East and
South Africa

Close to one million descendants of immigrants from the Indian subcontinent now live in Africa.[1] Some 95 per cent of them are found in South and East Africa. A little over half a million Asians live in South Africa, mostly in Durban, Pietermaritzburg, the coastal belt of Natal, and the industrial complex of the Witwatersrand in and around Johannesburg. Kenya, with an Asian population of some 160,000, comes in second place, the largest concentrations being found in the country's two largest cities, Nairobi and Mombasa. Uganda and Tanzania each have Asian communities of 80,000 to 100,000, which are likewise heavily concentrated in the urban areas, principally Kampala and Dar es Salaam. Much smaller groups are also found in Zimbabwe, Zambia, Malawi, Mozambique, Ruanda, Burundi, Somalia, and the Eastern Congo, but, as all these communities together total less than 50,000 people, we shall not be concerned with them here. Only in Malawi where they number some 11,000 do they play a significant economic role.

The Indians of Africa are but a part of a much wider diaspora of people who, during the last three thousand years, have radiated from the subcontinent down the Southeast Asian peninsula, across the Indian Ocean, and beyond. There is a reference in the

Periplus of the Erythraean Sea to Indian merchants and seamen trading on the coast of East Africa as far back as the first century A.D.[2] Along with Arabs, Persians, and Malays, Indians have in- fluenced the history of the East African coast for many centuries. In numerical terms, however, the Indian diaspora was principally a nineteenth- and twentieth-century phenomenon. Indians fol- lowed the British flag, usually under three- to five-year indenture, wherever their colonial masters found the need to replace slaves with cheap and reliable "coolie" labor in order to grow sugar or build railways. Thus, groups of peasants and townsmen seeking to escape the poverty and hunger of colonial India became the unwitting auxiliaries of British imperialism in as far-flung places as Guiana, the West Indies, Fiji, Mauritius, South Africa, and Kenya.

In some of the island societies, such as Mauritius and Fiji, Asians came to outnumber the indigenous population. But in Africa, these stepchildren of the British Empire were left stranded as tiny, powerless minorities at the mercy, in South Africa, of a tyrannical albinocracy, and in East Africa, of equally hostile black majorities. In South Africa, Asians constitute 3 per cent of the total population and are by far the smallest of the four racial castes.[3] In Kenya, Asians, although over three times as numerous as the Europeans, make up only about 2 per cent of the total. In Uganda and Tanzania, Indians number a bare 1 per cent.

To refer to the Asians of Africa as a "community" is rather misleading, because they are fragmented into a multiplicity of religious, linguistic, and caste groups. They include Hindus, Sunni and Shia Muslims, Sikhs, Jains, Roman Catholics, and Protes- tants, not to mention the sects and subsects. They speak North Indian languages like Hindustani, Urdu, and Gujarati and South Indian tongues like Tamil and Telugu. Among Muslims, sectarian membership forms the basis of communal organization; among Hindus, *varna* and *jati,* while less important than in India, still constitute lines of cleavage between endogamous groups.[4]

Yet, there is a sense in which African Asians are, in fact, a community. In colonial days in East Africa, they were a racial caste of intermediate status between the colonial masters and the

"Natives." In South Africa they are still in that position. By now, it is a tired cliché to refer to Asians as the "Jews of Africa." Many complex, stratified societies have their "Jews"—their scapegoated, pariah minorities of "middlemen." Indonesia has its Chinese; Northern Nigeria had the Ibo; East and South Africa have "their" Indians. (Only destitution, I suppose, saves the Palestine Arabs from becoming the "Jews" of Israel; as it stands, they are just its "aborigines.")

The Asian "community" of South or East Africa is, thus, almost entirely a product of outside forces in the larger society. The common burden of racial segregation and other legal disabilities; the fear of possible violence; the shared experience of rejection, prejudice, and scapegoating on the part of Europeans and Africans; the broad similiarity of socioeconomic position halfway between the affluent Europeans and the destitute Africans—those are the bases of what little solidarity and group consciousness exist among Asians. Still, the homogeneous image which most Europeans or Africans have of Asians is a very inaccurate one. Even fear of violence and political uncertainty have not been sufficient to overcome sectarianism and narrow communalism.[5]

In this chapter, we shall review briefly some of the similarities and differences between the positions of Asians in South and East Africa.[6] In spite of substantial dissimilarities between East and South African Asians in history, religious and linguistic composition, occupational and economic status, and political make-up of the host society, the fundamental likeness of their socioeconomic position is nevertheless striking. At the risk of belaboring what is already well known, let me list some of these similarities.

Both groups went from one part of the British Empire to another. The majority of the South African Asians came as unskilled or semiskilled workers under contracts of indenture of three to five years' duration. In East Africa, some 32,000 indentured workers were brought in to build the Mombasa-Kisumu railway between 1896 and 1902, but only 6,000 of them elected to stay in Africa after completion of their term of service, and the vast majority of East African Asians are descendants of skilled free immigrants.[7]

In both regions, Asians experienced, for the most part, a substantial rise in economic and social status. Many came from destitute and low-status groups in India, and, in relation to the British, they were mere "natives." In East and South Africa, their living standards gradually rose, and they came to occupy a middle position in the racial hierarchy between the Europeans and Africans.

The host societies were in both cases virulently racist colonial regimes with an entrenched white-settler community. Consequently, Asians found themselves in a new type of caste system based on skin pigmentation. Although they experienced "upward mobility" vis-à-vis their position in India, they also encountered a ceiling on that mobility; they became the victims of legal and customary discrimination and of a strong "anti-Semitic" type of prejudice. They were allowed to move up into the middle echelons of society, but only to become prisoners of their new ascribed caste status. As an intercalary group, Asians became a buffer between Europeans and Africans, a convenient scapegoat for both, and a highly visible stumbling block in the way of African "advancement."

The Asians of Africa became a highly urban group. In all four countries under consideration, Asians are between 80 and 90 per cent urban. In this respect, they are like the European group and unlike both the Africans and the parent population of India and Pakistan. Some South African Indians became small cane growers or market gardeners, and a few East African Asians gained a foothold in sisal and sugar-cane plantations. However, stringent restrictions on land acquisition by Asians and concentration in mercantile, service, clerical, and industrial occupations combined to make most African Indians urban dwellers. This is even truer in East Africa, where there is no equivalent to the South African class of small farmers and market gardeners in coastal Natal.

Demographically, the Asians remained small minorities, in part because of severe limitations on immigration once Africans replaced them in low-skill occupations. However, the combination of a high degree of urbanization, relative wealth (especially in East Africa), physical distinctiveness, enforced ghettoization, exotic culture and style of dress, and exclusivistic familism and sectarianism made Asians in Africa a highly *visible* minority. Thus, tiny minorities of 1 to 3 per cent of their respective countries' population have so profoundly influenced the appearance of large cities such as Kampala, Nairobi, Dar es Salaam, and Durban as to create the impression of "little Bombays." Paradoxically, a group as geographically, economically, culturally, and socially hemmed in by the larger society has unwittingly created the impression of physical omnipresence, economic affluence, and occult omnipotence. Such is the power of distortion of racial prejudice.

Rejected and hated by Europeans and Africans alike, denied assimilation into the *Herrenvolk,* and disdaining assimilation into an indigenous culture which they regarded as inferior, Asians have been thrown back on their own resources to provide basic services such as education, and they have sought security and self-respect in introverted ghetto existence, thereby further reinforcing anti-Indian stereotypes of clannishness, exclusivism, conservatism, and inadaptability. Treated as a pariah caste, Asians organized their ghetto existence along preexisting lines of solidarity: religion, language, and *jati.* Hindus maintained, albeit in simplified form, a caste system within a caste system. Within the Asian ghetto, walls of religious sectarianism, regional and linguistic chauvinism, and caste snobbery fragmented the minority into a bewildering diversity of little endogamous and mutually mistrustful groups. The Asian "community" is, in fact, a culturally modified (and often impoverished) microcosm of the great Indian kaleidoscope. This sectarianism in the Asian community was further fostered by colonial policies of "communal representation" in East Africa and "separate development" in South Africa. Each segment of the Asian group developed its places of worship, its schools, its voluntary associations, its charitable organizations—in short, its own set of self-contained institutions. The challenges of white racism and the influence of Mahatma Gandhi have sometimes led Indians to transcend sectarianism in the political sphere, and certain groups such as the Ismailis of East Africa have been known for their more open and cosmopolitan outlook. Generally, however, the Asian response to prejudice and victimization has been in-drawn fragmentation and withdrawal to the security of the primary groups: extended family, religious sect, and caste. Common victimization and stigmatization were not enough to draw people together.

In the last analysis, whichever way Asians reacted to outside conditions mattered (and continues to matter) very little as far as either Europeans or Africans were concerned. To be Asian in Africa means that one is always wrong. Hopes that this state of affairs might change after independence in East Africa have not materialized. In politics, when Asians collaborated with the Europeans they were blocking African aspirations; when they sided with Africans, as they frequently did, they were being opportunistic in anticipation of independence; when they tried to keep out of the conflicts, they were sitting on the fence. After independence in East Africa, Asians who did not opt for local citizenship were accused of disloyalty; those who did were suspected of opportunism and were still discriminated against on racial grounds.

Such then are some of the main similarities between East and South African Asians. As we have seen, these similarities are, to a large extent, the product of the external constraints imposed by the racially stratified and pluralistic societies in which African Asians found themselves. Later, we shall examine the crux of the "Asian problem," viz. the historical reasons for the socioeconomic position of Asians in Africa, the vicious circle of anti-Indian prejudice and discrimination, and the complex dynamics of race relations in the plural societies of East and South Africa. But before we do so, we must turn briefly to some of the salient *differences* between East and South Africa.

The "historical depth" of the Asian population is different in the two regions. In East Africa, the Indian presence dates back some two to three thousand years. However, until the nineteenth century, it was confined to the coastal strip and probably did not involve more than small scattered groups of merchants in the seaports, plus transient sailors. Nevertheless, by the mid- to late nineteenth century, Zanzibar and Mombasa each had a few thousand Indian residents. Many of their descendants today are fluent in Swahili and have adopted some of the coastal Swahili culture.

In South Africa, on the other hand, there is no evidence of Indian influence or immigration prior to 1860, and today South African Asians bear scarcely a trace of indigenous culture. Unlike the many East African Asians who speak at least some Swahili, very few South African Indians know Zulu, Xhosa, or Sotho. In another respect, however, South African Indians can be said to have deeper roots in Africa than East African Indians. Large numbers of indentured Indians began to enter South Africa to work on the sugar-cane plantations of Natal some forty years before Asian workers were brought in to construct the Uganda Railway. Restrictions on Asian immigration were more stringent in South Africa, and, consequently, from the time of World War I, the Indian community of South Africa grew almost entirely by natural increase. In East Africa, substantial Asian immigration continued until the early 1950's, and Dharam Ghai estimates that immigration may have accounted for as much as 60 per cent of the Asian population increase from 1948 to 1963.[8] Over 90 per cent of South African Indians are African-born, compared to only 60 to 65 per cent of East African Asians. Considering the relatively young age of the population, this means that a large majority of East African Indians over thirty years of age were born in Asia.[9]

In terms of place of birth, the Asians thus resemble the Europeans in both regions. Most of the non-African population of South Africa can trace its ancestry on African soil much longer than can most Asians and Europeans in East Africa. This is true in spite of the very deep historical roots of a few thousand Asians along the East African coast.

The consequences of this difference in the length of African experience are readily apparent. If one excludes the Goans who were already quite westernized in India, and the Ismailis with their dynamic modernist leadership, East African Asians are much less westernized and more traditional than their respective groups in South Africa. In the latter country, most Asians below the age of forty speak English as their home language, and seldom is any language other than English used between Indians in public places. Children have all but forgotten Indian languages and are sometimes barely able to converse with their grandparents. Hindu religious practices are mostly limited to rituals performed by women at home, to weddings, to funerals, and to the celebration of Diwali. *Jati* (caste) endogamy is breaking down fast. For example, in a coastal town of Natal which is probably among the more traditional in South Africa, it was found that in a sample of 308 Hindu marriages, 26 per cent were between spouses of different castes, and 8 per cent were between people of different *varnas*.[10]

This situation is in sharp contrast with the more traditional behavior of East African Asians. Among them, Hindustani, Punjabi, and Gujarati are commonly spoken both at home and in public places. English is, of course, the lingua franca of professionals and intellectuals, but many Asians speak only limited English. Caste endogamy and Hindu religious practices are reported by Bharati to be observed in a much more orthodox manner than in South Africa, although commensality restrictions have largely disappeared in both regions.[11] Insofar as East African Asians have departed from traditional Indian culture, they have become Africanized as well as Europeanized, whereas in South Africa the African influence is negligible and the European one very strong. The spread of Swahili as the most widely understood lingua franca of Eastern Africa and the official tongue of Tanzania is perhaps the most important factor in the gradual Africanization of East African Asians, especially those who live in the coastal and island communities of Mombasa, Dar es Salaam, and Zanzibar. South African Asians, on the other hand, are increasingly becoming English-speaking South Africans.

A second important difference concerns the internal linguistic and religious composition of South and East African Indians. In terms of religion, both regions have a majority of Hindus, but East Africa is far more diverse than South Africa. In addition to Hindus, Muslims, and Christians, who are represented in both areas, East Africa also has substantial Sikh and Jain communities. Hindus, who number over two-thirds of South African Indians, constitute a bare but growing majority of the

East African Asians. Muslims are proportionately more important in East Africa, but sectarian splits between Sunnis and Shias and, among the Shias, between the Ismailis, Bohras, and others are far more pronounced than in South Africa. East African Sikhs and Goan Catholics also constitute skilled and influential sections of the Asian population which have no counterparts in South Africa.

Linguistically, South Africa is the more diverse of the two areas. In East Africa, the related North Indian languages (Gujarati, Urdu, and Hindustani) are by far the most important. In South Africa, the Hindi and Tamil each account for 35 to 40 per cent of the Asians, with Telugu, Gujarati, and Urdu as relatively small minorities. These linguistic differences, especially the split between the unrelated Northern and Southern Indian languages, has probably accelerated anglicization in the absence of a common Indian language. Thus, English was adopted quite early as the medium of instruction in Asian schools. The North-South distinction splits the South African Hindu community down the middle because, beyond language diversity, there are also important differences in religious ritual and in systems of kinship and marriage. For example, the Tamil and Telugu have preferential cross-cousin marriage, a custom which North Indians regard as highly incestuous under the rule of *sapinda* exogamy.

In simplest terms, it might be said that East African Asians are more fragmented along sectarian lines, while among South African Indians, linguistic lines of cleavage have greater salience. The Muslim-Hindu split is also important in South Africa, but is somewhat mitigated by the fact that language communities cut across religions. There are both Muslim and Hindu Gujarati, and Urdu and Hindi are mutually understandable. It is as if each of the two overseas groups had "specialized" in one of the two major sources of conflict in the mother country.

Socioeconomically, there is a marked difference in both the relative and the absolute positions of East and South African Indians, in spite of the fact that they are both in an "intermediate" status. In absolute terms, East Africans are much better off than their South African counterparts. This is immediately apparent if one compares the Asian occupational structure of the two areas. In South Africa, only some 25 per cent of the Indians in the labor force engage in commerce, and 3 per cent in the professions. Nearly 30 per cent work in secondary industry, a third of those being unskilled and another third semiskilled. Some 10 per cent are domestic servants, and 17 per cent engage in agriculture, mostly as small-scale market gardeners or small cane growers. South African Asians constitute only 8 per cent of the total labor force employed in commerce, compared to 86 per cent for the Europeans. From these figures, it is obvious that the Asian merchant class controls only a small proportion of the country's trade and makes up only a fourth of the Indian population. Most South African Asians are small farmers, industrial workers, and domestic servants whose economic standing is only marginally above that of the Africans. The Asian professional and semiprofessional class is proportionately larger than the African one, but very small in relation to the European one. As to the clerical and white-collar occupations and the skilled manual trades, Asians are virtually debarred from them by "custom" or legislation.

In terms of per capita or family income, South African Asians are closer to the Africans than to the Europeans. They earn on the average some two and a half times as much as Africans, but only one-sixth as much as the Europeans. Most of the social services, welfare grants, educational expenditures, and the like are based on a racial scale whereby Asians and Coloureds receive approximately twice as much per capita as Africans and one-fifth as much as Europeans. Numerous pieces of discriminatory legislation such as the Group Areas Act, the Asiatic Land Tenure and Indian Representation Act, the Mines and Works Act, the Extension of University Education Act, and many others have restricted Indians from purchasing land or residing anywhere except in small segregated areas; prevented them from entering all universities except a segregated and government-controlled college; expropriated and evicted owners and tenants who lived in the white parts of towns; attempted to restrict traders to an

Asian clientele; prohibited entry and movement of Asians through several parts of the country such as the Transkei and the Orange Free State; debarred Asians from many occupations (including skilled manual trades) which are reserved for whites; and generally subjected Indians to a multitude of crippling and humiliating apartheid restrictions. (Yet, compared to the legal status of Africans, Asians are well off, for they do not have to carry "passes" and they have *some* freehold rights.)

Thus, South African Asians have been sandwiched in between the Europeans and Africans, but the squeeze has been much tighter than in East Africa. The major reason is that the much larger European population (nearly one-fifth of South Africa's total, and six and one half times as numerous as the Indians) has deliberately tried to prevent the upward mobility of all non-Europeans; in the process of reserving for itself virtually all the best jobs, it has kept Asians as well as Coloureds and Africans in a lowly, noncompetitive position. The very size of the European population has meant that the ceiling on nonwhite mobility has been much lower than anywhere else in colonial Africa, in spite of much greater opportunities created by an advanced industrial economy. Consequently, Asians found themselves squeezed in a narrow zone slightly above the Africans, in those occupations in which they could compete favorably with the Africans but which were too lowly to be attractive to the Europeans.

By comparison, the lot of East African Asians was enviable during the colonial era, and, in some respects, it has become even more so since independence. In the British territories, Asians were subjected to the humiliation of racial segregation, to discriminatory restrictions on immigration and land purchase, and to a tyrannical government which granted them a mockery of representation along communal lines. They were debarred from the top administrative positions and, in Kenya, from cash crop agriculture, but the broad middle range of urban occupations and the whole commercial sector was theirs to conquer. There was a racial ceiling, but it was quite high, if only because there were so few whites to sit on top of them. Thus, in South Africa, all

Indians have been pushed down by the dominant Europeans and confined to a narrow and depressed intermediate stratum. In colonial East Africa, the British allowed the Asians to fill the broad occupational vacuum between themselves and the Africans; and by rapidly filling that vacuum, the Asians effectively blocked African advancement and unwittingly lowered the ceiling for Africans to a level which, until the 1950's, was nearly as low as it still is for black South Africans.

The present socioeconomic position of East African Asians is still much as it was during the colonial regime. Asians earn approximately six times as much per employee as Africans, and, considering that proportionately many more Asians are in wage employment than Africans, the actual discrepancy is much greater than this. Compared to Europeans, Asians earn a little over one-third as much.[12] If one compares the position of Asians in East and South Africa, *relative to the other racial groups in these respective countries,* one finds, in gross terms, that East African Asians are economically twice as near to the Europeans and twice as far from the Africans as their South African counterparts. In East Africa, Asians are truly in a middle-class position; they are not, as in South Africa, a somewhat less underprivileged segment of the helotry.

The occupational structure of East Africa makes this difference with South Africa quite clear. In 1961, the Asians, who consituated a little over 1 per cent of the East African population, occupied an estimated 40 per cent of the professional and 50 per cent of the semiprofessional, technical, and managerial manpower of the three countries. Between 45 and 50 per cent of the Asian working population engaged in commerce, banking, and insurance. The rest were found as skilled artisans in manufacturing and construction, as clerks, typists, and other white-collar workers in the public services, as managers, professionals, and semiprofessionals, and in a variety of nondomestic services.[13] Until independence, Asian merchants virtually monopolized East African wholesale and retail trade (compared to a share of at most 5 per cent of South African commerce); Asian entrepreneurs controlled substantial sectors of industry and finance; and in Uganda

and Tanzania they played important roles in the sugar and sisal
plantations and in the marketing of cotton. So far, attempts by
independent governments to alter this situation have met with
only limited success. The Asians still hold the key to East
African economic development. They occupy a greatly disproportionate place in both the entrepreneurial and mercantile
bourgeoisie and in the white-collar and managerial middle class,
even though most of the *largest* firms are still under European
(mostly British) control.

Politically, the response to the two Asian communities has
also been rather different. South Africa has, by far, the longer
history of organized resistance to oppression. Under the towering
influence of Mahatma Gandhi, South Africans of Indian ancestry
have opposed white minority rule since the 1890's. One year
after Gandhi's arrival in Durban in 1893, the Natal Indian Congress (which later became the South African Indian Congress)
was founded, and in 1907–1913 thousands of Asians took part
in the world's first *Satyagraha* campaign. South Africa was in a
real sense the birthplace of Indian and Pakistani freedom, as
well as an important source of influence in the United States
civil rights movement and the political emancipation of Africa.
It all began in 1893 when Gandhi was rudely told to get out of a
first-class train coach in Pietermaritzburg, Natal.

Ironically, even militant opposition to apartheid in South
Africa has been along racially segregated lines, and the Indian
Congress was no exception. However, the Indian Congress collaborated with the African National Congress from the time of
its foundation in 1912 and consistently subscribed to the democratic aims of the African leaders. After World War II, the Indian Congress became one of the five constituent organizations
of the Congress Alliance, the main freedom movement of the
1950's. Indian leaders exerted considerable ideological influence
on radical South African opposition politics; most leaders have
consistently rejected the principle of communal representation
and boycotted elections on segregated rolls. Instead, they joined
African leaders in demanding one-man-one-vote in a nonracial
South Africa. In spite of its militancy and its small active mem-

bership, the South African Indian Congress has been broadly representative of the Asian population.

Naturally, not all South African Indians are radical and militant. Some joined groups to the right of the Congress Alliance, such as the Natal Indian Organization and the Liberal party. Many are politically apathetic or fearful to become involved, as is true of the majority of most human groups. Collectively, however, South Africans of Indian origin have a distinguished heritage of courageous, nonviolent resistance to injustice and tyranny. South African Indian politics also have a record of universalism and nonsectarianism which contrasts sharply with white politics in that country.

East African Asians also organized themselves politically along racial lines. The Kenya Indian National Congress was founded in 1914. In Uganda and Tanganyika, Asians constituted respectively the Central Council of Indian Associations and the Asian Association. As in South Africa, these movements have generally opposed racial discrimination and favored more democratic institutions. And, as in South Africa, these organizations were politically self-defeating in that to the extent that they were successful in achieving their goals, they could look forward not to political power but merely to a change of masters. This predicament was inherent in the political organization of a tiny minority along racial lines.

Yet, despite the fact that in neither region did Asians ever hope to gain power for themselves, their politics were rather different. With some individual exceptions, the mainstream of Asian politics in East Africa was more conservative and sectarian than in South Africa. It is true that, in the 1920's, Kenya Asians boycotted elections on the basis of communal representation and that, as independence was approaching, some radical Indian leaders identified with African demands, as shown for example by the creation of the Kenya Freedom Party for the 1960 election.[14] Generally, however, the Asian leadership opposed the white settlers, but followed a policy of extracting concessions from the colonial government by collaborating, however grudgingly, with it. By 1931, Kenya Asians had reluctantly accepted communal representation (not only qua Asians but also along religious lines) and made whatever use they could of their small, undemocratic representation in the Legislative Council. The colonial government, on its part, officially dealt with the Asian organizations as intermediaries between itself and the Asian communities. The South African Indian Congress was a radical movement; its East African counterparts were reformist.

Sectarianism and sectionalism in East African Asian politics were, of course, in good measure a product of the British policy of divide and rule and of communal representation along racial and religious lines. Thus, Indian Muslims, as a minority within a minority, came increasingly to favor sectional representation in the 1940's. The independence and partition of India in 1947 further exacerbated these divisions, and the Indian National Congress itself split along religious lines as a consequence. By contrast, the South African Indian Congress, by consistently refusing any "representation" along communal lines, avoided sectarianism in politics.

The Kenya war of independence and the accelerating pace of change in the late 1950's led a few Indian radicals to side with Africans, but the dominant reaction was one of increasing fear and ambivalence toward African demands. The British colonial government was discriminatory and racist, but it was a known antagonist which had allotted the Asian group a definite and somewhat privileged pigeonhole in the caste society of East Africa. The future under African rule, on the other hand, was uncertain. Thus, the Indian National Congress began to favor special constitutional and electoral entrenchment to protect the position of racial minorities. Even where leaders found it expedient to endorse publicly the cause of majority rule, they shared, for the most part, the private misgivings of most Asians.

There are two main reasons for the different political reactions of South and East African Indians. The first one, and perhaps the main one, is the contrast in their class position. A mercantile and professional bourgeoisie, to which most East African Indians belong, can scarcely be expected to be very radical. East African Asians were pariahs in the colonial society, but they were privileged pariahs who were given a fairly free hand to trade and grow moderately prosperous. They had more to lose to Africans than they had to gain from the British. In South Africa, this is not the case for most Asians. Most Indians have little to lose and much to gain from the abolition of apartheid. Interestingly, the small Natal merchant class which *does* have something to lose formed the Natal Indian Organization which, in its policy of accommodation and conservatism, is a closer analogue to the Kenya Indian National Congress.

The second reason for the political differences between South and East is that, in South Africa, Indians were offered so little in the way of franchise and representation that there was little temptation to accept it. The ludicrous parody of "representation" they were offered in 1946, for example, meant that they could boycott the elections without any practical cost and thereby avoid the plague of sectionalism. In East Africa, Asians had numerical preponderance vis-à-vis Europeans. They could exercise somewhat more pressure on the colonial government, and the latter was in turn distinct from the white settlers. There was the possibility, which did not exist in South Africa, of turning toward the government while opposing the white settlers. In other words, in East Africa, and especially in Kenya, there was more to be gained by compromise. Certainly, at the stage of evolution in the late 1940's and the 1950's, when the principle of racial parity among the unofficial members of the Legislative Council was introduced, the colonial framework had become relatively attractive by giving Asians vast overrepresentation vis-à-vis Africans, albeit underrepresentation vis-à-vis Europeans. In fact, that period marked the heyday of what little political power Asians ever had in East Africa.

The last major difference, and the most obvious one, between East and South African Indians is that the former now live under an African majority government and the latter are still under white minority rule. What differences has independence made to the status of Asians? Was the change of political masters to their benefit? The answer is that, although there have been substantial changes, some of them have been for the better and some for the worse. On balance, the Asians are still a pariah group caught between the white devil and the deep black sea. Independence has meant the abolition of the color bar in public and semipublic places. Asians in Kenya, Uganda, and Tanzania may now enter clubs, schools, hotels, and other amenities formerly closed to them. They are no longer subjected to the constant petty humiliations of European racism and apartheid. This has been the principal gain since independence, but, for practical purposes, only the intellectual, professional, and managerial elite have benefited from the change. The small shopkeeper, the artisan, and the clerk care very little whether they can join the golf club or have a gin and tonic at the New Stanley Hotel. Another benefit of independence to Asians has been the opening up of the former "white highlands" of Kenya which made it possible for a number of Asians to buy previously European farms.

In practice the amount of interaction between the three racial groups in East Africa remains almost as low as before *Uhuru,* except for some formal social mixing at the elite level. Racism in all three main population groups is probably as high as ever, although the outward expression of anti-African prejudice by Europeans and Asians has become much more subdued. Europeans have probably become somewhat more tolerant of Asians, since they themselves are no longer politically dominant. But anti-Asian feelings on the part of Africans are as virulent as ever. East African governments claim to discriminate on the basis of citizenship, but, in fact, there is a great deal of specifically racial discrimination against Asians in employment and trade licensing. Racial discrimination and anti-Asian statements by M.P.'s and high government officials are especially blatant in Kenya.[15] Even the threat of physical violence looms as large as under white rule, and these threats have materialized in the 1964 Zanzibar revolution.

The economic and occupational position of East African Asians is certain to deteriorate, and a number of Asians have already emigrated mostly to Britain, Canada, and India. Whether the Asians are being squeezed out through socialist policies as in Tanzania or through the kind of racist capitalism practiced in

Kenya (where the aim is to change the skin color of the merchant class, not to eliminate it), the results will be much the same for most Asians. Even under the best of circumstances, and assuming that anti-Asian prejudice would vanish, the privileged socioeconomic position of Asians is such that the majority of them are unlikely to be willing to "find their place" at the African level in an open socialist society. Their achieved position incapacitates most of them for life on terms of equality in poor, underdeveloped countries. That is why most emigrants choose affluent but alien Britain over familiar but destitute India or Pakistan.

Indians in East Africa are still in a much better position than in South Africa. Racial discrimination is much less blatant and is not legally entrenched; compulsory racial segregation has disappeared; political rights are based on citizenship rather than color; and, economically, the new restrictive policies on immigration, employment, land acquisition, and trade licensing are only beginning to have an effect. Even if economic restrictions were fully implemented, they would still be less racist and crippling than those imposed under South African apartheid. On the other hand, East African Asians, because they have more to lose, may prove less adaptable to changed conditions than South African Asians would under African government. In both cases, however, high visibility and cultural distinctiveness are additional obstacles to assimilation and acceptance into the African host society, whose tolerance for a privileged alien minority can be predicted to remain quite low. Arguments about contribution to nation building are likely to cut very little ice in a system where the greatest determinant of economic status still appears to be skin pigmentation. When affluent societies like the United States, Britain, and Australia have shown such intolerance of underprivileged minorities in their midst, how much less likely it is for underprivileged majorities to tolerate affluent alien minorities.

In conclusion, we must turn to the crux of the "Asian problem" in Africa. Its fundamental features are common to those of all "middlemen" communities. Economically successful groups which are disproportionately represented in mercantile activities and also have the misfortune of being culturally alien and physically identifiable almost invariably attract the hatred and envy of the host society. But, even within that general category of middlemen groups, African Asians constitute an extreme case, because they were caught in the racist dynamics of colonial or white-settler societies. The almost inevitable antipathy of the underprivileged masses was further exacerbated by the racism of the dominant minority, as well, of course, as by the Asians' assumption of cultural superiority over Africans.

Of all the "racial" groups of East and South Africa, Asians have probably exhibited the least *racism,* but their intense pride in their cultural heritage has led them to look upon European culture with ambivalence and accept as axiomatic their ethnocentric belief in their *cultural* superiority over Africans. Even as tolerant, cosmopolitan, and universalistic a person as Mahatma Gandhi shared that attitude of cultural condescension vis-à-vis Africans. Indeed, most of the first generation of mission-educated Africans were brainwashed into accepting the derogatory European view of their own traditions. Asians could hardly have been expected to react to their situation in terms of modern anthropological relativism at a time when even anthropologists were for the most part ethnocentric and even racist. Nevertheless, the quiet, self-assured cultural condescension of a powerless minority like the Asians was even more galling to Africans than the much cruder racism of the Europeans, who had power to back up their arrogance. (There is a parallel in Gentile resentment against some Jews' assumption of intellectual superiority.)

More specifically, the question is: How did the Asians come to occupy their present place in the racial hierarchy of East and South Africa, and how did the complex system of race relations of these countries develop? In spite of the fact that many Asians (especially the South African ones) came to Africa as unskilled indentured laborers, they had certain advantages over the indigenous population which favored their upward mobility. Many first came without families and thus found it somewhat easier to accumulate some savings. More importantly, Indians came from an urbanized, literate, monetized society which had already been exposed to long technological, cultural, and linguistic contact with the West. Of course, many of the Asian immigrants were poor, illiterate peasants of low status in India. But they had nevertheless been exposed to a money economy and were familiar with a technologically more developed society than those of East and Central Africa. While these advantages were objectively not very great, they were sufficient to give Asians a head start over Africans. In addition, of course, a number of immigrants especially to East Africa were already literate, skilled persons with some capital when they first arrived in Africa, and quite a few had been merchants and clerks back in India.[16]

Not only did the Asian immigrants have certain cultural advantages and commercial experience which gave them a competitive edge over Africans. Their place in the new society was also largely ascribed to them by the dominant Europeans. In many ways, that place was a limited and restrictive one, as we have seen; but, insofar as Europeans regarded the Asians as more "advanced" and more "intelligent" than the Africans, they gave preference to Asians in those skilled manual, supervisory, and clerical occupations which they regarded the Africans as incapable of performing and yet which were too lowly to be attractive to Europeans. Thus, by virtue of the European stereotype of Asians being an especially clever and crafty group, a whole range of intermediate occupations came to be *de facto* reserved for Indians.

This leads us to the whole set of racial stereotypes and prejudices which became the matrix of race relations in the plural societies of East and South Africa. I have argued elsewhere that systems of race relations fall broadly into two different types, the "paternalistic" and the "competitive."[17] Both South and East Africa show the simultaneous operation of both types. These racial caste societies, and, more specifically, the position of Asians in them, were to a significant degree the product of European attitudes; the colonial regime and the white settlers had the power to translate their prejudices into actual policy.

Paternalism was an important ideological ingredient of

colonialism. What better rationalization for colonialism could there be than the theory that the "natives" were backward, irresponsible, happy-go-lucky savages with a primitive, childish mentality who had to be patiently and slowly led up the path of Christianity and civilization by their white fathers? In its more benevolent form, this paternalism took the form of the "noble savage" theory: the "raw native" lived in a stage of mental simplicity and innocence; he was a noble, unspoiled child of nature, who had his pride and could become angry if ill-treated, but who could be relied upon to respond with gratitude to the just and enlightened rule of the colonial administration. In its cruder form, paternalism regarded Africans as incurably stupid and childish, or indeed as arrested specimens of human evolution between the chimpanzee and the European. The important thing was to keep the natives unspoiled, because with education they became cheeky and worthless, in fact inept and maladjusted caricatures of their white masters. Also, because natives were so naïve and incompetent, they had to be protected against unscrupulous characters who wanted to exploit them.

Then came the Asian to complicate this European intellectual image of the colonial society and this master-servant model of race relations. Asians were clearly different from Africans. For one thing, they were held to be heirs to a "great" civilization and, hence, could not be dismissed as simple-minded savages. So, naturally, the European image of Asians fell into the "competitive" model. A long tradition of anti-Semitism was adapted to local conditions and applied to Asians in Africa. Asians were defined as crafty, underhanded, dishonest, out to exploit the poor Africans and to compete unfairly with Europeans, clannish, unhygienic, and dangerous because of their intelligence and their propensity to reproduce like rabbits.[18]

The "Jew of Africa" was born, in the mind of his oppressors. But in the colonial situation, he was even more useful than the anti-Semitic myth had been in Europe where there were no "natives" to contend with. I am not suggesting here that the development and use of these racial attitudes were the product of a Machiavellian plot to divide and rule, as a vulgar Marxist might. Conspiratorial theories generally err in attributing to ruling classes more collective intelligence than they, in fact, possess. Certainly, the intelligence of a ruling class which distinguished itself by the crudity of its racism ought not to be overestimated. In any case, the social consequences of racism are of far greater significance than the motives of the bigots.

Given the European stereotypes of Africans and Asians and the theory of paternalism, it became the self-assigned duty of the Europeans to protect the naïve, helpless natives against the rapaciousness of the "Asiatics." Thus a justification was found for passing discriminatory legislation to debar Asians from purchasing land, from trading in certain areas, from selling liquor to Africans, and so on. In a number of ways, colonial policy did, in a self-fulfilling way, reinforce behavior patterns which in turn could be used to validate the stereotypes. What better way, for example, could there be to make Indians clannish and sectarian than to put them on a separate voting roll and to grant them representation along communal lines?

The great triumph of European racism was the way in which it succeeded in deflecting African hostility from the Europeans to a safely helpless scapegoat. Africans have taken over from the whites the entire battery of anti-Asian prejudices, adding to it the virulence of the frustrated underdog. After decades of humiliation, oppression, and exploitation, after the blood oath of Sharpeville and the concentration camps of the Kenya war of independence, the Europeans have achieved the miracle of being less hated by Africans than the powerless Asians whose worst crimes were a bit of cultural snobbery and some sharp business practices such as are inherent in any system of private enterprise. African governments continue to extend preferential treatment to Europeans and prefer to pay high salaries to expatriates rather than hire equally qualified Asians at much lower cost. The position of Asians in clerical and civil service occupations was largely the result of systematic discrimination by Europeans against Africans; yet it is the Asians who are accused of blocking African mobility. Asians are simply too good scapegoats not to serve that function. They are easily identifiable and alien; and, most importantly, they cannot bite back.

A study which I conducted among students at the University

of East Africa reveals a high level of anti-Asian prejudice among African students. Of a group of sixty-six students in a first-year sociology class, 65 per cent regarded the contribution of Asians to East Africa as "mostly negative," 41 per cent regarded it as "mixed," and only 3 per cent as "mostly positive." Over three-fourths (76 per cent) advocated racial discrimination in employment in favor of Africans, irrespective of citizenship. At the same time, 80 per cent denied that there was any racial discrimination against Europeans and Asians in East Africa. (Interestingly, of the twenty-three Asian students in the same sample, 87 per cent thought they *were* being discriminated against on racial grounds.) Asked in two separate questions what the positive and negative traits of Asians were, half of the African students mentioned no positive traits or explicitly stated that Asians did not have any. Only three positive traits were reported by more than 10 per cent of the sample: business ability, professional skills, and contribution to economic development. On the other hand, 41 per cent accused Indians of exploiting Africans; 22 per cent of dishonesty or deceit; 22 per cent of clannishness and unwillingness to mix with other groups; 19 per cent of superiority feelings vis-à-vis Africans; and 15 per cent of conservatism.[19] Even the "positive" responses were sometimes indirectly negative. Thus, one student said, "Some are honest." In the Durban study conducted in 1960, the attitudes of black South African students toward their Asian fellow citizens were quite similar, in spite of an ideology of nonracial opposition to white tyranny.[20]

Paradoxically, the long-run prospects for Asians are probably better in South Africa than in East Africa. Being, for the most part, already so close to the African standard of living, they will probably find it easier to accept conditions of equality with Africans after the revolution. Besides, the present system is so oppressive and humiliating for Asians, Coloureds, and Africans alike that majority rule will almost certainly be accompanied by an improvement in the position of Asians, barring, of course, the ever present possibility of a pogrom.

East African Asians, on the other hand, are the victims of

their success. As a mercantile bourgeoisie and a white-collar class, most of them are unlikely to adjust to life on the African level if they have any option of emigration to greener pastures. At worst, they are going to be squeezed out by racial discrimination, as is now being done in Kenya. At best, nonracial policies in socialism are going to have much the same adverse effect on most Asians. Intellectuals and highly skilled professionals will probably be least affected and ideologically best prepared to accept change, but since they also can most readily sell their skills on the international market, they are likely to be among the first to leave.

Even if racism, by some miracle, were to disappear from the East African scene, two things are nearly certain: Africans will not tolerate the perpetuation of an alien bourgeoisie; and most Asians will not want to stay at an African level of subsistence. Acute political crises, such as the Uganda one in 1967, or short-range economic expedients may give Asians some respite, but the handwriting is clearly on the wall: "Stay here on equal terms or leave."

Ironically, the predicament of East African Asians is much the same as that of South African whites. Neither group has a place in Africa at the economic level to which it has grown accustomed. That is why, quite independently of racism, it is so unrealistic to expect the Europeans of Zimbabwe and South Africa to relinquish or even share power voluntarily. If they did, most of them would no longer find life in Africa tolerable. Having for so long protected their privileged economic position by maintaining a monopoly of power and having jealously preserved a largely artificial gap between themselves and the Africans, relinquishing power would in fact also mean a drastic reduction in the European standard of living through the simple operation of a free economy. The whites would then have to discover for themselves what inhuman conditions they have so long imposed on their "happy natives." But white Africans scarcely need or indeed deserve any sympathy. They will easily find homes in Europe, Australia, or the Americas. Besides, their predicament is of their own making, and they have too long flaunted their arrogance against their fellow men to elicit much commiseration.

The Asians, on the other hand, are the victims of a historical process in which they played an insignificant role. They are the flotsam of the British Empire. The British crew all found room on the lifeboats. The Asian passengers have been left adrift in the currents of African nationalism. And the Indian ship whence they once came is nearly sinking under the weight of its present occupants.

NOTES

NOTE: I am grateful to Dharam P. Ghai, Yash P. Ghai, and J. S. Mangat for their constructive criticisms of this chapter.

1. Since the partition of India and Pakistan, the people who were previously referred to as Indians have increasingly been called Asians in East Africa. The South African government and formerly the British colonial government used the word "Asiatic," but this term is disliked by most Asians and is no longer used in East Africa. In South Africa, the term "Indian" is still the most neutral and widespread one, as the overwhelming majority of Asian immigrants came in fact from within the present boundaries of the state of India. In nineteenth- and early twentieth-century sources, the word "coolie" is often used in reference to Indians, but today the word has become a racial epithet. Although there are small groups in Africa who come from other parts of the Asian continent, here we shall be concerned only with people of Indian or Pakistani descent. On the coast of East Africa, Arabs constitute a distinct group from the other Asians, and the latter term almost invariably refers solely to persons of Indian-Pakistani origin.
2. Cf. George Delf, *Asians in East Africa* (London: Oxford University Press, 1963), p. 1.
3. The ruling whites or Europeans number 19 per cent of the total, the Coloureds or people of mixed descent 10 per cent, and the indigenous Africans 68 per cent.
4. Cf. Birbal Rambiritch and Pierre L. van den Berghe, "Caste in

a Natal Hindu Community," *African Studies* 20, no. 4 (1961): 217–225.

5. Even on the verge of Kenyan independence with the new threat of African nationalism, Asian politics remained highly sectarian. Cf. George Bennett and Carl G. Rosberg, *The Kenyatta Election, Kenya 1960–1961* (London: Oxford University Press, 1961).

6. The most important works on South Africans of Asian descent are: G. H. Calpin, *Indians in South Africa* (Pietermaritzburg: Shuter and Shooter, 1949); Mohandas K. Gandhi, *An Autobiography: The Story of My Experiences with Truth* (Washington: Public Affairs Press, 1954); Hilda Kuper, *Indian People in Natal* (Durban: Natal University Press, 1960); Pierre L. van den Berghe, *Caneville, The Social Structure of a South African Town* (Middletown: Wesleyan University Press, 1964); and C. A. Woods, *The Indian Community of Natal* (Cape Town: Oxford University Press, 1954). Works on Asians in East Africa include: Anonymous, *Racial and Communal Tensions in East Africa* (Nairobi: East African Publishing House, 1966); Delf, *op. cit.;* L. W. Hollingsworth, *The Asians of East Africa* (London: Macmillan, 1960); Paul Theroux, "Hating the Asians," *Transition* 7, no. 33 (1967): 46–51; J. S. Mangat, *History of the Asians in East Africa* (Oxford: Clarendon Press, 1968); and Stephen Morris, "Indians in East Africa: A Study in a Plural Society," *British Journal of Sociology* vol. 7 (1956).

7. Delf, *op. cit.,* pp. 11–13.

8. Cf. Dharam P. Ghai, ed., *Portrait of a Minority* (London: Oxford University Press, 1965), p. 91.

9. According to the 1962 census of Kenya, only 27 per cent of the Asian men and women over thirty years of age were born in East Africa. Cf. *Kenya Population Census, 1962* 4 (Nairobi: March 1966): 18.

10. Cf. Rambiritch and van den Berghe, *op. cit.*

11. Agehananda Bharati, "A Social Survey," in Ghai, *op. cit.,* pp. 21, 28–47.

12. Cf. Delf, *op. cit.,* p. 45; and Delf, "The Changing Face of Kenya Politics," *Transition* 5, no. 25 (1966): 48. See also Dharam Ghai, *op. cit.,* pp. 97–100.

13. Cf. *ibid.,* pp. 94, 102.

14. Cf. Bennett and Rosberg, *op. cit.,* pp. 111–115; and Delf, *Asians in East Africa,* p. 40.

15. See Theroux, *op. cit.* Kenya Asians, for example, are almost totally debarred from the highest administrative positions in the civil service, irrespective of qualifications or citizenship. In fact, the government openly pursues a policy of Africanization, by which it means replacing Asians and Europeans with Africans, irrespective of citizenship. "Africanization" as a policy is distinguished from "Kenyaization" where the test is citizenship, irrespective of race. Of course, Kenyaization does *de facto* disqualify the vast majority of Europeans and Asians. The remaining Asians are discriminated against under the policy of Africanization, which is a kind of second line of attack where Kenyaization does not "work." It is true that the Kenya legislation regulating immigration, trade licensing, landownership, and employment makes citizenship the test and that racial discrimination is unconstitutional. But, in the application of these laws, the actual test is frequently racial. For instance, in February 1968, when some employers in Kenya began to dismiss Ugandan and Tanzanian workers in accordance with the "Kenyaization" policy, the Kenya government hastened to exempt "Ugandans and Tanzanians of African origin" from the application of the law. Similarly, Kenya followed Britain's lead in requiring of *Asian* holders of British passports entry documents not required of white Britons. Some 35 per cent of the Kenya Asians received Kenya citizenship automatically or applied for it within the legal delay of two years following independence. Most of the remainder chose to become British subjects, and some 3 to 4 per cent are nationals of India and Pakistan. The Kenya government has been dilatory in granting citizenship to Asian applicants, and, as of January 1968, there were still some ten thousand unprocessed cases. With the British parliament stringently limiting the entry of British Asians into the United Kingdom, many East African Asians will literally have no place where they can go and work.

16. In South Africa, a social distinction is made between "passenger" Indians who paid their own passage to Africa and persons of indentured stock. See Hilda Kuper, *op. cit.*, pp. 7–9.

17. See Pierre L. van den Berghe, *Race and Racism* (New York: Wiley, 1967).

18. See Chapter 11.

19. Percentages add up to more than 100, because a number of stu-

dents gave multiple responses. The questions were entirely "open"; that is, the subjects did not check off a list of adjectives, but answered in their own words.
20. See Chapter 11.

Index

DATE DUE

GAYLORD			PRINTED IN U.S.A.